PARTY CRASHING

PARTY CRASHING

How the Hip-Hop Generation Declared Political Independence

Keli Goff

BASIC
CIVITAS
BOOKS

A MEMBER OF THE PERSEUS BOOKS GROUP
NEW YORK

Published by BasicCivitas Books,
A Member of the Perseus Books Group

Books published by BasicCivitas are available at special discounts for bulk
purchases in the United States by corporations, institutions, and other
organizations. For more information, please contact the Special Markets
Department at the Perseus Books Group, 2300 Chestnut Street, Suite 200,
Philadelphia, PA 19103, or call (800) 255-1514, or e-mail
special.markets@perseusbooks.com.

Designed by Timm Bryson
Set in 11 point Adobe Garamond

Library of Congress Cataloging-in-Publication Data
Goff, Keli.
  Party crashing : how the hip-hop generation declared political independence /
Keli Goff.
     p. cm.
  Includes bibliographical references and index.
  ISBN-13: 978-0-465-00332-7 (alk. paper)
  ISBN-10: 0-465-00332-X (alk. paper)
  1. African Americans—Politics and government. 2. Political parties—United
States. I. Title.

E185.G55 2008
323.1196'073–dc22
                                        2007045697

10 9 8 7 6 5 4 3 2 1

For my mother, Opel Goff,
the most beautiful woman I know
inside and out.

When the Negro was completely an underdog, he needed white spokesmen. Liberals played their parts in this period exceedingly well. . . . But now that the Negro has rejected his role as an underdog, he has become more assertive in his search for identity and group solidarity; he wants to speak for himself.

—MARTIN LUTHER KING, JR.,
Where Do We Go from Here: Chaos or Community?

Contents

INTRO-
DUCTION

If you opened the *New York Times* and read that there was a candidate running for president whose platform consisted of railing against gun control, single motherhood, and high taxes, who would this candidate look like in your political imagination?

Would you imagine the candidate to be young or old? Black or white? Liberal or conservative? Republican or Democrat? Would you consider him (or her) mainstream or out of touch with the majority of Americans? Would you consider the candidate someone likely to be buddies with the Hollywood liberal elite, or embraced by leaders of the religious right? If you had to name real-life political leaders and/or activists that this imaginary presidential candidate resembles, would it be former Speaker of the House and architect of the Contract with America, Newt Gingrich? Or controversial religious conservative Pat Robertson? Or maybe a composite of rocker turned conservative pundit Ted Nugent, with a bit of Vice President Dick Cheney and Rush Limbaugh thrown in for good measure?

What if I told you the candidate also railed against homophobia and expressed a liberal position on prostitution? Does that change the image in your mind at all?

What if I told you that the candidate is named Chris Rock?

Yes, that Chris Rock—edgy comedian extraordinaire.

As unlikely as this scenario sounds, remember that in an age in which "the Terminator" can be elected governor of California, a wrestler who costarred in a film called *Predator* can be elected governor of Minnesota, and a B movie actor who costarred with a chimp in a movie called *Bedtime for Bonzo* was elected not once, but twice, to the presidency, the scenario is *not* that far-fetched.

And would a Chris Rock presidency really be so bad?

At least the presidential debates (not to mention the State of the Union Address) would be far more entertaining and would probably attract more viewers. In an age in which the campaign of Dennis Kucinich is viewed as comic relief on the campaign trail, just imagine what a Chris Rock candidacy could do. After all, look at what he did for the Oscars.

Chris Rock has never expressed a desire to throw his hat into the political ring (unless you count his 2003 foray on film in *Head of State*), but his politics have been at the heart of some of his most compelling stand-up material. And yet his politics are not exactly what you may expect from a young black comedian known for edgy material and for using as many four-letter words in one hour as the rest of us use in one year—possibly a lifetime.

In his stand-up special *Never Scared,* Rock describes his politics as follows: "I got some shit I'm conservative about. I got some shit I'm liberal about. Crime—I'm conservative. Prostitution—I'm liberal."[1]

In his 1999 comedy special *Bigger and Blacker* Rock covers a great deal of political ground, including taxes, President Clinton, and nontraditional families. Of Clinton, Rock says, "One thing Clinton did that I didn't like is raise taxes. . . . You don't even pay taxes they take taxes. . . . That ain't a payment that's a jack." Of single mothers, Rock says he gets sick of hearing women say, "You don't need a man to raise kids . . . yes, you can have a kid without a man. That doesn't mean it is to be done. You could drive a car with your feet. That doesn't make it a good idea." He later adds that it is easy to tell which children will grow up to be troublemakers: "If the kid call his grandmamma mommy and his mamma Pam—he going to jail."[2]

Rock's comments on subjects as diverse as abortion rights rallies and the burgeoning class schism within the black community (highlighted by one of his more infamous routines on "niggas" versus black people) earned him the moniker "The William F-ing Buckley of Stand-up" in a piece in the online magazine *Slate*.[3]

Rock's politics defy all convenient labels. That's what makes them interesting and funny. Clearly, a pro-prostitution platform—even when described with a wink and a nod—is not going to endear him to traditional conservatives, yet challenging the choice to become a single mother is not likely to win him any points with hard-core liberals. Rock has publicly claimed to be a Democrat, but he has made a habit of challenging the relevance of traditional party labels.

In *Never Scared* he announces that "Republicans are fu**ing idiots. Democrats are fu**ing idiots. Conservatives are idiots and liberals are idiots," and adds for good measure, "Anyone that makes up their mind before they hear the issue is a fu**ing fool. Be a fu**ing person. *Listen.* Let it swirl around your head. Then form your opinion. No normal, decent person is one thing."[4]

What also makes Rock's politics interesting is that they are not merely his own. Whether he knows it or not, through his social and political commentary Rock has emerged as the voice of a movement. As a young, successful black American who refuses to have his politics forced into a box, Rock is one of the faces of a seismic shift occurring in American politics. Young black Americans whose parents have comprised a substantial portion of the Democratic Party's base for nearly half a century are asserting their political independence—literally.

According to a 2001 study from the Joint Center for Political and Economic Studies, approximately 30 percent of black Americans ages eighteen to thirty-five identify themselves as political independents.[5] It is tempting to dismiss such provocative findings as a fluke, so in 2007, in conjunction with the Political Research Center of Suffolk University, I conducted a follow-up study of four hundred randomly selected black Americans ages eighteen to forty-five (the age range of respondents was expanded to incorporate the responses of those who would have been thirty-five at the time of the initial Joint Center study). Our findings confirmed that a definite shift has occurred in how younger black Americans are defining themselves politically. Most significantly, more than a third of younger black Americans no longer feel the need to conform to traditional party labeling.[6]

The reasons for this shift are varied and complex. In some ways it is part of the natural progression of the American Dream: immigration, followed by integration, followed by assimilation, followed by I-want-my-taxes-lowered. But for black Americans, who came to this country not as immigrants but as cargo, the story is more complicated than that. Unlike other ethnic groups, the Irish for instance, who also struggled with discrimination upon their arrival, black Americans found that their skin color made full assimilation in the traditional sense impossible. Therefore, regardless of any other differences that may have divided them, including ethnic origin or class, black Americans remained united in a singular political struggle. This unity was firmly solidified by the civil rights movement as blacks from all walks of life, including a West Indian entertainment superstar named Harry Belafonte and domestic servants from the segregated South, marched side by side, each in pursuit of the rights denied them both. But it is hard to imagine that today the political issues that matter to a young black entertainment superstar, like Usher for instance, and a young black janitor would be the same. In the eyes of one, the most pressing political issue may be "I need a job that provides a living wage," while for the other it may be "I want my taxes lowered." (You can probably guess which issue would most likely matter to which individual.)

Unlike their parents and grandparents, young black Americans no longer view their political identity as black and white, so to speak. Today, the politics of race that were once the defining political issue for all black voters have become one political issue among many for younger blacks, causing them to reevaluate their political involvement, activism, and partisanship.

That black Americans are Democrats has been one of the most reliable truisms of American politics of the past forty years. But black Americans born after the civil rights movement are challenging the notion of a singular "black vote." Instead, they are proving that black voters come in all shapes and sizes (politically speaking), and that the issues that matter to them are just as diverse as those that matter to white Americans from different ethnic, geographic, and socioeconomic backgrounds, and different generations.

Issues like racial profiling, not to mention the response to Hurricane Katrina, have proven that race remains an issue relevant to our political discourse, yet such issues are still a far cry from the days of legal segregation. In other words, most black Americans can draw a distinction between being pulled over under questionable circumstances by a police officer while at the wheel of their car, and being legally forced to sit in the back of someone else's bus. As the role of race in American politics has changed, so have the political attitudes of those who have long been expected to allow race to define their politics—namely, black voters.

While our parents and grandparents grew up in a world in which the Emmett Till tragedy symbolized justice for black Americans in this country, the post–civil rights generation grew up in a world of O.J. Simpson, Michael Jackson, and Kobe Bryant—a world where race may matter, but money, fame, power, and who your defense attorney is may matter even more.

Not only has the post–civil rights generation grown up in an America in which segregation is a distant memory, but it has grown up in an America in which black people and black culture are the defining arbiters of America's cultural landscape. While the civil rights generation grew up in an America in which *Leave It to Beaver* represented the ideal American family (and black families were simply nonexistent in popular culture), the post–civil rights generation has grown up in an America in which the ideal American family is black and goes by the name Huxtable, as in *The Cosby Show*. Whereas the most influential woman during the civil rights era arguably was First Lady Jackie Kennedy, who could single-handedly spark a fashion trend with a public appearance, today the most influential woman is named Oprah Winfrey. Not only can she spark a trend by featuring something or someone on her show, but she has a Midas-like touch for doing so that has become legendary. Forty years ago the term "professional athlete" denoted white male, whether you were discussing professional basketball, football, or tennis. Today the idea of watching a basketball or football game without seeing any black faces (or watching a tennis tournament without seeing the Williams sisters) sounds unimaginable.

And then there's hip-hop. No other form of popular music in history has become such a defining cultural force, influencing the language, fashion, music, and movies of Americans of all races.

All of these changes have had a profound impact on shaping the political attitudes of the post–civil rights generation. After all, when members of your race begin to define American culture, it becomes harder to believe that your politics should be defined by the suppression of your race, and yet that is just what has long defined black America's decades-long relationship with the Democratic Party; a relationship that some younger black Americans have begun to question.

This is not to say that all younger black Americans have signed letters of intent with the GOP; in fact, in this election cycle they have emerged as a crucial force in the early success of Senator Barack Obama's presidential campaign. But many of these Generation Obama voters are also emblematic of the generational shift occurring among black voters. Unlike their parents and grandparents, for many members of Generation Obama their political loyalty lies with Obama not necessarily because of the party he represents, but because he is one of them. There is a growing contingency of black voters who believe that a candidate's party label matters a lot less than the candidate himself. Additionally, there is a growing contingency of younger black voters, fueled by the 2000 election recount and other factors, who have grown increasingly suspicious of the American political process in general. By extension they consider the major parties and the politicians at the helm of them suspect as well. This means that while they may not be moving into the GOP column, they are moving away from the political process in general, which ultimately harms Democrats by default.

One prominent Democratic political operative interviewed for this book faults the Democratic Party for essentially being asleep at the wheel for an entire generation and not noticing that there was a burgeoning swath of young black voters whom their message was not connecting with. He predicts that this new generation of voters presents a golden opportunity for Republicans, not because they will ever win a majority of them but because they don't need to win a majority to do serious damage to Democrats, particularly considering how many high-profile, close races there have been in recent years.[7] All they have to do is peel away enough votes and the tide of an entire campaign—or even an entire election cycle—can turn. Just think back to the 2006 midterm elections, in which control of the Senate was ultimately decided by less than 10,000 votes, or to the state of Ohio in 2004.

In covering the 2004 presidential election, the *American Prospect* noted that Democratic strategist Donna Brazile, who in 2000 became the first black woman to manage the campaign of a Democratic presidential nominee, had chided the Kerry campaign for a lack of blacks in senior positions. Additionally the article noted that "the need for Kerry to personalize his relationship with the black community is a sentiment heard across a broad spectrum of black voters. He has yet to show any originality, for example, in reaching out to young blacks, who are by far the most politically independent group of black voters. Only 50 percent to 60 percent of African Americans aged 18 to 25 identify themselves as Democrats." Ronald Walters, a political scientist at the University of Maryland, was quoted as saying, "This is a figure that should shock Kerry into action."[8]

Apparently it didn't. And we all know how that election turned out.

One young black voter interviewed for this book says that both of her parents were Democrats and that while she is a registered Democrat, she believes that "Democrats have been pimping the black vote for years." According to her, the only way that will change is if her vote and that of others like hers become up for grabs. Many of them already have. Another young black voter, who interned for a prominent Democrat before switching her voter registration to independent, explains her political evolution this way: "We never had to sit at the back of the bus. I've never been bitten by attack dogs. I know that all of those things happened but that's not my experience. You have to learn to customize your message for a different audience and they [Democrats] are just not doing that."

General Colin Powell says that while he does not consider himself an expert on voting patterns, he does believe that "over time as more blacks enter the middle class; as more blacks become of means—and that is happening—they will vote their interests which may not be the same as blacks used to do in the past." This, he believes, could present an opportunity for the GOP.[9]

However, Reverend Al Sharpton speculates that any burgeoning generational gaps that exist politically among black Americans will ultimately be dwarfed by the realities of what it still means to be black in America. "The one problem that I never worry about is at the end of the day reality sets in. As long as you've got bias in this country, they will start uniting these generational problems for blacks."[10]

It remains to be seen which one of them is correct.

Chapter 1

HIP-HOP MEETS THE HUXTABLES

The Politics of the Post–Civil Rights Generation

Every generation is defined by something. For Americans born at the turn of the twentieth century, it was World War I. For their children, it was the Great Depression and World War II. And for their children's children—baby boomers—it was Vietnam, Watergate, and of course, the civil rights movement.

For black Americans, the civil rights movement was more than one defining moment among many. Regardless of wealth, social status, or geographic location, there is not a black American born anytime before 1960 whose life was not forever changed by it.

Now, nearly four decades after the right to vote became more than an impossible dream for many African Americans, we may see yet another impossible dream come true. A black man may actually be elected president. This reality (the very thought of which probably would have caused most southern politicians to laugh to the point of tears forty years ago) raises the question of what is the defining experience for the generation of black Americans who have come of age in post–civil rights America.

Unlike previous generations that were defined by one or two major cultural touchstones, the post–civil rights generation cannot point to a single unifying experience. Instead, it has been shaped by a variety of cultural landmarks, some triumphant, others tragic: the war on drugs, the war in Iraq, 9/11, the rise of hip-hop, the rise of Oprah, the deaths of Tupac and Biggie, and the presidential campaigns of Jesse Jackson and Barack Obama.

What it has not experienced is legal segregation. This single fact has had a profound impact on the way the post–civil rights generation views politics.

The success of the civil rights movement gained black Americans countless rights, big and small—from equality in access to education and housing to water fountains—and yet it stripped black Americans of one historic privilege: the ability to share an inherent social and political bond. As Bakari Kitwana notes in his landmark book *The Hip Hop Generation,* "The previous generation had the luxury (if you want to call it that) of a broad-based movement. In a climate that screamed for change, youth movements across race, class, gender, and ethnicity were part of the culture."[1]

That isn't so any more. Post–civil rights black Americans are not defined by a universal social or political cause or movement as their parents and grandparents once were. Despite the best efforts of political strategists and the media to pigeonhole them, younger black Americans are staking out their own social and political identities. For some, this means embracing specific labels. Others simply want to be recognized by a political label that has long eluded black Americans: voter.

Not black voter. Not young black voter. Just voter.

But labels are often irresistible, and Kitwana has helped name this generation for the music and culture that many believe most sets them apart: the Hip-Hop Generation. Born between 1965 and 1984, one could argue that this is a group for whom Public Enemy's "Fight the Power" is as much an anthem as "We Shall Overcome" was for their parents.

Love it or hate it, hip-hop has been one of the defining cultural forces of the last two decades. Once a staple of the inner-city streets, today the music of 50 Cent or Yung Joc is just as likely to be heard blasting in the suburban homes of affluent white kids, in some cases even more so. For some, hip-hop music and culture embodies the essence of their American experience—in which to struggle is a fact of life and protest and rebellion are the only ways to be heard. Therefore hip-hop embodies the essence of their political identity. Others view it as merely one aspect of African American culture, not the most important aspect or the one that defines their American experience or political identity. The struggle of young black Americans to reconcile these two views is at the heart of the politics of the post–civil rights generation.

Like the blues before it, hip-hop is more than an art form. It is the soundtrack to the triumphs and tragedies of this generation's experience; but unlike blues or rock, hip-hop transcends the boundaries of music. While some (like my mother) dismiss it as questionable words put to indistinguishable beats, it has left an indelible mark on American culture, from fashion and film to politics.

Hip-hop's reach into mainstream popular culture, as well as the lack of a definitive, unifying political movement among younger black Americans, may explain why a name initially limited to a section in a CD store has come to be applied to a whole generation. Following the first ever hip-hop political convention, the *Black Commentator* wrote, "In the absence of a mass Black political movement, the generation born after 1965 has been named for the culture it created, rather than—as with the preceding generation—the political goals for which they fought."[2]

This has turned out to be both a blessing and a curse. On the one hand, it has given a voice to a generation that might otherwise have been ignored by society altogether. On the other hand there are many who do not deem hip-hop's contribution to be especially positive. As Kitwana notes, "It is not uncommon to hear some of these community leaders dismiss rap music—the most significant cultural achievement of our generation—as ghetto culture. Most of our parents, and especially civil rights leaders and community activists, would rather ignore rap's impact—especially those lyrics that delve into the gritty street culture of the Black underworld—than explore its role in the lives of hip-hop generationers."[3] Today, however, the negative rap on hip-hop no longer falls strictly along generational lines.

The controversy surrounding radio personality Don Imus's comments about the Rutgers women's basketball team, in which he referred to them as "nappy headed hos," cast a spotlight on how increasingly divisive the content of hip-hop music and the image its culture represents have become among black Americans. The argument lobbed by Imus defenders, sometimes with excessive enthusiasm, went something like this: if a twenty-something rapper can call a black woman "ho" in a song, why can't a sixty-something white guy say it in good fun?

Yet long before the Imus controversy, a growing number of black Americans of the so-called Hip-Hop Generation had begun to question whether hip-hop was doing more harm than good. Students at historically black Spelman College have been among the most vocal critics of hip-hop's often negative depiction of young black women, although their crusade was overlooked by most mainstream news outlets until Imus made the issue of interest to mainstream America.[4] Following the Imus brouhaha, Oprah Winfrey devoted two episodes of her program to a town hall discussion among cultural critics of hip-hop, students at Spelman, and prominent figures within the hip-hop community such as Russell Simmons and Kevin Liles, one of the highest-ranking African Americans in the music industry.[5]

While critics like Stanley Crouch liken hard-core rap to a modern-day "minstrel show" in which white suburban teens go on "audio safari" to see "darkies in their element," Simmons and Liles argue that hip-hop reflects the gritty reality of everyday life in impoverished communities. As is often the case with controversial subjects, the truth is likely somewhere in the middle.

As hip-hop struggles through growing pains, its audience has already begun to move on. The latest music industry sales figures suggest that hip-hop's reign as a defining cultural arbiter may be coming to a close. According to Nielsen Soundscan, sales of rap music fell by 21 percent in 2006.[6] In our survey of four hundred randomly selected black Americans ages eighteen to forty-five, 19 percent identified themselves as *not* fans of hip-hop, while 47 percent said they listen to it but believe "most of it reflects negatively on black Americans."[7] A discussion regarding the current state of hip-hop music is relevant to a larger discussion regarding the state of political activism among young black Americans.

While hip-hop's emergence as a cultural force is indisputable, its success in the past ten years has been due in large part to a cult-like following among suburban white teens. Yet the political agenda that moves a nineteen-year-old white teen living in Beverly Hills is unlikely to be the same one that moves a nineteen-year-old black teen in the Bronx. Lumping the two under the same political umbrella simply because of similar CD collections is absurd.

Kitwana says he coined the term "Hip-Hop Generation" largely in reaction to media attempts to lump post–baby boomer black Americans under the label Generation X, a formula he considers inaccurate and irresponsible because the experiences and concerns of many young black Americans is so different from their white counterparts.[8] But just as the Gen X label and what it came to represent (grunge music, the dot-com boom, the film *Reality Bites,* and "finding yourself") cannot fully capture the diverse experiences of that generation, the term "Hip-Hop Generation" fails to capture the broad experiences of young black Americans, or the range of their political philosophies. How can the political ideology of an entire generation be defined by a music and a culture that many members of that generation believe does not represent them?

Alexis McGill is a political scientist and consultant who has worked extensively with "hip-hop voters," first with Russell Simmons and his political group, the Hip-Hop Summit Action Network, and later with hip-hop mogul and rapper Sean "Diddy" Combs and his political group Citizen Change. McGill is not surprised by the media and political establishment's efforts to paint all younger blacks with a broad brush. Historically, she says, "I don't think we've made the argument that the black community is not monolithic, and so the media cuts to representations they have easiest access to."[9]

While Kitwana recognizes that "there are many people within the quote unquote hip-hop generation who are not defined by that," he asserts that the labeling reflects "what hip-hop has done [to] organize young people at a national and international level." From Kitwana's perspective, hip-hop has served as a mechanism for mobilizing an entire generation around issues that matter to them, inspiring people on a national and international level in a way that "is unprecedented." Beyond providing a platform for artistic expression, hip-hop has "created a national political infrastructure."[10]

This infrastructure grew largely out of grassroots activism among young, predominantly black Americans who were brought together by a shared love of hip-hop but were also united by their distrust of the traditional political process and politicians. A lot of these people, says Kitwana, "see electoral politics as bullshit, a waste of time, orchestrated, not going to bring about any tangible change, and you hear that from artists like Talib Kweli or the rapper Nas, and they represent a sentiment that is out there."[11]

The sentiment is so widespread that it has sounded panic alarms among Democrats, not because they fear losing members of the Hip-Hop Generation to the GOP but losing them, period. "When you look at statistics among younger African American men, they are becoming a real hard target for turnout, because they are dropping out of [the] participation process at a higher rate than are young African American women. Part of that is their cynicism and frustration about politics is higher," says Cornell Belcher, head pollster for the Democratic National Committee.[12]

Basil Smikle, Jr., a member of the post–civil rights generation and a political veteran, concurs. A political consultant whose career has included stints as a senior aide to Senator Hillary Rodham Clinton and an adviser to the presidential campaign of Senator Joseph Lieberman, Smikle says, "People are falling out of the political process because nobody actually thinks politics helps them." While it is a problem for both major parties, he predicts that it will be an even greater problem for Democrats. Due to rising dropout rates, joblessness, and incarceration, young black men are becoming increasingly alienated from mainstream society as a whole, and thus their political involvement down the line becomes less and less likely. Smikle believes this combination of factors means that Democrats will end up "losing a significant part of the base."[13]

Assemblyman Adam Clayton Powell IV is a second-generation black elected official. His father, Adam Clayton Powell, Jr., was one of the first black congressmen of the modern era. Powell explains that part of the problem is that older black leaders and other elected officials struggle to reach young black voters. "The

Hip-Hop Generation," Powell notes, "has practically dominated everything from culture, music, economics" but adds that "they dominate everything except politics, because they generally have not been participating."[14]

Cornell Belcher, the DNC pollster, says that "the real issue is they're not seeing politics first and foremost as the most viable avenue for bringing about change in the community, in their community; the change they desperately want to bring about." He adds, "You have younger African Americans, particularly younger African American males, searching for viable vehicles to bring about change."[15]

Kitwana observes that many members of the Hip-Hop Generation feel that the mainstream political establishment ignores the issues that most affect them, like police brutality and what he terms "hip-hop profiling": young black men being targeted for the way they dress, a problem he says is even more prevalent than racial profiling. For many this sentiment has been reinforced by two recent high-profile cases.

The case of six teens from Louisiana, dubbed the Jena Six, galvanized young black Americans, as did the case of homecoming king turned inmate, Genarlow Wilson. While a far cry from the days of Emmett Till, both cases were steeped in racial overtones. In the case of the Jena Six, one black teenager initially faced nearly twenty years in prison after he and five others were accused of assaulting a white classmate. The incident followed a series of racially charged clashes that began when nooses were found hanging from a tree on their high school campus. In Georgia seventeen-year-old Genarlow Wilson, who is also

African American, was sentenced to a mandatory minimum ten years in prison after being convicted of aggravated child molestation for engaging in consensual oral sex with a fifteen-year-old.

Both cases prompted a public outcry and accusations of racial bias. While debate continues regarding the details of the Jena Six case, critics have noted that the white students accused of the noose incident faced minimal punishment for what was deemed a prank. The black students, however, faced the possibility of serious prison time. The national attention both cases garnered (fueled in large part by the efforts of young black Americans) is credited with pressuring local authorities to revisit the cases, resulting in Wilson's release in 2006 after more than two years behind bars. Mychal Bell, the only member of the Jena Six to have been tried at the time of this writing, had his initial conviction set aside on the grounds that he should have been tried as a juvenile, not an adult, for the reduced charges of aggravated battery and conspiracy. (Bell originally faced charges of attempted murder.)

Genarlow Wilson's attorney, B.J. Bernstein, who is white, discusses the role that "subtle racism" played in her client's case. Drawing a distinction between "overt" racism, Bernstein notes that contrary to some media reports Wilson's alleged victim is not white but African American. Despite this fact, Bernstein acknowledges that racial stereotypes ultimately played a role in her client's prosecution. In an interview with CNN she recalls hearing various lawmakers refer to Wilson, an honor student, as a "thug," a perception buoyed by video taken at the scene of the alleged crime. "They see the videotape. There is rap music. Genarlow had dreads at the time. He was a great student, but he looked like a thug on a music video. And, at the legislative session, you heard them say, oh, he is just a thug."[16] As Bernstein astutely observes, were it not for its amateurish quality, the video of Wilson really wouldn't look that different from your typical rap video—just a couple of guys chillin' with a couple of girls. The key difference of course is that the fantasy Wilson and the other young men appear to be living on camera turned into the ultimate nightmare. Wilson, in spite of his numerous non-thug-like accomplishments, became a victim of the "hip-hop profiling" Kitwana speaks of, because when many people viewed the video they didn't see Genarlow Wilson homecoming king or honor student; they simply saw a "thug."

In addition to being wary of law enforcement, Kitwana argues that many members of this generation are also inherently distrustful of traditional social institutions. Globalization, the increasing instability of the American workforce, and the war on terror have given them a sense of unease, as they have grown up in a much less stable world than the one baby boomers and the civil rights generation grew up in. "If you look at someone born in the mid- to late 1960s, if they are born to parents who are not college educated—and even some whose parents are—there are very few options. If they go to college they are already part of an elite group." But those not fortunate enough to go to college (and given that in some major cities as many as half of young black males do not finish high school, there are many) end up with "McJobs" (as in low-wage service jobs at McDonald's) or "working at Wal-Mart or something." Or they hit what many view as the ultimate jackpot and "become a rapper or a basketball player."[17]

But a more realistic possibility is that they will not end up in Wal-Mart or the NBA but in prison. According to a 2005 report by the National Urban League, "One in 20 black men are incarcerated, while one in 155 white men are, and for every three black men in college, four are incarcerated."[18]

Even ten years ago, Kitwana adds, joining the military was considered a viable option. He wryly notes that he was fortunate to attend high school in the "be all you can be" era, in which commercials made the military look like a great way to pay for college, meet girls, and make Mom proud. "There weren't any real major conflicts. You could go into the military and make it into a career and not have any real threat of war. Whereas for younger members of the Hip-Hop Generation, the threat of war is ever present."[19]

These limited opportunities contrast greatly with those available to this generation's parents, for whom the rules were relatively clear: work hard for the same employer for a lifetime and you will get a piece of the Americans Dream, maybe not a huge piece, but enough to buy a home and raise a family, and enough to retire on. "These things absolutely define our politics. If you grow up having a clear understanding of these limited options, it makes you feel very cynical. It makes you feel like the older generation of our country is not looking out for you." He believes that this cynicism will continue to have a profound ripple effect on the traditional political process, most notably in driving members of the Hip-Hop Generation farther and farther away from traditional politics. "One of the things that comes with this generation is cynicism about the government's ability to seriously intervene in the lives of everyday people. I think this generation has the idea that government is something that works for rich people; something that works for corporations because that's how we've seen the government."[20]

A study conducted by the University of Chicago entitled "The Black Youth Project" suggests that a majority of black youth share this perspective. This nationwide survey of 1,590 youth of different races, ages fifteen to twenty-five, found that a majority of young blacks and Hispanics agreed that government leaders care very little about people like them.[21] The end result, according to Kitwana, is that this generation has begun "moving away from parties altogether" and gravitating toward other forms of activism. These emerging forms of activism Kitwana refers to could be seen in the organized response to the Jena Six and Genarlow Wilson cases. In both instances, young people did not rely on traditional political and legal channels to precipitate change. Instead of simply contacting elected officials or relying on so-called black leaders (more on that in Chapter 5), they effectively leveraged their collective power as social networking activists.

Today, even more important than being able to get a group of people to show up for a rally is being able to get a major news outlet to cover it. Demonstrating a savvy understanding of the power of mass media as a tool for social change, young black Americans e-mailed, blogged, instant-messaged, and text-messaged the stories of the Jena Six and Genarlow Wilson into the national spotlight. Their efforts were bolstered by support from high-profile members of the hip-hop community, including rappers Mos Def and Ice Cube. Michael Baisden, a nationally syndicated radio host, who is also a member of the post–civil rights generation, has been credited with using his daily program and website to mobilize thousands of protesters who descended on Jena in fall 2007. [22]

While the response to both the Jena Six and Wilson cases cause some to recall the civil rights protests of the 1960s, they are also potent reminders of just how much things have changed for the better. Had six black teens been accused of assaulting a white teen in the South fifty years ago, concerns about a noose being offensive for appearing on a tree would have been the least of their problems. A much more realistic possibility is that the teens themselves would have been hanging from them. But there's another reason that both of these cases speak to the evolving political sensibilities of the post–civil rights generation. As Genarlow Wilson's attorney observed, his case touched upon the "subtle" racism in American culture. As racism becomes more subtle, finding effective ways to combat it through political and legal channels becomes tougher and the line between so-called racists and everybody else becomes blurred.

In Wilson's case, one of the key opponents to his release was not a tobacco-chewing white southern racist. It was Thurbert Baker, the Georgia state attorney general, who is black and a Democrat.[23] Similarly, Donald Washington, the U.S. attorney for the western district of Louisiana, received harsh criticism from many African Americans for his early assertion that there was no proof of unfair prosecution in the Jena Six case.[24] Washington, a Bush appointee, is also black. The unwillingness of either man to classify his respective case as a watershed moment for civil rights represents a telling shift in the ongoing quest for racial equality. Quite simply claims of racial injustice are no longer as black and white as they once were. Neither are the good guys and bad guys. The responses of Baker and Washington help explain why many members of the Hip-Hop Generation have grown distrustful of traditional political and legal infrastructures and the people who run them—regardless of political party or skin color.

Though the Jena Six and Wilson cases eventually garnered mainstream national coverage, Kitwana notes that much of the activism of the hip-hop community is largely ignored by the mainstream media and major political parties. According to Kitwana, organizations such as the Hip-Hop Congress, which began on college campuses and now has thirty-five chapters nationwide, the Hip-Hop Association, and the Hip-Hop Caucus have thousands of members and participants. But Kitwana feels their activism is often overlooked. "I think so much of what's happening in terms of organizing among young people does not subscribe to traditional electoral politics. So much organizing at a grassroots level is under the radar."

That much of hip-hop activism falls below the mainstream radar does not, in Kitwana's view, lessen its relevance. He believes that if grassroots activists, those working in electoral politics, and prominent hip-hop artists join forces, they will be an unstoppable political force. "When those three forces align themselves properly at a national level I think there's going to be a huge impact and I think that people in electoral politics don't see that. They just see Russell Simmons."[25]

Simmons, who has been dubbed the godfather of hip-hop, has been at the forefront of efforts to mobilize post–civil rights generation black Americans in a hip-hop voter movement. Simmons himself did not register to vote until he was in his thirties, and explains that many in the Hip-Hop Generation feel, as he once did, that politics offers no real incentives for them to be involved. It's a sentiment he is working to change. In his book, *Do You*, Simmons writes, "Like many people in this country, I felt disconnected from the political process. I was aware that the civil rights movement had fought very hard to ensure my right to vote, but I still didn't appreciate its value." Simmons explains that many young people who feel similarly disconnected end up disengaged from the process, not through callousness or a lack of "caring" but because they lack "connectedness." [26] He feels that empowering young people and letting them know they can have an impact is key to inspiring their involvement. Simmons himself was inspired by his desire to change what he saw as unfair laws targeting many of the same people he is aiming to inspire now, the notorious Rockefeller drug laws.

Named for former New York Governor Nelson Rockefeller, the laws, which were enacted in 1973, have been recognized as some of the harshest in the nation targeting drug offenders. The laws make the penalty for sale or possession of a range of narcotics (in varying quantities) a mandatory minimum fifteen years to life in prison—the same penalty one would receive for second-degree murder. With the advent of the crack epidemic in the 1980s, countless lives were destroyed by addiction as well as prison. Simmons's brother was convicted under them and an activist was born. The same mentality, he says, that inspires a young person to buy a CD or new sneakers can also inspire political involvement. "Unfortunately, many of us are sheep. And many of us do what our community does and what dialogue is in our community inspires us to join in. You know, we don't want to be misfits."²⁷

Simmons credits the rise in social consciousness among other high-profile members of the hip-hop community as being crucial to attracting more hip-hop voters into the process. "Now there's a climate that we could really push involvement with young people now. Every rapper has a foundation. If you name the rapper, I'll tell you what they're doing in their community."²⁸

In his book, Simmons chides both political parties for underestimating the power of the hip-hop vote. Lack of voter participation (and political contributions) among younger black Americans is often cited to explain the lack of attention paid to the hip-hop voter by mainstream political parties and candidates. While these factors are partly responsible, they are not solely to blame. During the Imus soap opera, hip-hop came under siege as much as Imus did, and it appeared as though anyone who wasn't a successful rapper or hip-hop producer had something critical to say. It became painfully clear that hip-hop has a serious image problem. What also became clear in the indignant and self-righteous tone affected by many of the networks and journalists covering the story is that while white kids may be huge fans of hip-hop, their parents are not.

When I asked Simmons if the criticism surrounding hip-hop music and culture has hurt its namesake generation's ability to emerge as a serious political force, he said without equivocation, "No."²⁹ But following the Imus debacle, two Democratic presidential candidates, Barack Obama and Hillary Clinton, were harangued about previously embracing support from hip-hop artists (Ludacris and Timbaland, respectively). [30] It is not uncommon for political candidates to draw criticism for accepting support from controversial sources; but usually if a candidate accepts money from a controversial source like Denise Rich, the wife of fugitive billionaire Marc Rich, no one attaches the controversy to an entire voting bloc. (Wealthy divorcées are as much in demand in fund-raising circles as ever.)

Kitwana argues that ultimately the labels become a moot point when it comes to accessing power. The Christian Coalition, he points out, was seen as a fringe group until it began to demonstrate its clout as a voting bloc. [31] But when an entire group of people is lumped under a political umbrella due to a cultural phenomenon, their political clout becomes tied to the strength of that cultural brand, and right now the hip-hop brand is battered. Naming a political movement for hip-hop is arguably no different than using the NASCAR label to identify white (primarily southern) male voters. But the term "NASCAR dads" is essentially a relabeling of a familiar demographic. "Reagan Democrats" were also primarily working-class white males who became valued swing voters. The main difference is that while Reagan Democrats were traditionally northern white males whom Republicans worked to lure across the political aisle, NASCAR dads are southern white males whom Democrats have worked to lure across the aisle in recent elections. But no one ever argued that NASCAR dads or Reagan Democrats account for *all* white male voters. No one would suggest that real estate mogul

Donald Trump and entertainer Barry Manilow are "NASCAR dads," even though they are both white and male.

Shannon Reeves, a former NAACP staffer who now works for the Republican National Committee, says that while he grew up on Doug E. Fresh and Run DMC and considers their music integral to his formative years, hip-hop should not be what defines black Americans politically. "My parents and grandparents tore down barriers. They put their mark on the world. Through the civil rights bill [and] the voting rights act, they paved the way for equal opportunities. They got rid of the Jim Crow South. People in foreign countries are singing 'We Shall Overcome' in their own language. History will show their contribution to the world. I am just not going to accept that my generation's contribution to this country will be hip-hop music."[32]

Hip-hop is clearly a part of the story of the post–civil rights generation, but it is not the whole story. By allowing a cultural touchstone that originated among black Americans to become the defining voice for who we are politically, we have in a sense allowed the media and political leaders to segregate us once again, this time with our blessing. The result has been that for years the political relevance of younger black Americans—the so-called hip-hop vote—has been discounted.

While Simmons emphasizes that hip-hop activism is about organizing around specific issues in an ethnically and racially inclusive manner, in reality no one visualizes a white teenager (even a poor one) when they hear the term "hip-hop voter." For most politicians and journalists, the phrase "hip-hop" conjures up thoughts of music they don't understand and images of a black youth they would probably cross the street at night to avoid.

McGill, the political scientist who worked with Simmons on voter registration at the Hip-Hop Summit Action Network, stresses the importance of young black Americans mobilizing around specific issues as opposed to a specific race. "I don't think it's effective to organize around being black. I think it's effective to organize around class, education, criminal justice—things that affect us disproportionately because we are black." [33]

But part of the political evolution of the post–civil rights generation involves a changing definition of what issues most matter to African Americans. When I talked with Simmons, he described the hip-hop voter movement as "led by poor people" but supported by people of many classes who care about the same issues, namely, poverty. [34] But as young black Americans increasingly assert their political independence and begin forging their own political identities, many issues have begun to matter to them, and there is no longer a consensus on which issues matter most. For instance, according to our survey, black Americans ages eighteen to forty-five consider the war in Iraq the most important issue facing America today, with more than twice as many respondents selecting it over economic equality (26 percent to 12 percent, respectively). [35]

As Kitwana notes, the options available to a black man with a college degree are vastly different from those facing a black (or any) man without one. As a result, these two voters will likely lead vastly different lives, and their political identities and the issues that most matter to them are likely to differ as well. Generational differences within the post–civil rights generation have also begun to have a noticeable political impact.

Activist and onetime presidential candidate Al Sharpton says that instead of one unified post–civil rights generation, there are now two, with different political outlooks. "There's a civil rights generation, which would be people sixty and up, because they were grown in the civil rights era. Then you have the immediate post–civil rights generation, which is my generation, between forty and sixty. . . . I was nine years old in the '60s. Then you've got the generation behind us, who are twenty to forty." [36] The politics of this youngest generation, he says, are the hardest to pin down and the least predictable.

Kitwana agrees, explaining that he would not label those born after 1984 as the Hip-Hop Generation. Just as members of the Hip-Hop Generation had different experiences than their parents and grandparents of the civil rights generation had, this younger generation has also had different experiences. [37] Alexis McGill explains that while she came of age at a time when hip-hop was antiestablishment, some of the college students she has taught have never known it as anything but a mainstream cultural norm, no different from pop or country music. [38] They were not around (or were not culturally aware) when songs like Grandmaster Flash's classic, "The Message," were providing social commentary on issues like poverty and urban violence. The hip-hop they know is more about lyrics full of expletives and videos full of scantily clad women.

The cultural differences within the post–civil rights generation have resulted in the emergence of two primary categories of political thought among younger black Americans. One school of thought believes that the promise of the civil rights movement has not been fully realized and that the mainstream political establishment has essentially failed them. The other school believes that the civil rights movement opened doors and has afforded them countless opportunities that they can continue to build on through political involvement. The former idea, the one defined by the politics of disenfranchisement, has been fundamental to much of hip-hop's most inspired work and has also been at the core of most hip-hop activism.

The other school, the politics of progress, has divided (some might say conquered) every major ethnic group that has come to the United States in the past two hundred years searching for that mythical Atlantis known as the American Dream. Whereas Irish Americans comprised a legendary voting bloc during the Tammany Hall era, today no one expects Pat Buchanan and Ted Kennedy to find much common ground politically despite their shared Irish Catholic heritage. While people love to pay lip service to ethnic pride, everyone knows that the ultimate American Dream is to become so American that you don't stick out. You blend in, and in spite of where you come from or where your parents came from or what your accent may be, you want to be just like the Joneses. Part of this transformation means that along the way one changes from a hyphenated American to simply an American. This also means that one changes from a minority voter to simply a voter.

For most black Americans, such a transformation was never within reach. Skin color made it impossible for them to blend in.

(Those who did pass for white had to completely forsake their ethnic identity.) And that made the idea of black Americans ever being seen as voters rather than minority voters seem out of reach as well. But that has begun to change. Younger black Americans no longer see black as the only political party that exists.

This is not to say that post–civil rights black Americans are oblivious to the reality that race still matters in America. But they have grown up in an America where it is not the *only* thing that matters. Cory Booker, the mayor of Newark, New Jersey, believes that race is still an important and vital aspect of America's political dialogue, but in a more nuanced way. For instance, he says, "Why in this nation have there been perverse obsessions with little white girls—JonBenet Ramsey, Natalie Holloway—yet there are little black children dying in my city and others, unsolved crimes, heinous actions, and they're not talked about years later. There are not CNN specials evaluating them. That speaks to the fact that we still do not live in the society of our dreams yet." He continues, "We cannot avoid the reality that there are still racial challenges. But to me, 'racial challenges' is an intermediate description of what I view as overall challenges of justice, challenges for us to become the country of our highest ideals and our highest aspirations."[39]

In an interview for this book, former Secretary of State Colin Powell noted that his "sense among young blacks, including my own three adult children, is that increasingly, to a large extent [unlike] their parents' generation, they don't consider themselves just as black politically. They are increasingly looking at politics as to how it best reflects their interests and desires and goals; therefore they are making different choices."[40]

While racial profiling and police brutality exist in the post–civil rights generation's America, so does O.J. Simpson. In this America, the greatest threat to black communities does not wear a Klan robe and have white skin but is more likely to be a neighbor, family member, or friend who sells the street poison that has destroyed the lives of countless black Americans. In this America, people's failure to use condoms presents a far greater danger to the black community than water hoses or attack dogs ever did.

It is an America where racism still exists, but so does Oprah Winfrey.

It is an America where there are still black families living in public housing like the Evans family of the 1970s sitcom *Good Times* but there are also black families whose experience mirrors the brownstone-dwelling power couple known as Dr. Heathcliff and Clair Huxtable on *The Cosby Show.*

In short, the experience of this generation is part hip-hop and part Huxtable and it is this combination of experiences that has defined this generation's worldview and its politics. Much as feminism experienced its second- and third-wave movements, today's young black Americans represent a generation in transition as hip-hop voters and Huxtable voters begin to share the political stage. The problem for Democrats is that hip-hop voters don't trust them (or any other politicians), and Huxtable voters don't feel beholden to them. Unless the party begins to alter its message to reach these groups, it will lose both, from the party and possibly from the political process altogether.

Assemblyman Powell cites icons like Russell Simmons as increasingly important to spurring the Hip-Hop Generation's involvement. He predicts that so-called hip-hop voters have the potential to dominate politics—as long as they can conquer their distrust and register in large numbers. [41]

Alexis McGill thinks there is nothing preventing Hip-Hop Generation voters from becoming just as powerful as the National Rifle Association. [42] Simmons confidently notes that young people and hip-hop artists alike are becoming inspired by "the idea of taking charge of their country, of their future, of having an opinion; it's right on the tip. It's right there. We're right there where we can actually get them to make a lot of steps. Just the right statement by the right artist, the right movement and the ball starts picking up speed. . . . I think that [in] the last election, we did a pretty good job having them discuss the election and then vote." [43] McGill points to the hundreds of thousands of new young black voters the Hip-Hop Summit Action Network registered for the 2004 election. She says that whether or not their registration translates into long-term political involvement remains to be seen, and notes that conservatives took nearly thirty years to emerge as a potent political force. [44] But there is one significant obstacle that may be standing in the way: forty-eight states have laws restricting the rights of convicted felons to vote. According to the *Village Voice,* "Blacks make up 40 percent of the nation's disenfranchised, even though they are only 12 percent of the general population. At least 1.4 million black men—13 percent of all black men—cannot vote because of state felon disenfranchisement laws." [45] This means that even before Democrats worry about convincing younger black voters to vote for them, they must first contend with the fact that a number of them cannot vote at all.

Basil Smikle, Jr., the political consultant, has some simple advice for Democrats seeking to connect with this increasingly difficult to reach demographic: talk to young black voters with the same level of attentiveness and same emphasis on a broad range of issues that you display with other voters. Identify the issues that matter to them *today*—not the ones that mattered forty years ago—and make the case for why you are better on those issues than the other guy. Unless a distinct shift begins in how candidates and political leaders reach out to the post–civil rights generation, Smikle predicts that the ramifications could be far greater than the party losing members of its base. Smikle says that while he hopes he is wrong, he predicts that "you'll start to see fewer blacks running for office and winning. You will start to see fewer blacks involved in the process" in general. He hopes the tide will turn but is not particularly confident that it will happen soon. "I think you will start to see things get worse before they get better." [46]

WHAT'S IN A NAME?

The Independent Voter Revolution

To the ears of most people the term "hip-hop Republican" may sound like an oxymoron, but it's a label that has been used to describe Michael Steele, a Republican and former lieutenant governor of Maryland. During his 2006 Senate campaign, Steele received an endorsement from what struck many as an unlikely source, hip-hop icon Russell Simmons. What made the endorsement so surprising is not only that Simmons was known for his support of progressive causes and candidates (mostly Democrats) but that he had campaigned *against* Steele just four years earlier.

Simmons's high-profile support of Steele sent shockwaves through Democratic circles, particularly among those who had simply begun to expect the support of Simmons and other influential black Americans like him. Democratic strategist Donna Brazile called the moment "extremely significant." The *Washington Post* noted with amusement that Steele was likely the only candidate to have fund-raisers hosted in his honor by both Russell Simmons and Dick Cheney.[1]

Simmons eventually stepped forward to clarify his political loyalties. They lie with specific issues and people, not specific parties. In his recent book *Do You*, Simmons admits that his endorsement of Steele "shocked" and "saddened" some of his liberal friends, but he goes on to explain: "When it comes to politics, I try not to focus on labels—instead, I try to focus on finding the high notes in politicians and then working on pushing those notes to the forefront." He adds, "I don't represent any party. I only represent hip-hop, which not only transcends race, class, gender, geography, religion and national boundaries but transcends political parties as well."[2]

While it's easy to dismiss the activism of a celebrity as being out of touch with the everyday people who buy their albums or see their movies, Simmons's politics are representative of a growing movement among younger black Americans. Unlike their parents, who have maintained unwavering loyalty to the Democratic Party, younger black Americans increasingly identify themselves as politically independent. A 2001 study by the Joint Center for Political and Economic Studies reported that 30 percent of young black Americans ages eighteen to thirty-five identified themselves as independents, while 62 percent identified as Democrats.[3]

When the Joint Center released its report, I was more than a bit skeptical of its findings. "I am a young black American and my friends are young black Americans, and all of us are Democrats"—or so I thought. Shortly thereafter I had my first encounter with the Joint Center's 30 percent. I invited a friend—a young African American—to a Democratic fund-raiser. When she declined, I assumed it was because she was not supporting that particular Democratic primary candidate. The possibility that she might not be supporting any Democrat at all struck me as about as likely as the existence of unicorns and leprechauns. When she explained to me that she had switched her registration to independent because "Democrats need to get their act together," I was stunned, in part because this revelation was coming from someone I met when both of us had volunteered for a Democratic candidate only a few short years before.

Later a family member in my home state of Texas informed me that two of the younger ministers at their predominantly black church were also registered independents (something they had discussed to the chagrin and consternation of their membership). When two other acquaintances informed me that they also were registered independents, I began to realize that the Joint Center's 30 percent might not be so mythical after all.

In 2007, with the help of the Suffolk University Political Research Center, I decided to revisit the subject of party affiliation and young black voters. I wanted to find out if nearly ten years later the 30 percent had turned out to be a fluke or had flourished. Our study, which surveyed four hundred young black Americans between eighteen and forty-five, found that partisanship is decreasing with every generation. Among respondents eighteen to twenty-four (who would have been children at the time of the Joint Center report), 35 percent identified themselves as independents. [4] Perhaps more significantly, 41 percent of all respondents said they were registered Democrats but declined to identify themselves as "committed Democrats." Instead they identified themselves as registered Democrats who are "politically independent."[5]

The decline of partisanship among young black Americans was the subject of a 2003 article in the *New York Times* in which former Democratic National Committee Chairman Terry McAuliffe was quoted as saying, "This is very disconcerting for us going forward . . . It is critical that we do a better job of connecting." [6] For Democrats, the article went on, "the downside of weaker partisan ties" was "twofold."

> Unlike older blacks, many of whom vote consistently because they remember a time when they could not, younger blacks are more prone to sit out an election if no candidate grabs their interest. And even if they are not registered Republicans, younger blacks are more open to supporting Republican candidates and issues than older blacks.[7]

According to Cornell Belcher, head pollster for the Democratic National Committee, younger black Americans are increasingly identifying themselves as independents due to a combination of factors, including the perception, particularly among young black men, that the system is not fair. They see it as ineffective and therefore choose, in a sense, to opt out.[8] Opting out can mean not voting or choosing not to participate in the traditional two-party system, instead identifying as an independent.

Shannon Reeves, who was named chairman of the Republican National Committee's African American Policy Council in 2007, believes many young African Americans identify as independents because they "don't distinguish Republican or Democrat as philosophical groups. They distinguish both of them as being white groups. And they don't want to be associated with white groups in power. They will try to use their independence and if they see a candidate, they'll vote for him. They don't want to be considered as controlled by either group, and they don't see them philosophically that much different. They have summed it up to believe that they're both just white and so whichever white group is going to speak in the direction I'm going, then that's who I'll vote for."[9]

But conversations with young black independents reveal that their reasons for declaring independence from traditional party structures are just as varied as the reasons for taking a position on a specific issue. Some registered as independents because they were not impressed with the crop of candidates emerging from the mainstream parties and were therefore reluctant to commit to one party over the other for the long term. Some don't like the idea that just because they are a certain color they should be expected to align themselves politically with a particular team. Others believe that Democrats take black voters for granted, a perception shared by many of the black Americans interviewed for this book, including a number of Democratic elected officials. And others, like Russell Simmons, believe that to make a difference on the issues you care about, you have to vote for the best people regardless of their party.

When asked if he senses an independent streak emerging in younger black Americans' politics, Simmons answers, "I hope that there are more people who are independent and who are making choices as individuals and are thinking for themselves."[10]

Charizma, a black woman in her twenties, says that is precisely why, despite being raised in a household of lifelong Democrats, she is now registered as an independent. "I'm a registered independent because I'm an independent thinker. I don't want anyone counting on my vote. I think you should work for it."[11] Camille, another registered independent in her twenties, explains that there are a range of issues that shape her political outlook. On some issues she considers herself conservative and on others more liberal, so it makes little sense for her to be a Democrat like her parents.[12]

But some see the growing independence movement as merely an extension of the open-mindedness that is a hallmark of this generation. David Bositis, senior political analyst for the Joint Center for Political and Economic Studies, observes that "for many people it is more modern to think of yourself as independent."[13]

Rebelling against the identity of the previous generation is a notion as American as apple pie. The Greatest Generation liked big band music so their kids had to love something called "rock and roll." Boomers loved the Beatles so their kids had to worship Kurt Cobain and something called "grunge." Now members of Gen X are finding themselves on the receiving end of this rebellion as their tweens blast the profanity-laced lyrics of Eminem, among others.

Politics has long been an effective tool for carving out an identity that's separate and distinct from your parents. (The fact that it also happens to be one of the most effective tools for driving them nuts is usually just icing on the cake.) In response to the *Leave It to Beaver* Eisenhower politics of their parents, baby boomers became free-loving, protesting hippies. The idea of such rebellion among black Americans has in many ways been underappreciated by history, due in large part to the fact that blacks have had a separate, segregated American existence. However, just as boomers clashed with their more old-fashioned parents, shocking them with their hippie hair and liberalism, younger blacks in the 1960s and 1970s also shocked mom and dad by rocking sky-high afros, and a more in-your-face political consciousness to match.

The post–civil rights generation has continued this tradition. As discussed earlier, for some members of the post–civil rights generation, hip-hop music and culture has been a defining part of their rebellion. Hip-hop by its very nature is antiauthority and antiestablishment. In other words, anti–mom and dad. But this generation has also demonstrated a level of open-mindedness when it comes to issues of race that was virtually impossible for their parents to possess. For instance, while a black man in his sixties may view all white females through the prism of the Emmett Till tragedy and therefore as strictly off-limits, a young black man in his thirties may view them through the prism of Tiger Woods, Barry Bonds, Cuba Gooding, Jr., and countless others. In other words, not off-limits at all.

For teenagers growing up in an increasingly multicultural America, discussions of race are no longer limited to black and white but increasingly include brown or biracial and every color of the rainbow in between. Their circles of friends have begun to reflect this. A 2004 article in the *New York Times* notes how much the attitudes of younger minorities have evolved when it comes to discussions and perceptions of race. The article observes that Hollywood and the fashion industry have become increasingly racially ambiguous, as evidenced by growing numbers of models, actors, and sports superstars whose racial or ethnic backgrounds are difficult to discern. In addition to the likes of Tiger Woods, Yankees superstar Derek Jeter, actress Jessica Alba, and actor Vin Diesel, the article features a number of lesser-known models finding themselves increasingly in demand because they defy easy racial categorization. According to the article, their popularity has been fueled by the increasing purchasing power and influence of a generation of Americans with more fluid attitudes about race. "With the country's increasingly multiracial character, especially among the young, more and more Americans are unwilling to see themselves as bound by a single racial category, and Hollywood and Madison Avenue are taking notice."

The article goes on to discuss the impact this outlook is having on the political process: "Nearly 7 million Americans identified themselves as members of more than one race in the 2000 census, the first time respondents were able to check more than one category." It continues, "The more fluid way that Americans are viewing their racial identities has stumped the Census Bureau, whose counting of the population and collection of data on Americans every 10 years affects everything from antidiscrimination and voting-rights laws to health and education policy." The article contends that this notion of bucking traditional racial categorizations is particularly prevalent among young Americans, with those under eighteen at the time of publication "twice as likely as adults to identify themselves as multiracial on the census—helping to make the under-25 members of Generation Y the most racially diverse population in the nation's history."[14]

It is not surprising that a generation that flouts traditional notions of race would also challenge traditional racial boundaries. A 2003 Pew survey found that 68 percent of those between eighteen and twenty-nine feel that it's "all right for blacks and whites to date each other," while only 42 percent of respondents thirty and older feel that way. An unwillingness to conform to society's age-old racial definitions and boundaries is characteristic of an independent streak that is resonating politically. Just as this generation has defined its own racial and cultural identity, it seeks to define its own political identity as well. And just as perspectives on racial definitions and racial diversity have become more fluid among this emerging generation, perspectives on political labels have become more fluid as well.

Cory Booker, the Newark mayor who has been heralded as a rising star in the Democratic Party, sees the emergence of an "independent streak" within the black community as a good thing, "because to be captured by one party undermines the ability to negotiate and leverage change. If every political leader, Democrat or Republican, just assumes 'that's a black voter they're going to go that way,' then they're not going to answer to that constituency's interests," which "undermines the very nature of democracy."[15]

The idea that your vote is yours alone is a cornerstone of our democracy, yet if you belong to a racial minority you have long been expected to share your ideology, and thus your vote, with other members of your minority group. While some community leaders have argued that pooling political resources is the key to political power, others believe that unvarying unity eventually becomes a detriment. As former Congressman Floyd Flake once noted in an interview on PBS, "Most ethnic groups outside of African Americans have come to the realization that if they can get 30 percent or so of their people voting for whatever the opposition party is, it means that the door still opens when somebody goes, as opposed to us doing 95 percent for one party and if we lose that election, the door shuts because they don't need us." Flake described spreading a minority group's vote among different parties as "smart politics" and said that it is in the interest of black Americans to start practicing such smart politics more than they have.[16]

Erika Harold, who gained notoriety for her support of conservative issues like abstinence-only sex education during her reign as the 2003 Miss America, echoes this sentiment. According to Harold, if one party automatically expects to receive a particular group of votes and another party knows it will never receive that group of votes, then that group of voters ends up disenfranchised by default. Harold, who is multiracial but says she most closely identifies as African American, headlined a series of outreach tours targeting black voters on behalf of the Republican National Committee during the 2004 election. Calling the tours "an opportunity for dialogue," she explains that voters benefit most when both parties are forced to compete for their votes. "I challenge people to challenge both candidates—regardless of party—to answer hard questions."[17]

Alexis McGill, the political scientist and consultant who worked with Simmons's Hip-Hop Summit Action Network, says that while a community should not haphazardly split its vote, she does believe the evolution of young black Americans' perspective on party labels is a positive thing, for them and for the political process. "I think just the philosophical argument of young people declaring themselves independent is generally a good thing. It's talking to the party apparatus and saying you're really not speaking to me and you're really making me want to say that I don't want to be a Democrat and I don't want to be a Republican."[18]

When I asked Reverend Al Sharpton, the former presidential candidate, if he thinks the growing independent movement among younger black Americans benefits black voters, he argued that it is more effective to influence the process from within a major party. Independence, as he sees it, weakens those voters politically: "I think the solution is that if enough of us organize in either party, we can be the leverage to take over the direction of either party. To form an Independent Party takes us out of the process of either party." And at the end of the day, "you can be just as independent and be a member of either party. I can vote as a Democrat for a Republican or a Democrat. I don't have to register as an independent to do that, which means that if I see somebody in the primary that I like, I still reserve the option of voting in the Democratic primary because I'm a Democrat. But just because I'm a registered Democrat doesn't mean I have to vote Democratic." Sharpton stresses that since it is nearly impossible for third-party candidates to gain traction (unless they are billionaires), it is crucial to maintain a voice in the two major parties' primaries.[19]

Sharpton has spent much of his career as an independent voice challenging the status quo—from within the Democratic Party. Maintaining that independent voice is "why I ran for president and tried to form a bloc. Jackson did it. I hope others do it this time, because outside of that, you're going to choose between two guys. Unless you have a multibillion dollar Independent Party, how do you even have leverage?" He adds that "no independent could have been harder on Howard Dean than I was. And the only way I was doing that is I was in the Democratic primary. You couldn't say that I was a go-along Democrat. I jumped on Dean and I jumped on Kerry."[20]

Bakari Kitwana, author of *The Hip-Hop Generation,* notes that this philosophy has become an ongoing issue of debate among younger black Americans. As an example he cites the differences in perspective among the leaders of the Hip-Hop Political Convention. "You have a couple of trains of thought. One train of thought is let's use the Democratic Party to push our agenda, and we'll work ourselves inside and we'll make the Democratic Party change." The other school of thought is, "We would be independent and make the Republicans or Democrats offer us something. Rather than going along with the Democrats where we're not going to get anything and when you just go along with the Democrats, then what happens when they're out of power? Then you're just sitting on the sidelines."[21]

Kitwana believes that the majority of young Americans are politically to the left of both major parties, but he adds that "there is more of a tendency for people in that age-group to be independent in their outlook because they don't believe, as previous generations have, in unabashedly committing themselves to the Democratic Party. Why [would they]? What has happened with the Democratic Party with this generation of young people that would make them committed to them?" He describes the emerging independent perspective among younger black Americans as "good for the country."[22]

Amaya Smith, a spokesperson for the Democratic National Committee who is African American and a member of the post–civil rights generation, thinks increasing competition for the votes of young black Americans has forced the Democrats to improve, much as having a strong competitor in any sport would. According to Smith, it has encouraged Democrats to step "up our efforts considerably. So it's not only good for African Americans outside the party. I think it's good for the party, too."[23]

Jeff Johnson, a popular television personality known for his work on BET, describes his political philosophy as "politically free," which he defines as having the freedom to evolve politically. Johnson, who began his career working with organizations such as the NAACP and the Hip-Hop Summit Action Network before beginning his own political consulting firm, explains that his firsthand experience with partisan politics convinced him of the growing irrelevance of labels. "Working with left leaning organizations for nearly a decade in a formal capacity led me to feel imprisoned because there were areas where I could be labeled traditionally liberal but there were a whole lot of areas where I would be labeled traditionally conservative," says Johnson. "I got tired of feeling like I had to fit into somebody else's box who in many cases didn't have a real political agenda either way for my community."[24]

Johnson is not the only black American who has come to believe that an obsession with party labels has been detrimental not only to black voters but to the political process as a whole. Michael Steele of Maryland, whose support for raising the minimum wage and opposition to the death penalty have put him at odds with other members of the GOP, says that political labels are primarily used to divide and conquer. "I certainly learned in my campaign for the Senate as well as my campaign for the lieutenant governorship that these labels are often used to peg you. And you can't define me by just a conservative label because I bring to the table a lot of experience, which in some communities may be considered conservative and others may be considered moderate or even liberal." When asked if he believes labels are relevant today, Steele argues that they are becoming less so, noting that when he ran for office he was endorsed by five sitting Democratic members of his county council, a Democratic county executive, along with Simmons and others who had traditionally supported Democrats. "They weren't endorsing the party label," Steele says. "They weren't endorsing all things Republican. . . . What they were endorsing was a vision that I had talked about and laid out during the campaign. . . . Certain principles that I hoped to bring to the table and execute as a United States senator."[25]

In his first campaign for mayor of Newark, Cory Booker received support from both sides of the political aisle. Former Democratic presidential candidate Bill Bradley and former Republican vice presidential candidate Jack Kemp cohosted an event for him. Focusing primarily on party labels, Booker says, is no longer conducive to effective leadership. "My loyalty, ultimately, is to the communities I seek to serve. . . . I'm not going to be limited or constrained by party loyalty from finding ideas that work and make a difference. I do have a loyalty to the Democratic Party . . . but ultimately my deeper fealty is to the community. So I just don't want to be boxed in whatever I do."[26]

He adds, "If you are stuck in narrow party politics, you often quickly undermine your ability to serve the larger cause in which we all fight. There are more things that unite us as Americans—whatever you call yourself [politically]—than divide us."[27]

This sentiment is particularly strong among those coming of age in the era of 9/11. Divisive issues that were once partisan powder kegs have begun to drift into the background. Whether you believe that there are not enough affirmative action or diversity initiatives within your company, or you believe that there are too many, becomes a moot point if you're worried that a terrorist who doesn't know what affirmative action is (and doesn't care), may blow the office building up.

Erika Harold explains that growing up in a world dominated by national security issues has made her conscious of the importance of voting for the most qualified candidate, even when she doesn't agree with him on other important issues. "I am pro-life," she says, "but when you are considering a candidate for higher office, there are so many issues that are important to consider, including national security and also education." This is what inspired her to support Barack Obama over conservative Alan

Keyes for U.S. Senate in her home state of Illinois in 2004—the same year she spoke at the Republican National Convention.[28]

As Harold's support for Obama demonstrates, the burgeoning independent streak among young black voters may occasionally prove detrimental to Republicans, but overall it is more harmful to Democrats. Black voters have comprised a substantial portion of the Democratic base for nearly four decades, and the prospect of losing 30 percent—or at least not being able to count on it—is potentially devastating. Brazile labeled Simmons's endorsement of Steele "a shot across the bow" for Democrats. "This should be a wake-up call. You cannot take your most loyal base for granted. You cannot assume that just because people are black they will vote Democratic."[29]

But according to some young black voters, that is precisely the expectation Democrats have been operating under for far too long.

A young black woman who interned for Democratic candidates and elected officials before changing her registration to independent feels that Democrats simply assume that if you are "downtrodden" you will vote for them. "It's as though their entire campaign message is, if you're gay you should be a Democrat. If you're black, you should be a Democrat. If you're handicapped, you should be a Democrat." What she hates most about this is the implication that there are no black voters, just a "black vote," an idea she finds patronizing.[30]

Clyde, another independent voter in his early thirties, echoes that sentiment, explaining that when he walks into a voting booth, he doesn't think of himself as a "black voter" but as a voter who has specific issues that affect his everyday life, and therefore is willing to vote for the candidate who most benefits his interests, regardless of party. Describing himself as a Democrat on social issues and a Republican on fiscal issues, he explains that "I have a small business now, and am concerned about how taxes are going to effect me and whoever can convince me on that issue can have my vote."[31]

From his perspective the rise of the young black independent indicates growing political sophistication among black voters in general. "Now that we're two generations after receiving voting rights [we] should progress to the point where we vote according to our interests and not a party."[32]

Jeff Johnson, the television personality and political consultant, explained that it was partly this expectation that caused him to publicly cross party lines and endorse a Republican candidate after years of working on behalf of liberal causes. But Johnson did not endorse just any Republican. He endorsed Kenneth Blackwell. At the time of his 2006 run for governor, Blackwell, who is African American, was arguably one of the most reviled Republicans in the eyes of many Democrats and African Americans. Many held Blackwell, Ohio's secretary of state, personally responsible for the disenfranchisement of black voters that allegedly occurred during the 2004 presidential election. By extension they held him personally responsible for delivering another close election to Republicans.

Johnson, an Ohio native, said that while he was aware of the criticism it did not influence his opinion of Blackwell because he did not believe that one person was solely to blame for the disenfranchisement of voters. According to Johnson, "I thought there were things that Ken Blackwell did as secretary of state that added to the disenfranchisement of primarily black voters; however, I also know that in those districts where there were the greatest number of complaints those precincts were in counties with democratically controlled county election boards." From Johnson's perspective "everyone was complicit in those people in Ohio not being able to cast their vote so I thought it was interesting when I saw primarily white organizations from the left going into black communities telling them that this black man was bad for them when they didn't even have a black agenda. That to me is dangerous because as a community when you allow other people to come in and tell you who to support when they are not supporting you, that's a huge problem."

Ultimately the greatest influence in his decision to support Blackwell was Blackwell's Democratic opponent, Congressman Ted Strickland, whose campaign Johnson believed took black voters for granted, particularly younger ones. Johnson noted that after he reached out to both campaigns the Strickland campaign assigned some aides to meet with him who offered to send him materials outlining the congressman's plans for urban communities but never did. In contrast, Blackwell personally met with Johnson for two hours. Johnson explained that there are a number of issues on which he disagrees with Blackwell, including abortion (Johnson is pro-choice), but as Johnson noted, "I don't agree with my mother on everything." Furthermore, he felt strongly about Blackwell's plans for spurring economic growth in the state where the residents of large cities like Cleveland are struggling.

Johnson also noted that Blackwell had one of the strongest records of hiring minorities of any elected official in the state. "I just think if we're going to provide leadership for people then we need to be examples of leadership and that means not following people that others tell us to support and not just the liberal guy who smiles all the time," he said. "Just because there's a liberal that smiles all the time doesn't mean that he or she supports policy that ultimately transforms the community that you care about. We have to stop being concerned with personality and be concerned with transformation. I am tired of supporting people that smile and have great charisma but when they leave office nothing is different than when they came."[33] (Apparently Johnson is not alone in this perspective. Former Congressman Floyd Flake, a Democrat famous for demonstrating his own independent streak over the years, served as Blackwell's campaign cochair.)

Ken Blackwell lost his bid for governor. Jeff Johnson lost quite a bit too. "I was called everything from an Uncle Tom to a sellout." He also lost a number of lucrative consulting contracts, so many that it took his business nearly a year to recover. On a personal level, "there were people who stopped returning my calls who had been friends of mine for years." But while calling the experience "painful" Johnson also found it "liberating." The biggest lesson Johnson learned is that for most of the political establishment the idea of actual political independence is still a foreign concept. He explained that since he has not endorsed another Republican since Blackwell many are confused because they had written him off as a "Republican spy." "I think they felt like I was the black version of Anakin Skywalker," a reference to the *Star Wars* character, "being turned to the dark side and now that the 2006 race is over and I haven't supported another Republican they're confused." He continued, "Because so many people in this game are just robots and they don't understand people that are willing to think freely and for themselves." In spite of the personal and professional cost to himself, Johnson has no regrets. "If we allow the bottom line to drive our convictions then all we are is political tricks," said Johnson, using a slang term for prostitute. "Because all you're doing is tricking yourself for a political dollar as opposed to the power of your convictions driving what it is that you do and while that may not be the smartest business model I thought we were in this to change the community not to get paid."

The greatest threat to Democrats' long-standing hold on the "black vote" is not hip-hop Republicans or apathy but the passage of time. Forty years ago, when Dixiecrats like Strom Thurmond abandoned the Democratic Party over civil rights, voting for Democrats who supported major civil rights measures like the Voting Rights Act was tantamount to survival. When voting becomes equated with survival, the bond between a constituency and a party can be virtually unbreakable.

But a lot has changed in forty years. Few people are likely to feel as strongly about, say, affirmative action as they would about not being allowed to vote. While many life-and-death issues such as crime and AIDS disproportionately affect black Americans, they are not inherently race specific, and the political response to them (or lack thereof) cannot be blamed on a particular party.

For this reason fewer young black Americans are viewing politics through a race-specific lens.

As DNC pollster Cornell Belcher explains, with the number of younger black voters increasing disproportionately to the population in comparison to whites, finding a way to reach them is imperative for the Democratic Party. A particular challenge, he notes, is that younger black voters feel no great connection with the party's role in the civil rights movement. David Bositis of the Joint Center adds that young black Americans don't feel "the attachment to the Democratic Party that their parents and grandparents felt because they didn't experience the civil rights movement so they didn't remember Lyndon Johnson and what Lyndon Johnson represented for African Americans."[34]

This sentiment was reflected in my interviews with voters. Camille describes her parents as distrusting all Republicans because of their experiences living in the Deep South during the civil rights era, an experience Camille did not share. "They remember and they see things in a very different way than I do," she said. Her parents, coming from a line of sharecroppers, had a sense that "you were never given a fair shake. . . . That's the world that they come from." As a result, she explains, they became generally distrustful of white people, particularly those in power, but decided that politically "if they had to pick one, it's the lesser of two evils," and have remained loyal Democrats ever since.[35]

Robin, who interned for one of the nation's most powerful Democrats before switching her registration to independent, adds, "There is a growing disconnect and indifference among young black Americans because we have a different experience. . . . We never had to sit at the back of the bus. I've never been bitten by attack dogs. I know that all of those things happened but that's not my experience. You have to learn to customize your message for a different audience and they [Democrats] are just not doing that."[36]

The civil rights movement was successful because black Americans stood united, and consequently black voters have been reluctant to venture out on their own politically. But the civil rights movement not only gave black Americans the right to vote, it gave them the right to vote as individuals.

Someone once said that the American immigrant trajectory goes something like this: the first generation works the fields or the factories so that the second generation can become doctors and lawyers so that the third generation can study modern dance or work for a nonprofit.

In other words, there are rules that those in the very beginning must follow so that future generations can eventually achieve their version of the American Dream. While achieving some form of financial security is a big part of the American Dream, it is not the most important part; 99.9 percent of us go to bed every night and dream of winning the lottery because the money would buy us what every American really dreams of: controlling our own destiny. For some this would mean being able to tell that annoying boss what you really think of him. For others it would mean starting that dream career. The ultimate American Dream is about having the freedom to do what you want and to define who you are.

Most black Americans never had a "traditional" immigrant experience, yet they find themselves confronting some of the very growing pains that immigrants have. But there is a difference. The black version of the immigrant story did not begin at the turn of the century on Ellis Island. Instead, it began in the 1960s during the civil rights movement. Those at the forefront of the struggle—our parents and grandparents—worked the fields and the factories, so that our parents could integrate the colleges, so that we could study political science or film (or write books)—so we could live the dream. Since not following the rules that our forefathers had to is a big part of that dream, it is not surprising that it would become a predominant theme in every aspect of our lives; from our career choices, to dating and marriage, to politics. The political rules that our grandparents and parents were expected to follow were cut-and-dried: be a Democrat. After all there weren't a lot of options. You could vote for the guy who thought you were less than human and said so, or for the guy who at least pretended he didn't. But today our political calculations are no longer as black and white (so to speak) and therefore neither are our politics.

Adam Clayton Powell IV, the son of famed civil rights leader Adam Clayton Powell, Jr., says that while he is a lifelong Democrat, he feels it is important that black Americans not be handicapped politically by an obsession with labels. That is not what his father and others like him fought for. "In the '60s, the battle was for the right to vote," says Powell, "but it wasn't for black people to register to vote Democrat automatically."[37]

This is a political philosophy that younger black Americans have finally begun to embrace.

Chapter 3

SHADOW OF THE "FIRST BLACK PRESIDENT"

How the Democratic Party Lost Bill, His Sax, and Its Soul

There is not an educated black person in America (including me) who hasn't heard it said about them by a potential employer, teacher, or a fellow classmate.

The "it" is articulate.

"Articulate" is the fallback compliment used by some white Americans, particularly older ones, to describe a black person who speaks exceptionally well. Often, however, the person is not really exceptional at all. It's just that the speaker doesn't know many black people, especially in a professional context, and is therefore impressed by any black person who doesn't walk around shouting "Dyn-o-mite!" like the character J.J. from *Good Times*.

Obviously there are far worse things you could be called by a white person. The problem is that when "articulate" is used to describe a young black student but not his equally "articulate" white counterpart, it implies that any young black person who speaks proper English is an exception and therefore to be commended.

As a result, "articulate" ceases to be a compliment and instead becomes code for "I don't know many black people and the ones I do know don't sound educated, so I was relieved to meet one who sounded remotely intelligent."

This is the message Senator Joseph Biden conveyed when he notoriously referred to Senator Barack Obama as "the first mainstream African-American who is articulate and bright and clean and a nice-looking guy."[1] According to Julian Bond, chairman of the NAACP, "The person using it may think he's paying a big compliment but I have never heard anyone say, 'Gee, isn't Bill Clinton articulate, isn't Nancy Pelosi articulate, isn't Dick Cheney articulate.' People don't normally talk about how articulate other people are. It is only used in reference to racial minorities. And when I was younger, it was used about me all the time. You think of Obama as a graduate of Harvard Law School and being articulate in the proper sense, that's one of the things that you are almost automatically."[2]

Colin Powell notes that he heard it said about himself so often that it warranted a mention in one of Chris Rock's stand-up acts. Demonstrating a surprisingly adept Chris Rock impression, the former secretary of state recalls that the bit went something like,

"Colin Powell! Colin Powell! They all say the same thing—he's so articulate and well spoken. What do you expect? He went to school. What do you expect him to say: 'I's be the chairman?'"[3]

Now pause for a moment. Can you imagine former President Bill Clinton patronizingly referring to an African American as "articulate" and "clean?"

The Biden debacle illustrates a problem that has been brewing for Democrats for some time. As a younger generation of black voters emerges with no historic loyalty to the Democratic Party, the ability of individual Democratic leaders to connect with younger black voters becomes ever more crucial to the party's long-term success. Yet for a variety of reasons this is an area in which these leaders have stumbled continuously.

President Clinton's departure from politics (at least in an official capacity) has created a serious void for the party. From appointing a record number of black Americans to cabinet positions in his administration, to selecting a black artist to paint his official presidential portrait (the first black ever to do so), to including black Americans such as Vernon Jordan in his inner circle, to opening his postpresidency office in Harlem—Clinton demonstrated a commitment to inclusion that went beyond simply requesting a vote during an election year. Unfortunately this is a skill that not all of his Democratic peers have mastered.

When Nobel laureate Toni Morrison dubbed Clinton the nation's "first black president," the moniker drew more than a few chuckles and elicited a fair share of amens. It also sparked criticism. Morrison wrote, "Clinton displays almost every trope of blackness: single-parent household, born poor, working-class, saxophone-playing, McDonald's-and-junk-food-loving boy from Arkansas."[4] Some were offended by the idea that a white man could be anointed the nation's "first black president" simply for embodying some of the black community's less flattering stereotypes. But Morrison simply stated what had long been joked about privately: that Clinton didn't come across as your typical white politician and certainly didn't relate to black Americans as one. But even critics couldn't argue with the underlying message the essay reinforced, which is that former President Clinton does enjoy a unique relationship with black Americans. Even his fiercest critics acknowledge that his ease among black people and affection for black culture is one of his most genuine qualities.

To some degree Clinton's status as an honorary black American was solidified when he was inducted into the Arkansas Black Hall of Fame as an honorary member in October 2002. He made light of being called the first black president, stating in his remarks, "Thanks to you I now have proof." He added, "You have looked beyond the color of my skin to the work of my life and the color of my heart."[5] Former transportation secretary and Clinton appointee Rodney Slater remarked, "It's not about the skin. It's about the spirit and the soul of this soul brother. . . . Mr. President, you have given so many of us the opportunity to be the first black this, the first black that, and tonight we are going to give you the opportunity to become the first white inductee into the Black Hall of Fame."[6]

Perhaps the greatest testament to Clinton's unparalleled popularity among black Americans is that he was standing there at all, just six years after signing controversial welfare reform legislation into law. At the time, many liberals and leading black Americans viewed the legislation as an example of the Democratic Party caving to conservative pressure in an election year, on an issue full of overtones of classism and racism. Congressman John Lewis spoke for many—including some of the president's close black friends—when he said, "You cannot forget this. It's not something you easily dismiss. We have to go and stick with the president. But it's a very difficult calling for a lot of people."[7]

Yet unlike other Democratic leaders who also supported the legislation, like former Senate Minority Leader Tom Daschle, Clinton stood there that evening basking in yet another warm embrace from the community he had relied on throughout his political career. He readily expressed his gratitude, acknowledging what many political experts had long maintained: that he owed much of his political success to black Americans. "From living among you, I learned my simple political creed: Everybody counts, everybody deserves a chance, everybody has a role to play, and we are all better when we all work together. . . . I owe you more than you owe me."[8]

The give-and-take on display that evening between Clinton and a room full of black Americans encapsulated one of the Democratic Party's greatest political strengths and greatest political weaknesses in the twenty-first century. The strength is Bill Clinton's effortless rapport with the black community. The weakness is that despite the party's best efforts, he cannot be cloned.

In his book *Bill Clinton and Black America,* author and columnist Dewayne Wickham compiles first-person essays from prominent black Americans regarding President Clinton's special connection with the black community. Radio host Tom Joyner recounts how, while attending the ceremony in which civil rights icon Rosa Parks was awarded the Congressional Medal of Freedom, opera star Jessye Norman led the crowd in singing the black national anthem, "Lift Every Voice and Sing." Joyner notes that while every black American in attendance sang along with the first verse, by the final two verses Clinton and Norman were "doing a duet" because they were the only two people in the room who knew the words—and Norman had the words in front of her. For Joyner, the anecdote illustrates that "President Clinton may not have been all things to all Black people, but he was like no other president we've seen before. And unless by some miracle he's able to run again, I doubt we'll ever see one like him again."[9]

Unlike every other Democrat who has enjoyed popular support from the black community, like Jimmy Carter or Ted Kennedy, Clinton has an appeal to black Americans that is cross-generational. While black baby boomers see him as a southern son or soul brother who spent his career trying to right some of the wrongs he witnessed growing up in the South, young black Americans remember him as the first presidential candidate who actually seemed "cool," an image Clinton solidified by playing the saxophone on the *Arsenio Hall Show* (a talk show hosted by a young black American). This soul brother image has cast an impossibly long shadow from which other Democrats have struggled to emerge.

Think of the crowds of black Americans who swarmed the Hue-Man Bookstore in Harlem when the former president conducted his first book signing for his memoir *My Life*. One would be hard-pressed to imagine a similar sea of brown faces greeting Al Gore at the Magic Johnson Theater in Harlem were he to premiere *An Inconvenient Truth* there.

Former Congressman Floyd Flake, pastor of the megachurch powerhouse Greater Allen AME Cathedral in New York, notes that while the Democratic Party has run a number of qualified candidates in the years since Clinton left office, the comparisons to him have been a hurdle that is almost impossible to overcome. "The other candidates are good," Flake admits, "but everybody is measuring them against what they thought was the best. And in their minds, the best was Bill Clinton. Of the four or five presidents I've served with starting with Ronald Reagan, I consider him the best."[10]

Apparently young black Americans consider him the best too. According to our survey, Bill Clinton is the best liked political figure among young black Americans, with a favorability rating higher than any of the current Democratic candidates. Of the four hundred black Americans ages eighteen to forty-five surveyed for this book, 61 percent have a "very favorable" impression of him. This is compared to a 30 percent "very favorable" rating for his former vice president, Al Gore. It is also twenty points higher than that of current presidential candidate Hillary Rodham Clinton.[11]

What distinguishes him from other white elected officials, who have never been dubbed honorary black senator, honorary black congressman, or first black president? Why is it that even after supporting welfare reform (not to mention his handling of the Lani Guinier incident, in which he nominated Guinier, a black classmate from Yale Law School, to a cabinet post only to withdraw the nomination later under conservative pressure), his allegiance to black Americans was never once questioned? For one thing, the sincerity of Clinton's love of black culture and black people has come across throughout his career. No one thinks that the pure giddiness he exudes when watching someone like Patti LaBelle perform is anything but genuine. In fact his body language suggests he would probably have more fun at the BET Awards than at the Kennedy Center Honors. The same could not be said of any other president and few recent candidates (except maybe Al Sharpton). But that is only part of the story.

Bill Clinton was the first elected president since Nixon who did not come from any form of privilege. He was not born into money, did not marry into money, was not a movie star; his father wasn't a president (nor was his spouse), and yet he made it all the way to the White House. As corny as it may sound, he embodied the American Dream and surrounded himself with people who did likewise. And so he inspired people—particularly those, like him, born without privilege—in a way that few others have.

The Democratic contenders who have followed him (including his wife) have struggled to connect with black voters beyond the message of "I'm a Democrat, so you should vote for me." This has reinforced a sense among younger black Americans that the party has grown complacent in its quest to earn their support. When I asked a number of prominent black Americans if they believe the current Democratic Party takes black voters for granted, the consensus was yes. Russell Simmons is blunt. "They have and they do."[12] Alexis McGill, the political scientist and consultant who has worked for Democratic candidates, says, "Absolutely."[13] Even Democratic elected officials who hesitate to use the phrase "taken for granted" agree that there is a growing disconnect. Congressman Artur Davis (D-AL) says that at times the party has lacked an appreciation for the "seriousness of black voters. And when I say that I mean this: the black voters want to know what your positions are on issues. Black voters want to know what you're going to do. Black voters want to know what you've done and how you got it done. That's kind of the same thing white people want to know. And I think occasionally there's been a tendency on the part of Democratic candidates to not take seriously the seriousness of black voters."[14]

According to our survey, 32 percent of black Americans ages eighteen to forty-five do not believe "that the Democratic Party works as hard to earn the support of black voters as it does to earn the support of other groups of voters." Another 17 percent are unsure. This means that more than half of voters in this demographic are not confident that Democrats value the support of black Americans as much as they value that of other groups.[15]

While the issue of black voters feeling taken for granted by Democrats is not new, it is emerging as a defining political issue for one simple reason. Older black Americans may feel that politically speaking they have no other options (Julian Bond argued that our political system gives us "a bad choice and a better choice, not a bad choice and a perfect choice"), but younger black voters don't.[16] This is forcing Democrats to grapple with the reality that simply reminding people to vote for you just before Election Day is not the same as proving to them that you are deserving of their votes in the years between elections. It is also serving as a reminder that last-minute campaign tactics cannot take the place of a genuine long-term commitment to the communities whose support you are seeking.

As a child, Bill Clinton watched the primary customers at his grandfather's store—black Americans—and listened as his grandparents expressed their support for integration, an oddity among poor white southerners at the time. Clinton's relationship with black America was therefore cultivated over a lifetime and did not have to be created from scratch on the campaign trail. The immense influence of those early years can be seen on the dedication page of his memoir *My Life*: "And to the memory of my grandfather, who taught me to look up to people others looked down on, because we're not so different after all."[17] One cannot overestimate the role this early experience played in fostering his close relationship with the community through the years, and it stands in stark contrast to some who have attempted to follow in his footsteps, whose backgrounds are more like the *current* president's than the former president's.

Clinton's vice president and the 2000 Democratic nominee, Al Gore, is a fellow southerner but, unlike Clinton, the son of a senator. He grew up in a world of Washington privilege. As a graduate of the elite St. Albans School for boys in Washington, D.C., and Harvard University, Gore had little opportunity to interact with black Americans on a daily basis, especially not on an equal playing field. Furthermore, his father, Al Gore, Sr., had the distinction of being one of the Democratic southern senators who opposed the Civil Rights Act of 1964.

This is not to say that Vice President Gore lacks a genuine concern for black Americans and civil rights. In fact, he was the first major party presidential candidate to name a black American, Donna Brazile, as his campaign manager. But as many noted during the campaign, his background is remarkably like that of George W. Bush, who was also the son of a powerful politician, attended an elite private school, and then headed off to the Ivy League. In other words, no one would expect Al Gore to know all three verses of "Lift Every Voice and Sing." Like John Kerry but unlike Bush, Gore had at least some experience with black Americans during his service in Vietnam. Still, despite his best intentions, his privileged background created a cultural handicap for Gore in his interactions with black voters.

Ondre, a business student, admires Gore and would consider supporting him for president again—depending on who his opponents are—but feels Gore is severely lacking in his ability to connect with black voters. When asked to explain why, Ondre replies, "Clinton didn't come from a privileged background. Everybody else really came from a privileged background and I think that's key to being able to relate to a group of people, be they poor or black or whatever. Al Gore's father was a millionaire senator. All these guys were born with silver spoons in their mouths so I don't think they could relate to being black in this country or poor in this country."[18]

This privilege gap was evident among the Democratic primary candidates in 2004. The eventual nominee, Senator John Kerry of Massachusetts, unwittingly sparked a backlash by attempting to capitalize on Clinton's warm relationship with black Americans. In a March 2004 interview with the American Urban Radio Network, Kerry said that "President Clinton was often known as the first black president. I wouldn't be upset if I could earn the right to be the second." Instead of drawing flattering or at least humorous press coverage, Kerry found himself defending his right to inherit Clinton's legacy.

During the 2004 campaign, Donna Brazile said of Kerry's quest to become heir to Clinton's throne,

> That's a very steep hill to climb. Clinton bonded with African-Americans and they never, ever left him. I saw some internal polls recently. Clinton's favorable rating with black people was at 91 percent in 2000, 92 percent in 2002 and 94 percent this year. It will take years for John Kerry to build that kind of credibility with black voters. Clinton started in high school. He knew the verses at Baptist services. He knew the songs. He knew how to do the Electric Slide! Now, Kerry looks presidential and acts presidential, and African-Americans will be open to that. And if he can learn to dance and sway like Clinton, Kerry can get there.[19]

Paula Diane Harris, founder of the Andrew Young National Center for Social Change (named for civil rights legend and former Ambassador Andrew Young), was less kind. She responded to Kerry's statement by saying, "John Kerry is not a black man—he is a privileged white man who has no idea what it is to be a poor white in this country, let alone a black man."[20]

While Kerry's parents were apparently not rich, his extended family financed an upbringing for him that included summers at a Forbes family estate in France. The family traced its lineage to European royalty. Like Al Gore as well as George W. Bush, Kerry was educated at an elite prep school before heading off to the Ivy League, in his case Yale. But Kerry shared more than a fraternity brotherhood with the man who beat him to the White House: Bush and Kerry are distant relatives.[21] Kerry later married Teresa Heinz, heir (by a previous marriage) to the Heinz ketchup fortune. Like Gore, Kerry probably encountered few black Americans in his youth, especially poor ones. While he did not experience any "macaca" moments on the campaign trail, the skepticism his candidacy faced among black voters was evident in even the smallest campaign moments.

During an appearance on MTV's *Choose or Lose* Kerry was asked if there were "any trends out there in music, or even in popular culture in general, that have piqued your interest." Kerry replied, "Oh sure. I follow and I'm interested. I don't always like, but I'm interested. I mean, I never was into heavy metal. I didn't really like it. I'm fascinated by rap and by hip-hop. I think there's a lot of poetry in it. There's a lot of anger, a lot of social energy in it. And I think you'd better listen to it pretty carefully, 'cause it's important."[22] The ridicule this response garnered marked a rare instance when conservatives and fans of hip-hop found something to agree on.

Rush Limbaugh remarked, "Can't you just see old J. F. Kerry and Teresa Heinz riding around in the Range Rover at one of their mansions with hip-hop playing?" While it's hardly surprising that Limbaugh was critical of a Democratic candidate, it is surprising that his criticism echoed the hip-hop community's. (Limbaugh also seemed to be in tune with some high-profile members of the black community when he remarked, "Kerry goes to church every now and then for photo-ops, but he only goes to black churches. Why is it that Democrat candidates only show up at black churches during the campaign, yet never step foot in one after they're elected? I've answered my own question simply by asking it.")[23]

The hip-hop website SOHH dedicated an online forum to the subject "Is Kerry being truthful or just pandering to the youth vote?" While some responses were a little too colorful to reprint, a sampling summarizes the readership's reaction:

> "You know damn well he doesn't like hiphop. He's just saying it to gain votes. It's plain and simple."

> "It's not sincere if he just says he likes hiphop to gain votes, oppose to saying it because he really does get 'fascinated' by it. Full of [expletive]. . . ."

> "I heard on Hot97 this morning that John Kerry said he was 'fascinated with hiphop music.' LOL. What a bad way to gain the hiphop community's votes. VOTE FOR BUSH."

> "I agree he [Kerry] is full of **** for that and that botox work he did on his face really makes him seem insincere b/c he has no facial expression whatsoever. However, if Big Bird

were running for President with elmo as his VP, I still wouldn't vote for Dubya."[24]

(One post noted with amusement that another candidate, General Wesley Clark, claimed to be a fan of the hip-hop group Outkast.)

The whole forum spoke to the larger issue that Kerry's interest in a largely black form of music and culture was immediately deemed inauthentic and opportunistic—even by those who grudgingly said they would vote for him anyway. Now imagine that Bill Clinton had given the same interview and said that he found rap and hip-hop "fascinating." Let's say he took it a step further and specified that he liked a few songs by rappers 50 Cent or the Game. Would there have been criticism or controversy? Possibly. But it would not have revolved around whether his comments were sincere. More likely, conservatives like Rush Limbaugh would have criticized him for publicly endorsing artists whose lyrics and lifestyles do not sit well with much of Middle America. But no one would have questioned his authenticity. Ironically, Clinton helped solidify his positioning as a moderate by picking a fight with rapper Sister Souljah, when he criticized comments she made about white Americans. (The exchange gave birth to a political catchphrase, "Sister Souljah moment," defined by Wikipedia as "a politician's public repudiation of an allegedly extremist person, statement, or position perceived to have some association with the politician or their party. Such an act of repudiation is designed to signal to centrist voters that the politician is not beholden to traditional, and sometimes unpopular, interest groups associated with the party. Though, such a repudiation runs the risk of alienating some of the politician's allies and the party's base voters.")[25]

Kerry came across to many black voters as aloof at best and inauthentic at worst, a cardinal sin for someone who claimed Clinton's mantle as the "second black president." For many young black voters, the rationale for supporting Kerry became simply that he wasn't George Bush, not exactly the ringing endorsement a candidate hopes to hear from his alleged base.

Charizma, a twenty-something who once worked on Wall Street, says that what fueled her vote for Kerry was that she "didn't like George Bush. I felt like it was the lesser of two evils."[26] When asked to explain why he felt that John Kerry was less successful in connecting with black voters than Clinton was, Joel (a recent college graduate who was the first in his family to attend) says the answer is simple, "John Kerry is another son of privilege." Therefore he "doesn't know how" to relate to black voters. "He doesn't have any real experience. He spends his vacation on skis. He doesn't have the experience of a Bill Clinton. John Kerry doesn't have a Vernon Jordan as a friend."[27] Ondre, the MBA student, adds, "He was born with a silver spoon in his mouth" and therefore could not be "in the trenches" with blacks "like Clinton could." Ondre adds that Kerry "could probably tolerate" blacks enough to include them in his cabinet or policy decisions, but the word "tolerate" makes it clear that he doesn't think Kerry would necessarily be comfortable doing so.[28]

But if Kerry's performance on the campaign trail demonstrated that he was out of touch with black voters, one of his competitors demonstrated that he was practically out of this universe. Like Kerry, Howard Dean was born into a world of privilege, a fact that contrasted greatly with his campaign trail image as a small-town doctor turned small-state governor. A scion of a wealthy New York family, Dean attended the elite St. George's School, whose alumni include George W. Bush's grandfather Prescott Bush, before heading to Yale University. Given their nearly identical backgrounds, it should come as no surprise that Dean had something else in common with the president he was seeking to defeat. George W. Bush's grandmother was a bridesmaid in Howard Dean's grandmother's wedding.[29] This fact speaks volumes about how the world that shaped Howard Dean differs from the world that shaped Bill Clinton.

This is not to say that those from privileged backgrounds should not be welcomed into the political process. None of us has any control over the circumstances of our birth. But Senator Kerry and Governor Dean both struggled to grasp the idea that connecting with people who are different from you requires a strong commitment to doing so.

During his run for the 2004 Democratic nomination, Dean sparked a firestorm when he was quoted as saying, in an interview with Iowa's *Des Moines Register*, "I still want to be the candidate for guys with Confederate flags in their pickup trucks."[30] While references to the Confederate flag are a known sore spot for the black community, many black Americans were even more disturbed by Dean's response to the criticism his comment ignited, which showed that he was not even aware of having said anything controversial. His staff initially tried to squelch the matter by pointing out that Dean had said this before without garnering extensive media attention. This could possibly be one of the few instances in which a presidential campaign attempted to improve a candidate's standing by volunteering to reporters that he exercised poor judgment not just once but multiple times.

The response from his opponents, who rushed to seize their first real chance at knocking Dean off his front-runner perch, was almost as much of a train wreck as the comment itself. Dripping with moral indignation, they all played a variation on the same theme: "I may be out of touch, but I'm not as out of touch as *that* guy." (Which is a little like someone who doesn't approve of his daughter dating interracially pointing to a Klan member and saying, "At least I'm not him.") Dean's closest competitor, eventual nominee Senator John Kerry, said, "Howard Dean is justifying his pandering to the NRA by saying his opposition to an assault weapons ban allows him to pander to lovers of the Confederate flag. It is simply unconscionable for Howard Dean to embrace the most racially divisive symbol in America. I would rather be the candidate of the NAACP than the NRA." [31] Al Sharpton, one of two black candidates in the race (the other was former Senator Carol Moseley Braun), said, "If I said I wanted to be the candidate for people that ride around with helmets and swastikas, I would be asked to leave." [32]

For nearly a week—an eternity in the media-saturated world of presidential campaigns—Dean refused to apologize for the remarks. At the next presidential debate, when asked by one of his opponents if he was wrong for his initial statement, he looked into the cameras and replied, "No, I wasn't." He then attempted to defend his stance by adding, "People who vote, who fly the Confederate flag, I think they are wrong because the Confederate flag is a racist symbol. But I think there are a lot of poor people who fly that flag because the Republicans have been dividing us by race since 1968 with their southern race strategy. I am tired of being divided by race in this country. I want to go down to the South and talk to people who don't make any more than anybody else up North but keep voting Republican against their own economic interests."[33]

Sharpton, in a rare moment of measured calm, said of Dean, "I don't think the governor is a racist. I think some of his positions would have hurt us. When Clinton was found to be a member of a white-only country club, he apologized. You are not a bigot, but you appear to be too arrogant to say 'I'm wrong' and go on."[34]

The debate over Dean's remarks struck a particular nerve in South Carolina. For years, the NAACP has been leading a nationwide boycott of South Carolina because it continues to fly the Confederate flag over its capitol, a practice that became "traditional" in 1962 as the state's official answer to the civil rights movement. Moreover, South Carolina is the only state in the Deep South that is truly in play in the early primaries. It solidified its place as a make-or-break state when John McCain lost a bitter primary contest there to George W. Bush in 2000.

The *New York Times* called the state's battle over the flag "a second civil war." Lonnie Randolph, the South Carolina state NAACP chairman, said he was not offended by Dean's remark, as he believed that the former Vermont governor "didn't understand his own comments." Randolph added, "Probably more damaging than anything else is that he didn't want to apologize. It shows a degree of arrogance that I don't think people in public office can afford to have."[35]

Six days after the controversy began, Dean appeared on CNN's *American Morning* and said, "I think I made a mistake," a remark profound for its level of understatement. He continued, "I apologized for it. I think it's time to move on. The people who are most concerned about this are the people who are with us. I think we'll be fine."[36] But South Carolina State Senator John Matthews, a black Democrat, told the *New York Times* he considered Dean's apology less than sincere: "I think he only apologized after he checked the polls and with his supporters in this state." He also argued that the white voters Dean was attempting to woo with his flag comment were unwooable. "I don't think it'd bring anything to the table to go after those voters. They will never support Howard Dean. Most of the people supporting the Confederate flag tend to be right-wing, anti-African-American, anti-Jewish, anti-everything. Believe me—I live here. I know."[37]

This really gets at the heart of what was so discouraging about Dean's flag debacle. No one believes he harbors any ill will toward black Americans. But his inability to grasp some of the most fundamental emotional triggers associated with America's complicated racial history showed how out of touch he is with the African American experience. Even a black voter with no strong opinion about politics in general is likely to have a strong opinion on the Confederate flag.

As Sharpton pointed out, as soon as Clinton received criticism for belonging to an all-white country club, he immediately apologized, acknowledging the weight of his actions, and thus allowed his campaign to move on. Furthermore, he never would have carelessly (or callously) tossed around Confederate flag symbolism. As a southerner who grew up in Arkansas and saw the flag used by the crowds protesting the Little Rock Nine as they attempted to integrate Central High School, he would have known that no matter what audience he was trying to reach, the flag is not an acceptable bridge because its very essence is divisiveness.

Two months later, when the issue was raised during the primary's so-called Black and Brown Debate emphasizing issues pertinent to black Americans and Latin Americans, it became clear that the Confederate flag issue represented more than an isolated political misstep. Al Sharpton had made campaign fodder of Dean's comments since the media firestorm around them began. (Sharpton lobbed one of his more colorful zingers while campaigning in Washington, D.C., commenting on how Dean's record as governor might translate into Supreme Court appointments. "We don't know exactly what the Supremes would look like under his watch, but I am betting it won't be Diana Ross. If we are not careful, those guys with the Confederate flags on the back of their pickups could be wearing black robes instead of white ones.")[38]

The Black and Brown Debate allowed candidates to pose questions to one another, and Sharpton challenged Dean on his record of hiring minorities for senior positions within his administration as governor of Vermont. He orchestrated one of the evening's defining moments by getting Dean to admit that his administration had no African Americans or Latinos in cabinet or senior policymaking positions: "In the state of Vermont—where you were governor '97, '99, 2001—not one black or brown held a senior policy position, not one. You yourself said we must do something about it. Nothing was done."[39] Sharpton concluded, "I think if you're talking—if you want to lecture people on race, you ought to have the background and track record in order to do that. And I think that clearly people—governors import talent, governors reach all over the country to make sure they have diversity. And I think that, while I respect the fact you brought race into this campaign, you ought to talk freely and openly about whether you went out of the box to try to do something about race in your home state and have experience with working with blacks and browns at peer level, not as just friends you might have had in college."[40]

What was particularly ironic about this exchange is that while two Democrats debated whether or not one of them was committed to diversity in his administration, a sitting Republican president was watching the intraparty fighting flanked by two black Americans he had appointed to historic positions—secretary of state and national security adviser.

Howard Dean did not become the Democratic nominee, and mistakes made on the campaign trail tend to fall under an honorary statute of limitations after which the media move on to the next story and the public forgets. But few could have predicted just how relevant Dean's record on staffing would become. A year after his presidential campaign came to an end, Dean succeeded Terry McAuliffe as chairman of the Democratic National Committee.[41]

This is significant because one of the greatest, yet least talked about, obstacles to the post–Clinton Democratic Party's ability to connect with black voters is its lack of diversity in senior staffing and leadership. In a February 2005 interview with the *Minnesota Spokesman-Recorder,* K. C. Morrison, a political scientist at the University of Missouri, observes that black Americans have not enjoyed real power within the Democratic National Committee since the late Ron Brown was chairman from 1989 to 1991. "I think it remains to be seen, the extent to which blacks will become leaders, at least at this iteration of the party. We haven't achieved that level of leadership since [Brown's tenure]." He adds, "The party is in a desperate situation in trying to find a way out of its minority situation. We should expect to have a greater role and greater presence." The same piece quotes Howard Dean as making greater diversity within the DNC a priority of his tenure. "My thought is on how to fully integrate on every level. The way we'll deal with that is the same way that we deal with diversity at the DNC. When you put people in charge of operations at the DNC who are people of color, then you'll have a much better likelihood that people [of color] will be hired."[42]

To his credit, Dean has made efforts to follow through on this commitment. After months of discussions, the Democratic National Committee failed to make Dean available for an interview for this book by deadline but permitted me to talk with Amaya Smith, a DNC spokesperson who is African American. Smith commends Dean for demonstrating a commitment to diverse staffing practices during his tenure. She credits him with recognizing the "brilliance" of Cornell Belcher (the DNC pollster) and appointing him to such a historic role, along with others. Belcher echoes this sentiment, pointing to the Democratic National

Committee's current communications director, Karen Finney, who is African American, and deputy political director Rodney Shelton.[43]

Belcher acknowledges that achieving diversity remains a challenge. He says that if you're African American and working in America, you may have to try harder than the next guy to get ahead—even in Democratic politics. "It is part of the larger struggle. When I was working at the DCCC [Democratic Congressional Campaign Committee], I had to fight. When you're working on a campaign, you've got to fight. Where in America, corporate America, political America, where in America don't African Americans have to put up this fight?" When I asked him if perhaps the Democratic Party should be held to a higher standard than, say, Morgan Stanley when it comes to demonstrating a commitment to diversity (particularly since Morgan Stanley has never claimed to represent the interests of black Americans), he paused before answering. "I think the Democratic Party wouldn't say we are representing black interests. I think we'd say we are trying to represent all American interests, particularly that of working families."[44]

A 2007 article in the online magazine *Politico* notes, "Given how black voters overwhelmingly support Democratic candidates, the dearth of black national political consultants is remarkably low, say several top African American consultants."[45] One African American political operative who has worked on presidential campaigns (he requested anonymity due to his ongoing relationships with various Democratic candidates and leaders) describes the problem as an intrinsic part of campaign culture.

"There is a small group of political operatives and consultants that work on these statewide and national campaigns and they are almost exclusively white."[46] This sentiment is shared by Cornell Belcher, who was quoted in the *Politico* piece as saying, "You'd be hard-pressed to find more than four or five consultants of color, black or Hispanic, at the top levels of the field. It's still a very closed, closed world."[47]

The anonymous source goes on to explain that campaigns often have no African Americans in senior campaign positions, or if they do, they tend to hire one black senior staff member and give him or her a deputy title, as in deputy communications director or deputy field director. Often this means the staffer is given responsibility for handling all issues related to the black community.[48] Campaigns (and some high-ranking elected officials) are sometimes nervous about putting an African American in a sufficiently prominent position where they will become the visible face of a campaign because they fear this might alienate other voting groups. In other words, a black campaign spokesperson may not play so well with white male swing voters in Ohio.

An even bigger problem regarding staffing diversity is the same one that plagues other competitive fields. People like to think of politics as an idealistic realm, but just as in other professional domains, most hiring decisions are not based on how qualified you are but who you know. Just as in every other industry from banking to law, if you are an upper-middle-class white person and most of the people you surround yourself with are the same, then the network from which you receive referrals will be primarily white.

A former DNC official (who also requested anonymity due to ongoing work in national politics) adds that there is another hurdle to diversity in politics that no one likes to talk about: the financial instability that is often part of the climb up the political ladder. Like many other competitive, glamorous fields such as fashion or filmmaking, politics favors those who can live on next to nothing and be prepared to move at the drop of a hat. "Politics is sort of like the equivalent of working in the mailroom waiting for your big break in Hollywood." Often you can't "pick up and move to different states unless you have a financial cushion to do so."[49]

Dean's recent efforts are a step in the right direction, but to fully remedy the diversity dilemma, Dean and the rest of the party leadership must be willing to put their money where their mouths are. A fundamental problem in the political hiring process is that jobs on campaigns, and even in the offices of elected officials, are extremely low paying or even no paying, beginning as voluntary positions or internships. (This problem is not exclusive to the Democratic Party but exists throughout politics and government and other ultra-competitive fields, including media. A 2004 report from the Congressional Management Foundation noted that blacks hold less than 5 percent of the policy jobs in the U.S. Senate and less than 7 percent of Washington-based staff positions in the House of Representatives.) The result is that those who are able to secure entry-level jobs and begin the long climb up the campaign or legislative ladder often have the financial support necessary to do so. In other words, those whose parents can subsidize their son or daughter's idealism (or their own personal dream of saying, "My kid works at the White House") have a built-in advantage. On high-profile campaigns, where the competition for jobs is particularly fierce, overwhelmingly these individuals are neither minorities nor poor.

Just as Sharpton challenged Dean over the lack of minorities in his administration, he could have challenged any of the other candidates on the absence of minorities on their field staffs in Iowa and New Hampshire, or in senior positions on their national staffs. Had he posed the question, "Can you point to a *senior*-level spokesperson, foreign policy adviser, or communications director on your campaign staff who is black or brown?" to any of the other candidates, Dean's record would hardly have been the only casualty in that evening's debate.

The former DNC official says the Kerry campaign was emblematic of this. This source describes the Kerry campaign as, "Very white. Not diverse at all." But the source adds, "It was not out of malice. They're doing what they know. You find this sometimes with liberal whites because their voting record is good and the work that they do and public service is good, so they say judge me by my record and what I do not by who I hire." The source comments that while the issue was raised with Kerry's campaign by influential black Democrats, it was not taken seriously, at least not before it was too late.[50]

It is worth noting that among the current crop of Democratic presidential contenders there is a noticeable measure of staff diversity—at least among two of them. According to the Associated Press, "Not unsurprisingly, those campaigns with the most women and minorities among top staff members are Democrats Hillary Rodham Clinton and Barack Obama." Senator Clinton's closest circle of advisers is a diverse group of women who include an Indian American and an African American, among others. Her campaign manager, Patti Solis Doyle (who has worked for Senator Clinton since the 1992 presidential campaign), is Hispanic. Obama's senior team includes six minorities, including an African American policy director, pollster, and political director. Additionally, his national field director is Hispanic and his spokesperson, Bill Burton, is biracial, like the candidate himself. Unfortunately, according to the article, the campaigns of the other candidates pale in comparison—literally. The diversity of the Clinton and Obama campaigns reinforces a larger point: diversity in leadership tends to manifest greater diversity, an idea the party as a whole has at times struggled to grasp.[51]

The issue of staffing diversity is not merely a philosophical debate. A candidate's staff sets the tone for how that candidate will approach the issues relevant to a particular community, especially if the candidate has limited personal experience with that community.[52] The former DNC official notes that when a campaign lacks diversity, minority communities "tend to get treated as an afterthought." The official specifically points to how media buys on stations targeting predominantly black audiences were not addressed until the very last minute.[53]

Congressman Davis explains, "There's been a tendency [among Democrats] to think, 'Oh we can mobilize black kids to vote if we send out a rapper.' Or, 'We can mobilize black people to vote if we just hire some people to go out and get some absentee ballots.' Or, 'If we do some hip-hop ads basically and if we come up with a theme for our candidate that people might want to dance to, well, they'll vote for that person.' Every now and then there's been a tendency to think that you can practice those kinds of politics in the community." From his perspective, "most Democratic candidates don't think that but there are always a few who think that and sometimes it's very easy in the final weeks of a campaign just to do what you've done before with respect to get out the vote activity."[54]

Russell Simmons, the hip-hop mogul who has been a prominent donor to Democratic campaigns, cites the lack of diversity among Democratic leaders as one of the party's greatest problems, and one that has caused it to fall short in the policy arena. In his book *Do You,* he criticizes the party's commitment to policies to uplift the poor: "I attribute the Democrats' lack of will to the fact that their leadership is still too far removed from the people they want to help." He notes how stunning the lack of diversity has been at events he has attended over the years: "When I go to Democratic fund-raisers, I'm often alarmed by how few black people are there. Or by how few Asians or Latinos are either. I once walked out of a very big Democratic strategy meeting in New York City because of the nearly one thousand people there, almost all were white. They were talking about empowering people, but none of the people they were going to empower were present to hear them. A barbecue at Dick Cheney's house would probably look more inclusive than that fund-raiser!"[55] I asked Simmons if he feels a lack of diversity is still hindering Democrats and he replied, "Of course it is! Because the people always want to help the people, but don't want to hang out with us. You can't help people if you don't know them." He adds, "You can help them some, but you can help them more effectively, if you know them and if you know the issue. . . . You can have a general idea, but you can't have a real understanding, without talking to the people."[56]

While candidates can continue to shape their personas to appeal to various voting blocs, at the end of the day, if they are not surrounding themselves with people who are representative of the voters they are seeking to represent, they will fail. For instance, it is highly unlikely that if African Americans had been holding *senior* campaign staff positions, Dean would have handled the Confederate flag debacle so poorly. Senator Biden would probably have been less inclined to use "clean" as a term of endearment for a black candidate, particularly a fellow senator, or to follow that comment up with an equally embarrassing blunder months later. According to the *Washington Post*, "Biden attempted to explain why some schools perform better than others—for instance, in Iowa, as compared to Washington, D.C. 'There's less than one percent of the population of Iowa that is African American,' said Biden."[57]

Source A goes on to say that the Democratic Party has begun to lose the interest and loyalty of younger black voters because of its failure to notice that the issues that matter to that audience have begun to change. The reason it failed to notice is that it does not have enough post–civil rights generation black Americans in senior staffing positions to convey this. He adds, "The issue is not so much there are not enough black faces. There are not enough black faces in high-ranking positions as key decision-makers. There's nobody running anything." When I asked him what—if anything—might turn the tide, he said that one of two things has to happen. Either candidates will begin to lose black votes, or a cadre of prominent black donors and fund-raisers will need to emerge who begin to ask why they are raising $250,000 for a candidate who is not spending any of that money on minority consultants or strategists.[58]

There were many prominent black staffers in the Bill Clinton era, he explains, not only because of Clinton's commitment to diversity but also because of Jesse Jackson's campaign. "If you look at people who were there before, most of those folks came out of Jesse's camp: Mignon Moore, Donna Brazile, Alexis Herman—a lot of those folks came from Jesse. Jesse did something that most black elected political folks have not done since, which is mentor young leadership." But over the years Jackson's protégés have begun to do what most seasoned political operatives eventually do. They leverage their political experience into lucrative career opportunities, including some beyond the political arena, and with each passing year their presence becomes less visible in the day-to-day operations of high-profile campaigns. This, combined with the fact that President Clinton has been out of office for nearly a decade, has resulted in young black Americans beginning to lose a pipeline into the political field.[59]

This disconnect, the source says, is evident in the messages the party uses to try to reach black voters. "I think when people have traditionally campaigned in our communities, they consistently talk about schools and crime—and all that's important, but now there's a much greater need . . . to have the same conversation they do in white communities, around property taxes, education but talked about in a different way, investment opportunities, home ownership—all the things that you would not necessarily come to our community to discuss, you now have to talk about."[60]

Congressman Davis shares an anecdote that illustrates this point. In response to a question about whether the party's ability to connect with black voters has suffered since Bill Clinton left the White House, he tells a story of a prominent white Democratic politician (whom he declined to name) who was invited to speak before an audience of black investment bankers, stockbrokers, and other financial service professionals shortly after Hurricane Katrina. The politician was asked to talk about the Democratic Party's relevance to the audience's interests. Instead, he spent his entire speech "talking about reauthorization of the Voting Rights Act and about Katrina. At the end of the speech, the first question from an audience member was, 'Do you have any interest in addressing the things that people in this room are dealing with day in and day out?'" Davis says there is an important moral to the story. "It makes the point that every now and then our leaders tend to think that there's a 'black message,' and they frame a black message that is all-purpose and invariably consists of whatever is the issue that seems to be impacting black people," a type of stereotyping that he refers to as "lazy thinking."[61]

Cornell Belcher, the DNC pollster and a thirty-something member of the post–civil rights generation, believes the Democratic Party is slowly but surely undergoing an awakening. He explains that one of the most important steps has been convincing the leadership to see black voters as "persuasive voters" (voters in need of persuasion) rather than GOTV (get out the vote) voters.

As a testament to the difference diversity in staffing and leadership can make, Belcher notes that he and Donna Brazile have been instrumental in driving this message home to party leaders. Belcher and Smith, the DNC spokesperson, both credit Howard Dean with bringing people of color into the hiring process so that their voices can be heard on these issues.[62]

When I asked Sharpton how he would rate Dean's leadership as DNC chair, three years after he challenged Dean's record on diversity, he was not as generous. On a scale of one to ten, he gave Dean a five: "A lot of progressive people that supported Dean have said to me, 'You know, you were right about Dean. . . .' A lot of them said, 'You know, I thought you were too harsh on him. But now he's the chair of the party. Show me where we've gained in the black community.'"[63]

In 2005 Russell Simmons gave a similarly skeptical assessment, telling the *New York Daily News,* "When it comes to reaching out to poor people and minorities, I think there's no enthusiasm on Howard's part, while Ken [Mehlman, former chair of the Republican National Committee] shows a real willingness to listen." When I asked Simmons if he still feels that way, he responded, "I don't think any of the leading Democrats have proven that they are committed to lifting people out of poverty in a meaningful way."[64]

In the eyes (and hopes) of many, the Democratic candidates running in 2008 represent the best chance the party has had in years to recapture the Bill Clinton glory days. There's only one problem. Make that three.

In this election cycle, three candidates embody the characteristics that made Clinton so appealing to black voters over the years. One candidate has the Clinton southern charm. One has the Clinton name. And one candidate is actually black.

The problem of course is that only one can get the nomination.

Former senator and 2004 vice presidential nominee John Edwards, an attractive native southerner, comes closest to embodying Clinton's all-American, everyman, If-I-can-make-it-you-can-too persona. Like Clinton, he grew up in a working-class southern family that was atypical for its openness to black Americans, an experience that helped shape his outlook on the campaign trail, including his early denunciation of the Confederate flag during the 2004 campaign. While in almost any other election year he might have found himself the front-runner, this year his campaign has been overshadowed by two candidates who out-Clinton him—one literally.

When speculation began building that Senator Clinton would indeed run for president, some predicted that her candidacy would fulfill the dreams of black Americans who were still mourning the former president's departure from the White House, particularly after years of an increasingly partisan atmosphere and an increasingly draining war. It has long been apparent that however brilliant she may be, when it comes to personality and charisma, Hillary is not Bill; but the expectation was that since she is married to him, she doesn't need to be. His presence was supposed to be enough to inspire the hopes, dreams, and most importantly the votes of black Americans, thus ensuring that a president named Bush would again be followed by a president named Clinton. The only scenario the Clinton camp didn't anticipate was the emergence of a viable candidate who could out-black the former president. Someone like Reverend Sharpton they could prepare for; at best he would be a fringe candidate catering to a handful of black voters in the primaries. What they did not count on was the emergence of a black candidate with the sterling academic credentials possessed by both Clintons, and the charisma possessed by one.

Early polls showed Senator Clinton leading among black voters, but as the campaign began in earnest, these voters began to move toward Barack Obama. The prominent black political operative interviewed for this book noted that there is something very Clintonesque about Barack Obama that has helped fuel the excitement about his candidacy. After eight years of President Bush, whose intellect and communication skills have been the butt of so many jokes, people are thrilled to find a candidate who is bright and thoughtful yet also charming—like Bill Clinton. Obama also has Clinton's gift for communicating in a way that connects with people. "He speaks in paragraphs instead of sound bites, and that's a very subtle distinction. He has this very Clintonesque way of speaking, like he's talking to you across a dinner table, and that stimulates a way of thinking in his audience that a lot of politicians don't necessarily do." (This operative is not affiliated with one specific presidential campaign.)[65]

Senator Clinton, like her husband, has a solid record of appointing blacks to senior positions (including Maggie Williams as her chief of staff during the White House years), but she lacks her husband's easy rapport with black voters of all ages, income levels, and backgrounds. Instead she has struggled to find a natural voice in which to address black voters beyond her husband's shadow. The question has never been whether Hillary cares about black Americans but whether she can connect with them.

The differences between Bill and Hillary have been magnified at high-profile events. At a January 2006 celebration of Martin Luther King's birthday, Hillary drew fire for comparing the GOP–controlled House of Representatives to a "plantation." While Al Sharpton and Barack Obama defended the comment, it drew heavy media coverage and some pointed criticism. Republican Congressman (and fellow New Yorker) Peter King said, "It's definitely using the race card. It definitely has racist connotations. She knows it. She knew the audience. She knew what she was trying to say, and it was wrong. And she should be ashamed." First Lady Laura Bush called the comment "ridiculous."[66] As I watched the firestorm unfold, I asked, (1) Why is Laura Bush weighing in? and (2) If Bill Clinton had said this, would it have been a news story?

Journalists seemed less shocked by the word choice than by the source. Even those who agreed with the statement thought it had an odd sound rolling off of Hillary's tongue. On some levels, watching Hillary trying to whip up a black church into an amen frenzy seems about as normal as watching Laura Bush play the sax on a late night talk show—not out of the question but definitely unusual.

Saturday Night Live parodied the remark in a sketch that depicted it as a clear effort to pander to the black vote. The sketch insinuated that had Clinton been trying to pander to Latino voters she would have replaced the word plantation with "landscaping business," and had she been wooing Jewish voters she would have said "concentration camp." At one point there's a reference to figure skating and efforts to pander to gay voters. (You fill in the punch line.)[67]

If Bill Clinton had made such a comment, it might have warranted a brief flurry of comment in a few political blogs and maybe a couple of local news stations, but of all the things done and said during his presidency, *that* would not have warranted a *Saturday Night Live* sketch. It is doubtful that anyone would have accused Bill Clinton of playing the race card by mentioning plantations.

The contrast between the two Clintons was also on display at the funeral for civil rights icon Coretta Scott King. Their different speeches, and the reception each received, became the subject of a *New York Times* piece entitled, "On Podium, Some Say, Mrs. Clinton Is No Mr. Clinton." In the article, everyone from Republican pollster Frank Luntz to former New York Governor Mario Cuomo (a legendary speaker in his own right) assess the immense strengths of the former president's delivery and the weaknesses in the senator's. According to the piece,

> Like her husband, Hillary Rodham Clinton can work a room, remembering names and personal details, and dazzling acquaintances along the way. And like Bill Clinton, she can master arcane details of public policy, wowing experts in several fields. But as a public speaker, Hillary Rodham Clinton is no Bill Clinton, and that became all too

apparent at Coretta Scott King's funeral last week, when
the two made a rare public appearance together. The crowd
burst into boisterous applause and a standing ovation as
Mr. Clinton took the stage and delivered his address, off
the cuff, with what many said was the mellifluence of a
preacher. But when it was Mrs. Clinton's turn at the micro-
phone, the room became more subdued, as she offered
more formal remarks, in her characteristically deliberate
and measured style.[68]

The piece continues, "To her critics and admirers, the moment was a reminder that for all her skills as a politician, Mrs.
Clinton is not known for her ability to move people with the
power of her oratory, something that could prove a liability
should she run for the presidency in 2008."[69]

When Clinton began her run for the White House, the comparisons continued. Perhaps the greatest testament to how large
her husband's shadow looms was evident at the forty-second anniversary of Bloody Sunday, the day civil rights protesters were
attacked as they attempted to march from Selma to Montgomery, Alabama. The *New York Times* described the image as "an
extraordinary sight: the Clintons and Mr. Obama, two of them
competitors for the Democratic presidential nomination, walk-
ing—with two black congressman, and sometimes others, in
between them—down Martin Luther King Jr. Street to commemorate the footsteps of black demonstrators who were met
with violence as they tried to march to Montgomery to demand
civil rights in 1965." After the Clintons and Obama delivered

their remarks at two different locations, the *Times* christened the former president "arguably the most cadence-blessed speaker of the three."[70]

Where does this leave the Democratic Party's relationship with younger black voters? The consensus is that the answer rests heavily on how the 2008 primary season plays out. The former DNC official notes that Obama's candidacy could be one of the best things to happen to black voters in a long time, because it would force the Democratic establishment to devote more attention and more resources to appealing to black voters early on, rather than treating them as an afterthought. (This official is not affiliated with one specific presidential campaign.)[71] Some also speculate that what has fueled Obama mania among younger black Americans is largely his status as an outsider. It is no secret that the mainstream Democratic establishment had anointed Senator Clinton as its heir apparent. And while younger black Americans may not feel that her husband takes black voters for granted, he is not running.

Following the Democrats' devastating losses in the 2002 midterm elections, the online magazine *Salon* wrote that "the absence of Bill Clinton, who forged an extraordinary personal and political bond with African-Americans, may also be hurting the party when it comes to turnout." Morris Reid, a former Democratic Party operative (and now managing director of Westin Reinhart, a consulting firm), says of the 2002 losses, "Clearly Democrats were spoiled with Bill Clinton."[72] (It's worth noting that Democrats' wins in 2006 were due in large part to the apathy of conservatives, not the enthusiasm of black voters.)

In the *Salon* piece entitled "Did Blacks Stay Home?" Donna Brazile is quoted as saying, "My advice to Democratic candidates is: Stop the drive-by campaigns. Don't spend two years courting white voters and independents and the last two weeks courting black voters. African-American voters should not be taken for granted."[73] This is a sentiment shared by Mayor Cory Booker of Newark. Noting drive-by campaigns in his own state, he adds, "You see candidates that come by during the election and promise the world—I'm not going to talk about anybody—but literally, I remember some campaigns: 'Oh you're going to get universal health care, universal this, universal that,' and then find it very hard to deliver on the actual things they've been promising. I've seen people incredibly adroit and articulate in black churches getting communities going, preaching tired old phrases that I've heard for decades and then gone." He continues, "If you want to serve a community you've got to be connected to it in something more substantive than the flashy rhetoric of the campaign and I think the Democratic party has played some of the same records over and over again thinking my generation's going to dance to that beat and it's just not going to happen."[74] Shortly after our interview Booker endorsed Barack Obama for president. Months later he was joined by another up-and-coming black elected official in endorsing Obama—Massachusetts Governor Deval Patrick. (This endorsement was perhaps even more telling, since Patrick had served as Assistant Attorney General for Civil Rights in the Clinton administration.)

In the essay in which she calls Bill Clinton "the first black president," Toni Morrison explains the label this way: "African-American men seemed to understand it right away. Years ago, in the middle of the Whitewater investigation, one heard the first murmurs: white skin notwithstanding, this is our first black President. Blacker than any actual black person who could ever be elected in our children's lifetime."[75]

It remains to be seen if that will change in 2008.

Bakari Kitwana summarizes the feelings of many in the Hip-Hop Generation. While he has some criticisms of the former president's policies, he also feels that the he was one of a kind. "With Clinton, you can't bottle and reproduce that. It's like trying to have another Tupac."[76]

Chapter 4

THE RISE OF GENERATION OBAMA

How Obama Voters Are Reshaping American Politics

In politics there are certain people and organizations whose endorsements are so valuable that most candidates would readily sell their own mothers to get them. Some of the usual suspects include the National Rifle Association on the right and MoveOn.org on the left. There are also certain individuals from whom any candidate or elected official, regardless of political party, would be thrilled to get a personal thumbs-up.

They may not be political heavyweights, but you probably won't find any White House contender (at least of the male persuasion) who wouldn't love to have Halle Berry or Beyonce give him the time of day, let alone her support. Unfortunately for the other candidates, their hearts, at least politically speaking, belong to Barack Obama.

The 2008 campaign likely marks the first time in history that one presidential candidate has snared not one but two of *Maxim* magazine's Hot 100 Sexiest Women. In addition to charming both Catwoman and the Queen of Bootylicious, he also inspired one love-struck voter to create a song and accompanying video titled simply *I Got a Crush on Obama*. (Having viewed it, I am pretty sure Beyonce has nothing to worry about.) The idea of a heartthrob on the presidential campaign trail is amusing to both journalists and voters (mostly female) alike. Can you imagine someone broadcasting a declaration of love, in song or otherwise, for Bush or Kerry? Let's not even get started on Kucinich.

Entertainment value aside, this adulation of Barack Obama, a first-term senator whose name most Americans (including the president) struggle to pronounce, forces us to ask why.

In Hollywood they say an actor's career trajectory goes something like this:

Phase 1: Who is James Dean?

Phase 2: Let's see this James Dean kid.

Phase 3: Get me James Dean.

Phase 4: Get me a James Dean type—but younger.

Phase 5: What ever happened to James Dean?

Since it has long been said that politics is for people not attractive enough to make it in Hollywood, it's no surprise that political careers tend to follow a similar trajectory. A certain amount of dues paying—waiting tables and struggling—is supposed to take place between phases 1 and 3, but somehow Obama (at least on a national level) managed to pass seamlessly from a handful of supporting roles to his first Oscar nomination in record time. This accomplishment has confounded the political establishment, which despite Obama's growing momentum since his election to the Senate consistently assumed that he would idle in phase 2 at least long enough to make it convenient for the candidates waiting in the wings. (One political consultant remarks that while Obama's book may have been called *The Audacity of Hope,* to the Clinton camp it was more like "Who is this guy to have *The Audacity to Run?*")

To borrow a phrase from President Bush (something most Americans probably try to avoid doing), people woefully "misunderestimated him" and the growing Obama movement.[1]

Much has already been written about the many reasons Obama's candidacy has captured the American imagination. There is his diverse racial and cultural background, which allows just about every American to believe that he represents some part of them. There is his optimism, which is a breath of fresh air in a political climate ripe with name-calling and extreme partisanship. There is his forthrightness about his own weaknesses and flaws— something voters have become used to discovering through the media, not from the candidate himself. There is his apparently normal family life, not to mention his telegenic wife and young children. In other words, he's a likable guy. As my mom would say, he's "good people."

What has not been written about extensively is how Obama has inspired a new generation of young black voters, donors, and powerbrokers. For many of them, his candidacy has begun to restore their faith in a system they long ago dismissed as broken. Many had given up on ever making a tangible difference through the political process. The idea that a young black man could have a serious chance of becoming president has fueled a renewed sense of political purpose among many of these voters. If his candidacy fails, especially if he is the perceived victim of some injustice, the long-term effect on black political involvement could be devastating.

According to our survey research, one-quarter of black voters ages eighteen to forty-five say that Obama's candidacy has made them more likely to vote in the next presidential election, a notion that Obama appears to be well aware of.[2] According to the Associated Press, Obama was quoted as responding to a voter who questioned his ability to win a general election by saying, "I guarantee you African-American turnout, if I'm the nominee, goes up 30 percent around the country, minimum. . . . Young people's percentage of the vote goes up 25–30 percent. So we're in a position to put states in play that haven't been in play since LBJ."[3] The anonymous political operative (cited in the previous chapter) says that Obama has struck a chord with younger black voters in a way that no one—least of all the Clintons—had anticipated. He says that Obama conveys "a sense that he's the future of the Democratic Party and not something that we've seen before . . . rehashed in a different way." Obama effortlessly conveys the sense that "he represents the future in the fact that he's an African American, that he's young and the majority of this country feels that with all of the Sharptons and Jacksons of the world, this guy represents what we think the country has evolved into. I think that all of those factors create this since of hope and it inspires people. It's a look to the future instead of a rehashing of the past."[4]

Bakari Kitwana, who has written extensively on post–civil rights generation black Americans, recalls that Jesse Jackson's candidacy "was transformative in the lives of many young black men" and predicts that Obama's candidacy could prove similarly inspiring. He adds that Obama's candidacy differs from Jackson's in key ways. First and foremost, unlike Jackson and Sharpton before him, Obama is a sitting elected official, as opposed to an "activist," a term many Americans identify as code for "agitator." Second, Obama holds two Ivy League degrees, which demonstrates that he is not only intelligent but has the ability to succeed in elite environments. "When Barack first said he was going to run," Kitwana says, "I think within mainstream electoral politics many people felt 'this is just another black candidate' and the previous definition of what a black candidate is was Jesse Jackson and Al Sharpton. Now that the money is rolling in, people see that he is not just another black candidate. What we are seeing with Barack is unprecedented."[5]

A June 2007 *USA Today* article captures just how unprecedented the excitement among black Americans really is. While blacks have historically not comprised a large portion of the campaign donor pool (with some rare high-profile exceptions), Obama has inspired a great number of first-time black donors, including celebrities like jazz musician Branford Marsalis. But the article also reports that among a crucial group of donors—African Americans whose income is above the national average of $31,000 and are therefore more likely to contribute—Obama had carved out a sizable edge over Clinton. According to analysis of donations from six hundred zip codes nationwide (which *USA Today* describes as having "sizable numbers of black households with above-average incomes"), "Obama received about 70 percent of the donations that went to the two candidates from these areas." In some zip codes, the authors found, Obama received twenty-six contributions to six for Clinton.[6]

Clinton's campaign spokesperson dismissed the idea that such an advantage was significant, calling it unsurprising that Obama's candidacy would "tug on the heart" of black donors. He went on to add, "I'm taking nothing away from Obama as an emerging star, but if you look at this with heart and head, Hillary Clinton is the choice for African-Americans."[7]

Clearly it depends on whose heart and head are looking.

While Clinton has some high-powered African Americans in her corner (including Bob Johnson, founder of BET and one of the nation's first black billionaires), many of these supporters date back to her days as First Lady, some fifteen years ago, or to her first Senate campaign nearly a decade ago. Obama's donors tend to be people who were in college or grad school, or were still struggling with their first job during the Clinton administration. The race for donors in the so-called money primary, as well as the primary itself, has revealed a generational divide in the black political establishment, with those loyal to the honorary first black president and his wife in one corner, and those loyal to the man who may actually become the first black president in another. (Though it is worth noting that Bob Johnson's former wife and BET cofounder Sheila Johnson, who has previously supported both Clintons, has endorsed Obama.)

According to the anonymous African American political operative I interviewed, Obama's candidacy has benefited from a generational divide that has been festering for some time. But the old guard Democratic establishment, including the Clintons, has been slow if not inept at responding to it. This divide has allowed Obama to come out of nowhere and build the fund-raising apparatus that has kept him competitive—far more so than anyone initially expected—catching the Clintons off guard. He explains that the Clinton team always knew that a large segment of the population would never vote for her, with her unfavorable ratings consistently placing between 35 and 37 percent, but they were confident they could formulate a winning strategy in spite of that. What they did not count on, he says, was real competition among the population they most relied on to vote for her. "This is a group of people who would have voted for her were it not for him, but now you've got that core group who is either in his corner, or on the fence because of him, and it is a much greater number than [the Clinton campaign] originally thought."[8] This group of people includes black Americans who have been among her husband's most loyal supporters.

Among our research sample of four hundred black Americans, Obama had a distinct advantage with a 25 percent edge over Clinton in a head-to-head ballot test among respondents ages thirty to thirty-four and 20 percent edge among those ages twenty-five to twenty-nine.[9]

The operative explains that one reason Obama has emerged so quickly as a serious contender for the support of younger black Americans is that the Clintons were caught flat-footed due in part to their own inner circle. They have been relying on many of the same key players within the black community throughout their fifteen years on the national stage, but those players lack influence among the young black professionals who have been instrumental in Obama's rise. "What I think the Clinton campaign has done, it has relied on a lot of the old political linkages. They're going to the old guard machines—the Democratic bosses, the county leaders, the older elected officials, and so on. What they failed to understand is [that] a significant percentage of young professional African Americans don't care about those guys, don't care about those old political institutions, because most of us could not point to anything we've accomplished because of them. They haven't helped us do anything, so what difference does it make when you have Charlie Rangel, or Clyburn, or anybody of that era? You have all these people endorsing her that we have no connection to."[10]

While he (like others interviewed for this book) adamantly expresses gratitude for the gains achieved by prominent black leaders in the civil rights movement, he feels that some of these leaders are out of touch and unwilling to move forward to address current issues facing black Americans. This perception has created a gulf between some of the old-guard black leaders and the younger black Americans now beginning to take over the reins of political activism. "The people that we can relate to are now investment bankers, doctors, lawyers, they're other business types, people in the music industry, media folk," he said. "These are people that we have a closer connection to and aspire to be and if they talk, then we'll listen, but this old guard—they haven't really nurtured younger African Americans." As a result, "there's a whole group of African Americans that the Clinton campaign just hasn't connected to."[11]

Just as the Clintons in 1992 appealed to many young white baby boomers who wanted to vote for someone like themselves and not like their parents, Obama has struck a chord with young black voters and donors who are similarly thrilled at the opportunity to vote for a contemporary. And not just *any* contemporary, but a contemporary who represents the very best America has to offer—not just black America but America, period. Just as *The Cosby Show* displayed successful black doctors and lawyers to Americans whose only previous experience with black people may have been as maids and nannies, Obama has shown Americans a black presidential candidate who is smart, accomplished, and seriously competitive, whereas, previously they had seen such candidates only in the role of campaign agitators, running to highlight issues but with little hope or expectation of actually getting nominated. There is a pride in this—particularly since it has never been seen before—that has captivated many younger black Americans who have waited a lifetime to see themselves depicted accurately on the national political stage. The measure of pride Obama has inspired is something that other candidates cannot compete with. This explains why so many of my generation have gravitated to Obama's campaign in a way that they have not to others, including Senator Clinton's. One prominent black attorney I spoke with who has supported both Clintons in the past said he was supporting Obama this election because, "When I wake up and look in the mirror in the morning, I look a lot more like him than I do her [Senator Clinton]." A young black financial professional in her early twenties said of Obama that "he is the first candidate I ever felt compelled to give money to." She is not alone.[12]

While Clinton's low-dollar fund-raisers (fund-raisers in which the minimum contribution is $100 or less) tend to attract a relatively diverse audience of twenty-somethings and early thirty-somethings, the majority of the audience still tends to be white. (In previous election cycles I have contributed to the campaigns of Senators Clinton, Obama, and Edwards.) Obama's events attract a larger percentage of young black professionals. In March 2007, for instance, the Obama campaign held a low-dollar event on Clinton's home turf of New York at which they expected five hundred attendees. In the end, the event had to be relocated to accommodate the nearly 1,500 who attended. It raised $200,000 and the timing could not have been better. Thanks to that fund-raiser and others like it, Obama stunned the political establishment by revealing first quarter fund-raising totals in the neighborhood of $25 million, rivaling Clinton's $26 million. While $200,000 may not sound like a huge slice of a $25 million pie, the donors who attended that event will actually play an important role in determining whether his campaign succeeds over the long haul. While Hollywood superstars and the megarich get most of the media attention, campaign finance regulations essentially limit them to one four-figure check per campaign. The donors who give $100 here and $100 there, or $200 when you hit a really rough patch, constitute the real lifeline of a campaign. Ever since he emerged on the national stage, Obama has been cultivating young black professional donors of that caliber in a way that few other national candidates have done, with the possible exception of another black rising star, former Congressman Harold Ford.

Someone whom Obama and Ford have in common is Robert Smith, a longtime friend of Ford's whose fund-raising capabilities (particularly among a broad network of young black professionals in New York) made him the only African American included in a 2004 *New York Observer* piece on "baby bundlers."[13] The term "bundling" refers to the process of collecting a large number of political contributions from a large number of people in a relatively short time, a capability that campaign finance restrictions have made a crucial skill to have in the fund-raising toolbox and one at which Smith has proven particularly adept. Given Obama's current status as a political rock star, raising money for him is not difficult, but, as Smith explained in a recent interview, this was not true four years ago. At the time, Obama was a virtual unknown outside of his home state of Illinois. Yet Smith was able to organize a fund-raiser for him in the Big Apple with five hundred attendees, nearly all of them young black professionals, that raised $80,000.[14] Young black professionals have since become an important part of Obama's increasingly powerful campaign juggernaut—the primary obstacle standing in the way of Senator Clinton's coronation cum nomination (a.k.a. coro-nomination).

In addition to inspiring a generation of young black professionals, Obama has also spurred a generation gap among donors in the entertainment industry. While Clinton has the support of legendary producer Quincy Jones and Motown founder Berry Gordy, Obama has L. A. Reid, known for working with current music industry heavyweights such as Usher, and the music mogul Andre Harrell, known for giving another music mogul—Sean "Diddy" Combs—his start.[15] Not to mention his support from Hollywood heavyweight Will Smith.

If their celebrity support were expressed in competing campaign songs, Clinton might be humming along to the Temptations's

"My Girl" while Obama would be grooving to Usher's "U Make Me Wanna." And then of course there are Halle and Beyonce, both of whom have been spotted at various Obama fund-raisers. The former was later seen sporting an "Obama for Change" T-shirt, while the latter allegedly caused the senator to forget his own celebrity status and request an autograph. Not to mention Rosario Dawson, Gabrielle Union, Sanaa Lathan, and countless other members of young Hollywood's brown beauty brigade.[16] (Instead of "Obama for Change" perhaps a more appropriate slogan for Obama's campaign T-shirts would be "It's good to be Barack" or maybe "Don't hate the player. Hate the game.")

These supporters were instrumental in helping Obama shock the political establishment for a second time. In July 2007 it was announced that Obama had out-raised all of his Democratic counterparts, including Clinton, with a record $32.5 million. CNN posted a headline reading "Obama's Money Puts Clinton's 'Inevitable' Nomination in Doubt."[17] According to the anonymous political operative, selling the public on a candidate is in some ways no different from selling it on anything else. If your neighbor gets a new car, the next time a commercial for that car comes along you're more likely to take a look. The same goes for candidates. "There are a lot of people, African Americans in particular who had said 'I'm supporting Hillary but I'm not certain,' but then [Obama] starts to surge ahead, particularly on fund-raising, and then they start to think 'wow, if he can go toe to toe with her then there must be something about this guy. Let me pay attention to him.'"[18]

Lauren Williams, the editor of Stereohyped.com, a news and entertainment blog targeting young black Americans, has not formally endorsed Obama or any other candidate but admits, "I just really like him. I love the idea of him." She told me this sentiment is shared by much of her social circle, most of whom she said are supporting him. It also appears to be shared by many of her readers, who have begun to look forward to Williams's regular feature, "Obamarama," which reports the latest happenings on the presidential campaign trail with particular focus on Obama's candidacy.[19]

Alexis McGill, the political scientist and former political director for the Hip-Hop Summit Action Network, said that Obama has indeed created excitement among younger black Americans, especially among those with similar educational and social backgrounds. It is among this group, she said, that discussions of his candidacy most often feature the refrain, "It's our time."[20] Bakari Kitwana believes that Obama's support is not so class-specific but inspires blacks of all income levels. He notes, however, that the generational divide Obama's candidacy has highlighted runs deeper in some circles than others. According to Kitwana, the people most threatened by Obama are not those of less privileged class backgrounds but older black Americans who are already in power. "You have people who are steeped in electoral politics continuing to work the way they are in terms of race, and Barack upsets the balance a little bit. It's forcing people out of their comfort zone." He speculates that some older so-called black leaders worry that Obama's rise will mean that they're no longer "the only go-between [linking] black people and national electoral politics."[21] That his leadership is not rooted in racial politics is precisely what makes him so appealing to many younger black Americans. One young black voter interviewed said of Obama, "I love the fact that he's different and I hope he doesn't become a black leader. I hope he becomes a leader." But this possibility is also what makes some older blacks uncomfortable.[22]

This fear of the Barack factor, as Kitwana labels it, can be seen in attempts to question Obama's blackness. Since he became a serious presidential contender, media outlets have obsessed over whether Obama is "black enough" to connect with black voters. Much of the coverage has focused on Obama's atypical background: his African father, white mother, Indonesian stepfather, and Hawaiian upbringing. Columnist Stanley Crouch wrote a piece entitled "What Obama Isn't: Black Like Me." Crouch does not claim that Obama is not a black man but argues that his heritage and experience are not something the average black American can relate to. Crouch writes that "when black Americans refer to Obama as 'one of us,' I do not know what they are talking about. In his new book, *The Audacity of Hope,* Obama makes it clear that, while he has experienced some light versions of typical racial stereotypes, he cannot claim those problems as his own—nor has he lived the life of a black American." Crouch concludes that "if we then end up with him as our first black President, he will have come into the White House through a side door—which might, at this point, be the only one that's open."[23]

Debra Dickerson, writing in *Salon,* goes farther, saying that Obama's lack of connection to the black American slave experience in essence makes him *not* a black American.

To say that Obama isn't black is merely to say that, by virtue of his white American mom and his Kenyan dad who abandoned both him and America, he is an American of African immigrant extraction. It is also to point out the continuing significance of the slave experience to the white American psyche; it's not we who can't get over it. It's you. Lumping us all together (which blacks also do from sloppiness and ignorance, and as a way to dominate the race issue and to force immigrants of African descent to subordinate their preferences to ours) erases the significance of slavery and continuing racism while giving the appearance of progress. Though actually, it is a kind of progress. And that's why I break my silence: Obama, with his non-black ass, is doing us all a favor.[24]

It is no coincidence that Crouch and Dickerson both belong to the civil rights generation, not the Hip-Hop Generation (and clearly not Generation Obama). Their assessments of Obama's black Americanness are perfect examples of the generational divide that has been so instrumental in spurring the Obama movement. While it may not have been their intention, by essentially rating Obama's black Americanness like an Olympic sport (five points for geographic origin, ten points for having American-born black wife, eight points for effort), Dickerson and Crouch hit on a sore spot for many young black Americans. Dickerson is right that there are a range of experiences that make black people different and therefore we should not all be lumped under the same ideological umbrella, but debating Obama's authenticity is, for a lot of younger black professionals, reminiscent of playing the Oreo card. While it may take different forms, it boils down to this: criticism from other blacks that if you don't speak a certain way, think a certain way, act a certain way, and have parents who speak a certain way, act a certain way, or come from a specific place, you can't really be authentically black—except on the outside you are, so you must be an Oreo. While Crouch and Dickerson do not say this specifically, their criticism of Obama feeds into the black community's long-standing prejudice that there is only one way to be black.

This mindset has become particularly destructive among black youth, with kids who try to earn good grades being told they are "acting white." The result of this peer pressure, in some cities, is a dropout rate among black males approaching 50 percent.

For young professionals who have suffered the Oreo accusation, whether on the playground or in a college fraternity (as in, "Okay, you may be black on the outside, but how black are you *really?*"), Obama's story is a welcome reminder that no one has a lock on what it means to be black in America. Whether you have something in common with Obama's experience or not, if you are black in any way, shape, or form, his experience will reflect on you—like it or not.

Some members of the civil rights generation are buoyed by Obama's candidacy. Reverend Jesse Jackson was an early supporter, endorsing Obama shortly after he first announced his run for the presidency. However, Jackson sparked an Oreo controversy of his own when a South Carolina newspaper quoted him as accusing Obama of "acting white" for not addressing the Jena Six controversy more forcefully. Jackson later claimed he did not recall making the comment.[25] Another civil rights legend, NAACP chairman Julian Bond, calls Obama a "tremendously appealing candidate." (He can't resist a laugh at Senator Biden's expense, adding, "Isn't it obvious? He's so articulate.") Bond explains that in addition to his charming personality, Obama takes an approach to politics that is refreshingly different. As an example, he mentions an event where several of the Democratic candidates spoke. While the other candidates focused on the war in Iraq, Obama talked about the divisions in American politics that are harming our nation. "He took an entirely different approach than all of the other people, and I think that's both refreshing and appealing. I mean, he has positions on all these issues like all the rest of them do but he decided that there was something bigger than this. And that was the political divisions—and I'm guessing the racial divisions—in American society."[26]

This idea, that politics should be about more than partisanship or racial politics, has been one of the driving forces behind the Generation Obama movement.

It is a movement so passionate that one has to wonder what will happen if Obama doesn't make it to the promised land? The answer to that question has less to do with whether Obama loses than with how. In any campaign, there is always the possibility that the candidate you support may lose. But according to Bakari Kitwana, expert on the Hip-Hop Generation, Obama is not just any other candidate. From Kitwana's vantage point, young black Americans, many of whom are already suspicious of the establishment, have a vested interest in seeing Obama succeed, because there's a perception that if he, with his Ivy League credentials and winning smile and multiracial appeal, can't make it, then no one will—at least not to the White House.[27]

Even campaigns with the greatest momentum and media adulation can crash and burn (just ask Howard Dean), so if Obama makes a misstep—his own version of the Dean scream—his supporters will be disappointed and even heartbroken, but at the end of the day they will likely chalk it up to the fact that he is only human (one of his biggest selling points on the campaign trail) and maybe it just wasn't meant to be. It's also possible that Obama will have no missteps and will be fortunate enough to run the elusive "perfect" campaign—à la Harold Ford's Senate race in Tennessee—but, like Ford, still not win. Even then, his supporters will be disappointed but may hold out hope that perhaps he's destined to become the first black vice president before becoming the first black president. But there is another possibility.

Perhaps something—a negative advertisement, a cutting remark, the release of some questionable yet damaging opposition research—will derail his candidacy. As Ford learned the hard way, it only takes one provocative ad or questionable mailing to turn a "perfect" campaign into a losing campaign. If this happens (or is perceived to happen) during the Democratic primary, the Democrats will find it nearly impossible to convert Generation Obama supporters into general election supporters, not just in this election but for a lifetime.

The prominent political operative who requested anonymity says that in spite of all the hype surrounding Obama (much of which he says is deserved), Senator Clinton still has an advantage and will likely win the primaries. He credits the Clintons' long-standing relationships with some of the key players in local political machines in early primary states, but he explains that a no-holds-barred, victory-at-any-cost strategy would ultimately prove costly for both Clinton and the Democratic Party. "You really have to be careful," he says, "how you go after an African American candidate. Certain buzzwords, such as saying that he is 'not experienced,' or he's 'too young,'" are perceived as condescending; the modern equivalent of keeping an uppity black in his place. This perception will play particularly poorly among a generation of young black professionals who may have been passed over for that promotion at a bank or a law firm—not because they are black, of course, but simply because their white superior feels they are "too young" or "lack experience."[28]

The Clinton campaign has already showed signs that it is struggling to find the right tone to use in criticizing Obama. For instance, when they demanded an apology from Obama because mogul David Geffen (a longtime Clinton supporter turned Obama donor) criticized Senator Clinton's candidacy, most campaign watchers said the move fell flat.

Saturday Night Live, which has become notorious for skewering the presidential candidates over the years, spoofed the rivalry brewing between Clinton and Obama for the support of black voters. Comedian Amy Poehler, impersonating Senator Clinton, insinuates that she is half black during an interview with Chris Matthews (or rather another actor portraying him). When he attempts to question her about her alleged ethnicity, she argues that no one has questioned Senator Obama about his claims that he is half black. Chris Matthews then notes the apparent double standard. While the absurdity of it all clearly warrants a chuckle, the potential for fallout from a contentious primary is no laughing matter for Democrats.

The anonymous political operative feels that the primary will likely remain a horse race to the end, and he believes the Clinton campaign will give in to temptation and do something that either crosses a line or at least flirts with it. When that happens, he says, some younger black Americans will sulk for a bit before looking over at the GOP alternative, putting their bruised feelings aside, and coming into the Hillary camp. But for others who were already questioning their allegiance to the Democrats, an Obama defeat could be the straw that breaks the camel's back. Feeling taken for granted by a party is one thing. Feeling "screwed" (his word) is another.[29]

Kitwana is equally blunt. If Obama loses, he says, and there is a perception that the nomination was "stolen" from him by the Democratic political establishment, it will definitely move a large group of younger black voters even farther away from Democrats than they already are. "It would restore the belief that it [the political process] is all orchestrated," says Kitwana. "If the nomination is stolen from him, people will feel the same level of cynicism that they felt in 2000 with the Florida recount."[30]

In a sense, it would be a replay of the Jesse Jackson–Michael Dukakis primary, and we all know how Dukakis fared in the end. But Obama is, by all accounts, more qualified than Jackson was, which heightens the potential fallout from a primary perceived as unfair. According to the political operative, deep discontent among Generation Obama voters would present a golden opportunity for Republicans.[31]

As for the ever-present question, "Is the country ready for a black president?" perhaps the person best qualified to answer that is the only other one who has really been in Obama's shoes, General Colin Powell. For Powell, who has talked with Obama and says he is "proud to see him out there," the answer is *yes*. "If he can demonstrate the leadership the country's looking for and his positions are sound, then yes, the country's ready. I think, frankly, when I was thinking about it twelve years ago, there were a lot of people who said the country was ready then. You never know what some folks will do when they actually get into the booth, and that's something black people talk about all of the time—'Yeah, they'll say they love you, Colin, until they have to go pull the lever'—but I think that's less true now than it was twelve years ago. I think the country has matured to the point where a woman or a black could be elected."[32]

Another high-profile Republican believes Obama has the potential to be the first successful black candidate for national office. Ken Mehlman, the former chairman of the Republican National Committee and a Harvard Law School classmate of Obama's, said in an interview, "I think if Barack Obama were the nominee for president or vice president, he would be an incredibly compelling candidate, and I think he'd be compelling apart from his race." Mehlman then added, "But I think his race would be an asset."[33]

Mehlman explains that while he doesn't agree with Obama on many issues, he considers him a personal friend from their school days, and he hopes Obama's candidacy will have the same impact on Americans that Sandra Day O'Connor's appointment to the Supreme Court did. "The effect of Sandra Day O'Connor on the Supreme Court was to say to millions of women, 'You can too,' and more women entered the legal profession, which made our profession a better place and a stronger place. Having an African American president would say to millions of children all around this country, 'You can too.' Barack Obama as president would say to all Americans, 'Anybody can compete and anybody can win,' which is what America is all about. That's what's different with us. We're not perfect. No nation is perfect. But we constantly perfect ourselves."[34]

This sentiment is shared by one of Obama's early supporters, Representative Artur Davis (who entered Harvard Law School the year Obama began his historic tenure as the first black president of the *Law Review*). He says that Obama's "election would be a transformative event in this country. We have struggled with race for 217 years, and we have struggled with the notion of how we build one community in this country despite our racial differences. I think if Barack Obama were elected president of the United States it would mean that race was not an impediment to being elected to office in this country if you were a good enough candidate." He adds, "It certainly wouldn't guarantee that you would have a massive number of blacks being elected to office, but it would mean that for a good, talented candidate who could raise the money and who had the message, who had the talent, that race would not be an impediment. There is still a strong belief that race is a barrier to political advancement. If Obama got elected it would lift that barrier."[35]

It is this hope and possibility—not that *a* black man could be elected president but that a young, charismatic, and qualified black man could be elected president—that Generation Obama is counting on.

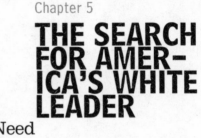

Chapter 5

THE SEARCH FOR AMER-ICA'S WHITE LEADER

Do We Still Need "Black Leaders"?

Suppose radio personality "John Imus" has just insulted members of the Dartmouth women's lacrosse team, referring to them as "stringy-haired hos." John Imus is black. The majority of the players on the Dartmouth lacrosse team are white. A massive public outcry erupts. America's white leaders are outraged. They demand that John Imus be fired and threaten to boycott the companies of any of his sponsors until he is.

But who exactly are America's designated white leaders?

Would it be George W. Bush, since he is the president whether you voted for him or not?

Or maybe Dick Cheney, who is, many believe, the true power behind the president?

What about Bill Gates, the richest man in the world, so rich that his wealth could easily subsidize a small country?

Or maybe Bono, the lead singer from U2? Over two decades he has demonstrated the power to fill stadiums with people who shout out the lyrics to nearly all of his songs (no president can do that) while also demonstrating the power to convince presidents, diplomats, and royalty to become more engaged in global issues from AIDS to debt relief.

How about Michael Moore? Love him or hate him, his books and movies have made him a one-man political empire. Or his counterpart on the right, the always provocative (and usually offensive) Ann Coulter?

Maybe Bill O'Reilly, culture warrior?

What about Senator Hillary Clinton? Some allege that she was to her husband's presidency what Cheney and Rove are to Bush's.

And we can't forget onetime presidential candidate and Klansman David Duke. He certainly has a constituency that values his leadership. They may hide themselves under white hoods and robes, but they're still a constituency.

Come to think of it, I can't recall the last time I heard the term "white leader." There is an understanding that white Americans are a diverse group, representing a diverse array of ideas, communities, and constituencies, and it is absurd to suppose they would all have one leader. If a poll were conducted asking who is the nation's "most important white leader" and the results named

George W. Bush first, Hillary Clinton second, and David Duke third—the inference being that they are all somehow representative of the same constituency—pundits and media critics would cry foul. Black leaders, however, are discussed under one umbrella based on skin color, irrespective of ideology.

There have been polls for the nation's "most admired woman" or "most admired man," but asking people who they admire is very different from asking them to anoint a "most important leader." Asking who someone considers the "most important leader" insinuates that he or she would be willing to *follow* that person. Posing such a question in a racial context is becoming increasingly questionable as the black community continues to become ethnically, socially, economically, and politically more diverse.

Yet for a black person in a leadership position, his race is assumed to be integral to how he leads and therefore integral to how he is viewed as a leader. This century-old idea is beginning to lose credence among a new generation of black Americans who are helping to redefine the concept of black leadership.

According to a February 2006 Black Voices poll conducted by the Associated Press and AOL, minister and activist Jesse Jackson is considered the nation's "most important black leader." He was crowned the reigning leader of black America with 15 percent of the vote.[1]

This designation is not particularly surprising given Reverend Jackson's high profile over the past decades, first in the civil rights movement and later in national politics. Jackson is without question one of the most recognizable black Americans in a leadership capacity. So the surprise of this poll is not that Jesse Jackson garnered 15 percent of the vote. The real surprise is the difference between this poll and a similar one taken two years earlier.

In 2004, Black Entertainment Television and CBS conducted a poll to find the nation's most important national African American leader. Again Jackson came in first, this time with 21 percent of the vote. He was followed by Colin Powell with 13 percent and Al Sharpton with 4 percent. Former Congressman Kweisi Mfume earned 3 percent, while Louis Farrakhan and Condoleezza Rice tied for last place with 2 percent.

While Jackson's lead decreased, he held on to the number one spot. The most significant difference between the two polls is not who came in first but who came in second and third. In 2006, Secretary of State Condoleezza Rice came in second with 11 percent, then Colin Powell with 8 percent and Barack Obama with 6 percent. Louis Farrakhan garnered 4 percent, while media mogul Oprah Winfrey tied with the late Martin Luther King, Jr., for 3 percent. Perennial presidential candidate Al Sharpton came in last with 2 percent.[2]

What a difference two years can make.

In the Black Voices poll, most of the leaders selected by respondents are not typically considered black leaders at all. Rice, Powell, Obama, and Winfrey are without question leaders and they are without question black, yet they are rarely thought of in popular culture as "black leaders." Unlike Jackson or Sharpton, the experiences and accomplishments of these leaders have not been tied exclusively to the black community. Nor have they sought to position themselves as voices of that community. Instead, they represent all Americans who share their political consciousness (or in Oprah's case, her social consciousness), regardless of skin color or ethnicity.

Perhaps the greatest testament to how the concept of black leadership evolved in the two years since the BET/CBS poll is that the people in the second and third spots for the nation's most important black leader are—gasp!—Republicans. More black Americans chose two black Republicans as their leaders than chose Jesse Jackson.

This is not to say that leaders like Jesse Jackson lack influence, power, or a constituency. It is simply an acknowledgment that their power to influence constituencies is not what it once was. The constituencies that Jackson and other black leaders relied on to fuel their rise to power are no longer the cohesive unit that once defined the black community. Instead, like other ethnic groups before them, the black community is undergoing a transformation from a cohesive social and political voting bloc to one divided by issues of class and politics. The result is a community divided, unable to agree on what constitutes an authentic, relevant, and effective black leader, or even on whether one is needed.

According to our survey, 51 percent of post–civil rights generation black Americans do not believe their community needs a "black leader," while 37 percent think it does. But one thing the respondents were almost universally united on is that the high-profile leaders often dubbed "black leaders" by the media do not represent them.[3]

During the civil rights movement it was accurate to anoint someone like Martin Luther King, Jr., as a black leader because the majority of black Americans, rich, poor, northern or southern, relied on him for leadership during the dark days of segregation. White politicians, in turn, recognized the political value of such black leaders. In one of the most remarkable moves of his 1960 presidential campaign, John F. Kennedy reached out to King's wife, Coretta, shortly after King was arrested for a protest in Atlanta. After Bobby Kennedy worked behind the scenes to get him released on bail, the King family proved instrumental in persuading other prominent black pastors to publicly endorse Kennedy's candidacy. The impact of their support in Kennedy's subsequent victory was crucial, in one of the closest elections in history. Since then, countless politicians have sought to replicate the black leader formula. But its power has significantly waned. Today, the idea that one black leader (or even two) can deliver the black vote is not only outdated but borderline absurd.

Bakari Kitwana says that for this generation, "the idea of the leadership model being one person is absolutely out the door. I think this is a generation looking for multiple leaders or group leadership. Not just erroneously thinking there's just one person and he's the leader."[4] This shift in perspective was evident in the organized response to the high-profile Jena Six case. While stalwarts like Jesse Jackson and Al Sharpton both attended protests on behalf of the Louisiana teens, they were not the driving forces behind them. A number of high-profile black Americans lent their support, financial as well as other, but it was without question a joint effort, one driven largely by members of the post–civil rights generation.

In his stand-up comedy special *Bigger and Blacker,* Chris Rock jokes that "I think we need a new black leader." Compared to

Martin Luther King, Jr., those who have followed have been "a bunch of substitute teachers." Al Sharpton "ain't Martin or Malcolm but if you get beaten by the cops he's the guy to call." (Ironically, according to media reports, Rock's mother turned to Sharpton when she faced discriminatory treatment at a restaurant.)[5] Rock also muses that the reason Jesse Jackson has been able to secure the release of American hostages in various countries over the years is because foreign leaders realize that the most effective way to antagonize an American president is by releasing the hostages to Jackson.[6]

For older black Americans who have followed Jackson's career from his days as Martin Luther King's trusted confidante to the time when he made history by becoming the first competitive black presidential candidate, Jackson is the epitome of a black leader. Similarly, for disenfranchised black Americans who live in communities where police officers are not viewed as those who protect you from harm but those who may harm you, your husband, or your son, Al Sharpton is a hero. But for a generation of young black professionals, their brand of leadership no longer resonates.

Julian Bond, the legendary civil rights activist and NAACP chairman, says that while he considers "black leader" an overused term, it can still be valid. But there are degrees. "I tend to think of people who are leaders as people who either have followers, that is measurable numbers of people who say, 'I'm following him or her.' But there are also leaders who don't have any actual followers, who are thought leaders. That is, their thoughts, their ideas are attractive to people or they help people think about things in different sorts of ways." He mentions as an example of a "thought leader" NAACP cofounder W.E.B. Du Bois, who didn't have a constituency of voters but did have a group of people who relied on his ideology and leadership nonetheless. He draws a similar comparison to Oprah Winfrey, an example of a present-day thought leader because of her immense influence on everything from what people watch to what they read. He also notes that because her reach goes far beyond the black community, it raises the question whether it is accurate to label her a black leader in the traditional sense, instead of perhaps a leader who happens to be black.[7]

The emergence of black Americans like Oprah, who lead without tying their leadership directly to their race, begs the question of what exactly the term "black leader" means today. If the criteria are to simply be black and accomplished, and to play a role in influencing the behavior of the masses, then Winfrey is clearly the nation's most important black leader. According to author Michael Silverstein, she "influences the purchase of 20–25 percent of *all* goods."[8] This means that she's more effective at selling *anything* than the most powerful politicians are at selling policy ideas to an often disengaged and distrusting public.

Let's say the requirements for black leaders are limited to those in politics, law, or government. Is Supreme Court Justice Clarence Thomas a "black leader"? He is inarguably one of the most powerful black men in the nation, and possibly in the world, since the Supreme Court makes decisions on laws affecting everything from abortion to the international war on terror. There was a time when being a conservative would immediately disqualify you from the title "black leader," but Colin Powell and Condoleezza Rice seem to have changed that. Their presence and their politics have helped reshape the way an entire generation of black Americans think of what it means to be black and a leader, and whether or not being both inevitably makes someone a black leader.

Traditionally the label "black leader" has been applied to a black American (almost always male) who uses his position to call attention to issues of particular importance to the black community and thereby becomes recognized as a voice of that community. Cory Booker, the mayor of Newark, New Jersey, who has been cited as one of the nation's up-and-coming leaders, explains that this definition no longer really applies. "I think the days of a single voice for black America, the days of the Booker T. Washington, the Fredrick Douglass, or the Martin Luther King, are long gone." But he adds that being a black American provides a unique experience that definitely shapes his leadership style. "I'm a leader of a city that's incredibly diverse and so I'm a leader, period. But when you describe me as a black leader it does have an important clarification in some ways. I think it points to a specific historical experience. I think it points to a level of personal experiences and understanding."[9]

He elaborates:

> I think of myself as a leader of the city of Newark. But the
> fact that I'm African American helps to add texture and
> depth to my experience. And not that you can't approach
> that from a different perspective, as a Catholic leader, as a

woman leader. So I think that there's probably a lot of layers and nuances to being a black leader. But for me, I come from a certain cultural context. I can't escape the fact that I'm a Christian, or a heterosexual, or growing up in the Northeast. They all inform the different balances that inform who I am and they empower me in what I do. I think it was Skip [Henry Louis] Gates had a wonderful quote—and I'll paraphrase it—where he talked about loving the fact that he was black, and loving everything black, luxuriating in black culture, black music, black food. But it was always for him a deeper portal to transport himself into a larger understanding of humanity. So much of who I am and the things I like about myself—my capacity for compassion, my drive for social justice—are all important human traits, but a lot of them have been deeply informed by my experience in this country as an African American.[10]

Booker also explains that the spectrum of blacks in leadership today is so diverse that it is impossible to pigeonhole the politics that are emblematic of a black leader because today it can theoretically include Al Sharpton or Condoleezza Rice. Julian Bond similarly notes that at the end of the day what defines a successful leader is varied. For instance, he says, it should not be limited to those who can get laws passed that improve the lives of black Americans, because by that criterion "most of the members of Congress are not leaders." He adds that "you can stand outside and shout and yell all day long and still be a leader." From his perspective, people as diverse as Barack Obama and Al Sharpton serve valid roles. "There are many, many ways and we need as many practitioners of the different ways as we possibly can have."[11]

In an article in *Ebony,* the nation's oldest magazine covering black issues, Reverend Grainger Browning, pastor of Ebenezer AME Church, defends the present-day relevance of Jackson and other past civil rights leaders: "The national issues that we are facing in 2006 are not that much different than what Dr. King faced in 1966." He adds, "To think that the issues we face have changed is to make a serious mistake."[12] Except that most young black Americans think the issues *have* changed. It is this fundamental disagreement that distinguishes their politics from those of the civil rights generation.

The civil rights battles that these young black Americans brace themselves for on a daily basis involve issues such as affirmative action and racial profiling, not lynching. Even when high-profile tragedies with racial overtones occur, such as the shooting of unarmed African immigrant Amadou Diallo by the New York police, there are class implications that allow young black professionals to avoid facing the reality that they too can become victims of the system. Any thought of what can happen to a poor black immigrant like Diallo is tempered by the fact that a wealthy black man like O.J. Simpson (regardless of what the DNA evidence might say) can go free.

While these young black Americans did not grow up witnessing the leadership of King or Malcolm X firsthand, they did grow up with a diverse array of black role models and leaders, including civil rights leaders like Jesse Jackson as well as pop cultural icons like billionaire Oprah Winfrey and Bill Cosby, who made family life look so fun that even white kids wished he were their dad.

For many in this generation, the idea that the pursuit of civil rights has to be confrontational and in your face does not ring true. Thus the idea that blacks in leadership positions must be confrontational to be heard no longer rings true either.

Any discussion of black leadership is fraught with historical baggage that does not burden white leaders. This baggage consists of the weight of an entire community's hopes, dreams, and expectations, as well as the harsh judgments that come with a failure to live up to all that is expected of you.

Erica, a twenty-six-year-old Alabama native, calls the idea of a singular black leader outdated and says that while she is grateful to leaders from the past, from Marcus Garvey to Martin Luther King, Jr., she believes that "to really do what we need to do as a community, everybody's going to have to take that individual responsibility."[13] Cary, a Morehouse graduate, makes a similar observation, saying he considers the whole concept of a single black leader "a dangerous misconception," the danger being the perception that the black community should look to just one key person for guidance and leadership. According to him, every black American has a responsibility to live up to his utmost potential as a leader in his day-to-day life, as a worker or parent, instead of waiting for a singular leader or savior. He adds that this perspective is shared by a number of his Morehouse classmates, who grow tired of hearing comparisons to the famed "Talented Tenth." This idea, set forth by NAACP cofounder W.E.B. Du Bois, asserted that the most talented 10 percent of blacks are crucial in leading and securing the future of the rest. As Cary sees it, all black Americans have responsibility for their own future.[14] He is apparently not alone in this perspective: 1 percent of respondents in the AP-AOL Black Voices poll identified *themselves* as "the nation's most important black leader."[15]

Historically this baggage has also consisted of a battle over the most effective strategies for securing the black community's future. While leaders and issues have changed over the years, the battle itself has largely remained the same, focusing on one key question—How aggressive should black Americans be in fighting for equal rights and justice? This is the question that divided someone like Nat Turner from Frederick Douglass. Turner, a slave, led a group of slaves and black freedmen in a revolt that killed more than fifty members of white slave-owning families in Virginia. Douglass was also born into slavery, eventually escaped, and became one of its most vocal critics. But he did not use violence to advance his cause, instead using his status among prominent white Americans, including President Lincoln, to advocate freedom for black Americans. At the turn of the twentieth century, this same issue divided Booker T. Washington and W.E.B. Du Bois. Washington was heralded for his contributions to the educational advancement for black Americans, but his unwillingness to aggressively press for integration and his strong ties to prominent whites put him at odds with Du Bois, who derisively labeled Washington "the Great Accommodator."

At the height of the civil rights movement this issue divided the two most revered black leaders who ever lived, Martin Luther King, Jr., and Malcolm X, at least early in their careers. King advocated working with like-minded white Americans through protest and a lot of patience, to secure the future of black Americans. Malcolm X believed that after two hundred years of patience, it was time for black Americans to take their future into their own hands.

Today, this issue continues to divide leaders like Jesse Jackson and Al Sharpton, who believe that the most effective way to secure black America's future is through protest and the press, from leaders like Colin Powell or Oprah Winfrey, who seem to believe that simply doing their jobs incredibly well and becoming powerful Americans helps black Americans, as well as all Americans.

Floyd Flake, the former congressman who is also a pastor of the megachurch Greater Allen AME Cathedral, says that first and foremost he considers the idea of a singular black leader ridiculous. "I think it's the most absurd thing in the world when it comes to the notion that there can only be one black voice that speaks for black people." He explains that while he has no criticisms for Sharpton or Jackson specifically, "leadership for me is no longer the rhetoric of civil rights, it is the understanding that civil rights has to go to the next level. And the next level is civil responsibility. So that this is not about one leader, it's about understanding that all over America there have emerged leaders who are delivering directly to people and those are who I consider to be the real leaders." Leaders like Sharpton and Jackson, he says, "have a role, but I think that ultimately the people that get the respect today are those who are giving directly to, or meeting directly the needs of the people. And as those people are empowered to become homeowners, to know that they have quality schools that they can put their children into, or being empowered to understand that values that are instituted will help their families to stay together and not become a part of the jail population. That's what people are responding to nowadays."[16]

As a testament to just how tenuous Jackson's influence has become, *Ebony* magazine recently ran a piece entitled "Does the Rev. Jesse Jackson Still Matter?" Such an article would have been unthinkable even a decade ago, but as the piece notes, today "some wonder whether Jackson's time has come and gone. Many question whether the former presidential candidate and Martin Luther King, Jr. protégé's traditional brand of civil rights activism is still relevant. Others say that Jackson and other black leaders of his generation—like Andy Young and the Rev. Al Sharpton—are out of touch with today's 30-and-under hip-hop generation."[17]

According to our survey research, the answer is resounding. Of the four hundred young black Americans we polled, 72 percent answered no to the question, "Do you believe Jesse Jackson speaks for you?" The same number said they do not believe Al Sharpton speaks for them.[18]

While there is without question a sense of gratitude for the doors opened by civil rights pioneers that have allowed younger African Americans the many opportunities they enjoy today, there is also a sense that some civil rights leaders are stuck in a leadership model of the past, one rooted in a near obsession with race consciousness at the expense of effectiveness. Stephen Ward, writing for the *Black Agenda Report,* describes the present-day role of Jackson and Sharpton as follows:

> Nostalgia for the 1960s can also be disempowering for young people who are searching for models of activism and organizing. It tends to re-inscribe the primacy of charismatic leaders like Sharpton and Jackson who take their place at the front of the march, draw the cameras and provide the sound bites. This type of leadership is designed for public spectacle, not serious movement building. Their talents and commitments notwithstanding, Sharpton and Jackson remain stuck in a mode of protest politics that is increasingly out of line with current realities and challenges.[19]

One of the greatest criticisms leveled at Jesse Jackson and Al Sharpton is that in spite of the good intentions with which they may have begun their careers, somewhere along the road their quest for publicity began to outshine their quest for making a real difference. The fact that both men have ended up on a sort of emergency speed dial for high-profile whites accused of racism (from Don Imus to Michael Richards of *Seinfeld* and bounty hunter Duane "the Dog" Chapman) has not made them appear more credible or relevant. To the contrary, it gives the appearance that they have morphed from true civil rights activists into professional apology-accepters for hire. This was not always the case.

Jackson was mentored by the best-known and most-exalted black leader in our nation's history, Martin Luther King, Jr. He was with King in Memphis on the day King was felled by an assassin's bullet. Since that time Jackson has emerged as an iconic presence within the black community. He made a name for himself as a champion of causes for blacks and the poor through his Rainbow PUSH Coalition. He is probably best known, however, for his 1988 run for the presidency, the second by an African American after the late Congresswoman Shirley Chisolm did it in the 1970s. Jackson shocked the political establishment by emerging as a competitive candidate, winning 55 percent of the vote in the Michigan primary and eleven primaries total.

Along with advocating on national issues, Jackson has achieved recognition as an international statesman for his role in securing the release of American POWs during the war in Kosovo and Americans held in Cuba during the 1980s, as well as for his role in securing the freedom of an American pilot captured in Syria during the Reagan administration. This firmly established Jackson as a formidable international presence, and his ability to influence leaders abroad increased his influence at home.

Despite his contributions to black America and America as a whole, Jackson is perceived by many as not always having altruistic motives. He is seen as a little too willing to interject himself into contentious, high-profile battles, including the controversial Terri Schiavo case. Margo, a self-described liberal, says of Jackson, "I see him in the press a lot. . . . I see him get behind issues that are visible." But she notes that while he is great at drawing publicity, she doesn't see him actually getting a lot done for the community. "I don't think he necessarily represents me," she said, adding that she feels the same way about Sharpton.[20]

Some elements of Jackson's personal life have also affected his standing among young black Americans. Many of those interviewed do not recall the days when Jackson marched with Dr. King, and they were children when he made his historic run for the presidency. However, nearly all recall the scandal that erupted when it was revealed that he had a child out of wedlock with a former aide. Camille, a twenty-five-year-old southern native, says of Jackson, "Black people in general are really conservative when it comes to cultural things, so one of the things that's really important about being a black leader is that you really have to be on your p's and q's all the time. And I think that he [Jackson] has done some things that are not looked too favorably upon, and black people as a community tend to be somewhat unforgiving."[21]

She then delivers her most stinging rebuke of Jackson: "I don't necessarily think that I would classify him as a black leader."[22]

Cary, the Morehouse graduate, adds, "I think he started off doing the right thing. I think he's done a lot of good things but he's human like everyone else. He's sort of faded out of the community. Now when you see him it's like 'There's Jesse Jackson who had an affair.'"[23] Kristen, a twenty-four-year-old, adamantly proclaims her respect for Jackson's work over the years but finds his personal woes troubling. "I respect Jesse Jackson but I am a spiritual person and I believe you should practice what you preach. He had illegitimate children." She reiterates that her generation wants leaders who are not hypocritical and adds, "If you say it we want to see it. When I don't see you living up to the things that you say, I'm going to lose morale. I'm going to lose trust. I respect Jesse Jackson but I wouldn't say he necessarily speaks for me."[24]

Interestingly, few of those interviewed offered similar criticisms of President Clinton. For some, Jackson's greatest sin was not his infidelity per se, but that as a member of the clergy he has a responsibility to set an example. While Charizma, a registered independent in her twenties, considers Clinton's infidelity and how he handled it is as much a part of his likable persona as his saxophone playing, she is less forgiving of Jackson: "I'm not a fan of Jesse Jackson. He's a hypocrite in some ways. As a reverend he preaches certain religious values that he doesn't abide by himself."[25]

In spite of the comparisons (both negative and positive) between Jackson and Sharpton, Jackson's career has been seen as more credible by the mainstream establishment. While Sharpton's runs for the presidency are mainly viewed as good entertainment that livens up the presidential debates, in the 1980s Jackson became to the Democratic left what candidates like Pat Robertson were to the Republican right. He forced the party to take stock and rediscover its conscience on social issues. And as much as Sharpton may garner accolades for his presence at domestic protests, he has never approached Jackson's recognition as an international force.

Sharpton first became a national figure through his involvement in the controversial case of Tawana Brawley, a black teenager who claimed to have been assaulted by a group of white men, including police officers, in the 1980s. The story was eventually revealed to be a hoax, and one of the men who was wrong-fully accused won a judgment against Sharpton for defamation of character.

In the past decade, however, Sharpton has rebuilt his image by positioning himself at the forefront of legitimate civil rights cases and has moved from the fringes of leadership to the mainstream. He established himself as a go-to critic of the New York Police Department and mayor-turned-presidential-candidate Rudolph Giuliani, becoming a voice for those who believed that they had been victimized by his administration. This included the family of Amadou Diallo, the unarmed African immigrant shot nine-teen times by four police officers.

Sharpton has also emerged as a perennial candidate and pop cultural personality, running for mayor, senator, and president and appearing regularly on television. As political observers have noted, if his goal were to become an elected official who passes legislation to improve the lives of black Americans, Sharpton could easily win any number of local offices, from city council to state senate. Instead of running for offices that are actually within his reach, however, Sharpton has chosen unwinnable races that heighten his profile. In so doing, Sharpton has managed to culti-vate a persona as activist and community leader without having to work with government bureaucracy or face the criticism that comes with casting a vote for an unpopular piece of legislation.

Consequently Sharpton has carved out a lucrative niche as a power broker: someone who may not be electable but can deter-mine whether or not others get elected by granting, or withhold-ing, his endorsement. The underlying assumption, of course, is that as a "leader" Sharpton has the power to dictate how black voters will vote.

Within the sport of politics, however, the endorsement game is one whose rules are complicated and where it is virtually impossible to keep score. Calculating the impact of endorsements is much less a science than an art form bordering on pure guess. Under certain circumstances an endorsement can definitely help. For instance, if you are accused of being a racist, it probably helps if the NAACP denounces the accusations and someone from the organization subsequently endorses you (since the organization itself is legally prohibited from endorsements as a 501c3). Or, as happened with then Governor Bill Clinton in 1992, if you have been accused of playing the race card by criticizing rapper Sister Souljah (and also criticizing Jesse Jackson for inviting her to speak at a Rainbow Coalition event), it helps if Jackson ends up endorsing your candidacy.

But outside those extreme circumstances, the calculation gets very muddy. Countless candidates have lost elections in spite of being endorsed by others more popular than they are. Former President Bill Clinton, one of the most popular Democrats living, endorsed Joe Lieberman in his 2006 Senate primary, which Lieberman ended up losing. Sharpton and Jackson endorsed Lieberman's opponent Ned Lamont, but no political analyst would seriously allege that Lamont's victory means Jackson and Sharpton are more influential than Bill Clinton. Furthermore, Lamont subsequently lost the general election to Lieberman—badly. (Political consultant Alexis McGill, who worked on the Lamont race, notes that he received so much criticism for Sharpton and Jackson's involvement that the campaign was forced to alter its post-primary strategy.)[26]

After discontinuing his own race for the presidency in 2004, Al Sharpton endorsed John Kerry. We know how that turned out. Kerry not only lost but struggled to connect with black voters throughout his campaign, even with Sharpton's endorsement.

In New York City, an endorsement from Sharpton is viewed as an even greater gamble with higher political costs. In the 2001 Democratic primary for mayor, Sharpton's endorsement became a defining moment in the campaign, and many say it determined the outcome of the election. Sharpton endorsed Fernando Ferrer, a former Bronx borough president who is Puerto Rican, over Mark Green, the city's onetime public advocate, who is white. During the campaign Green and Sharpton socialized, leading political observers to assume that Green was trying to secure Sharpton's endorsement or at least neutralize him so that he would not actively work against Green's candidacy. Sharpton subsequently endorsed Ferrer, as part of what was dubbed a "black-brown" political coalition meant to combine the power of black and Latino voters to win city hall. Shortly before primary day, fliers were distributed in predominantly white ethnic neighborhoods displaying a cartoon of Sharpton with an inflated posterior on which Ferrer was planting a kiss.

Green ultimately won the primary, but it was a case of winning the battle and losing the war. Despite his insistence that no one related to his campaign had anything to do with the fliers, the incident alienated Latino and black voters, many of whom abandoned him in the general election.[27] A group of prominent black businessmen, including Earl Graves, the founder of *Black Enterprise* magazine, the late actor and activist Ossie Davis and his wife Ruby Dee, and Ed Lewis, former publisher of *Essence* magazine, all endorsed Republican Michael Bloomberg shortly after the flier controversy and just before Election Day.

Bloomberg won.

This controversy illustrates the complexities involved in a Sharpton endorsement. While it is impossible to know how many votes the endorsement brought Ferrer in the primary, it is widely accepted that the derogatory flier cost him crucial votes in key white neighborhoods. The fact that a proportion of black voters abandoned Green in the general election perpetuated the idea, at least among some, that Sharpton influences black voters. But the truth is more complex. A black person didn't have to be a fan of Sharpton's to react against the flier. There is likely not a black person in America who would claim to be a fan of Willie Horton, the rapist and murderer who became the star of one of the most infamous political ads in history when George H. W. Bush used him in the 1988 presidential race to portray Democratic nominee Michael Dukakis as soft on crime. Yet to black Americans, the use of racial innuendo to play on white America's worst fears was incredibly offensive. The reaction of black voters in the 2001 mayor's race had much less to do with Sharpton's endorsement than with the fact that many Hispanic and black voters felt the need to teach a Democratic candidate and the Democratic Party that race-baiting tactics have no place in a party that claims to embrace minorities.

Some of the people I interviewed said that while they are not influenced by Sharpton's endorsements and don't feel he represents them as a leader, he does serve a purpose. One young black registered Republican compares Sharpton to a relative who shows up at Thanksgiving dinner and exposes certain truths that the family might not like talking about but that need to be stated.[28] Luke, a stylist, is even more blunt. While he does not always agree with Sharpton, he believes that the behavior of the NYPD toward minorities has improved since the Amadou Diallo shooting, and Sharpton deserves some credit for that.[29] The larger point being that whether he wins or loses or can adequately speak for a younger generation, there is value in having a voice out there that is not afraid to say . . . anything. Sharpton can antagonize just about anyone without fear of losing votes, precisely because he never runs in an election he plans on winning. Clyde, a lawyer and entrepreneur, says, "You know what he does. Al's an agitator. Al brings up issues. Al Sharpton ran for president just to bring up issues and he was very effective at doing so. He made the presidential debates worth watching."[30]

Sharpton delivered one of the most dramatic moments in the 2004 Democratic presidential primary debates when he forced Howard Dean, then the front-runner, to acknowledge that he could not name any high-ranking blacks in his gubernatorial administration. Sharpton also pressed Dean on his infamous Confederate flag comment. These moments were important because Dean's white opponents attempted to capitalize on the Confederate flag remark but came across as simply trying to capitalize on a flub. No one really believed that John Kerry was more in tune with the feelings of black voters than Dean was. Sharpton lent the issue a measure of authority the other candidates lacked, not only by virtue of his race but by the passion with which he articulated his feelings. No matter what one thinks of Sharpton, there is something inherently troubling about watching a white person try to convince a black person that he is overreacting to racially charged comments the white person has made. Sharpton's confrontation with Dean, and the unrelenting media scrutiny, eventually forced Dean to apologize.

While the exchange proves that Sharpton does have impact, it is much less direct than an ability to deploy thousands of voters on command. Like his role in the mayoral election, his persona in national politics remains controversial among both white and black Americans.

The Imus controversy is a perfect example of how Sharpton can cast a cloud over causes he supports, no matter how worthy. While Sharpton certainly bears some credit for increasing public awareness of Imus's remarks and thus some credit for his eventual dismissal, his involvement also drew intense criticism that distracted from the issue at hand. Though practically no one was willing to publicly defend Imus's remarks, many were indignant that Sharpton and Jackson would attempt to paint themselves as voices of moral certitude on any subject, and particularly on what does or does not constitute appropriate speech. Instead of focusing on why it is not acceptable for anyone, particularly the host of a political news program for a major network, to call young women "nappy headed hos," the conversation became about how a man who once referred to New York as Hymietown and another with a history of using race to inflame contentious situations were in any position to judge someone else's ethics.

Regardless of their recent accomplishments, Jackson and Sharpton both have histories that have made them persona non grata among a number of white Americans. For Sharpton it will forever be the Tawana Brawley incident. For Jackson it was Hymietown, a derogatory reference to Jews made early in his 1984 presidential campaign. This is the issue that provides one of the greatest measures for comparing and contrasting older leaders who are black to those being looked to by a new generation of black Americans. In considering what makes an effective black leader, one must ask how effective a leader can be while perceived as a lightning rod by many whites, particularly when whites still constitute the majority of those in power.

Erica, the Alabama native, likes Sharpton because his "political voice is uncompromising," but she doesn't "think he's effective." She explains that he's "an intelligent man" who lacks the ability or willingness to maneuver successfully in mainstream America, or among mainstream American leaders, the way Barack Obama does. "We still have to leverage powerful white people to get what we need and I think Sharpton doesn't have the finesse to do it."[31]

I read Erica's quote to Reverend Sharpton and asked him to respond. He called her analysis "a very reasoned answer" but added, "The problem with that is at the end of the day, one would have to say, 'What are the goals and the achievements?' If my goals were to try to get racial profiling laws there and I did, and put

people in jail that broke the law and we did, and open up corporate America and we did, then where do you say is the lack of ma-
neuvering? You can't compare that to Barack's goals of getting
legislation passed because that was not my goal, that was not my
role. I think you always have to judge people by the basis of what
they do. Just like it would be unfair to say has Barack done anything about police brutality or has he been able to do some of the
stuff I do. He's not a civil rights activist. So it's almost like saying
I like Sharpton as a boxer but he doesn't hit enough home runs
because he don't play baseball." He added, "A friend of mine—
conservative, Republican, black—called me this morning and
says, 'Every time I say that we no longer need an Al Sharpton
then Imus opens his mouth and I say, you know what, we still
need guys like Sharpton.'"[32]

Although Sharpton is often cited by the media as well as critics
as the epitome of the black leader phenomenon, he considers it "a
biased term" and wonders why people want to limit the scope of
his leadership. "Why am I not a leader, a political leader, or a civil
rights leader? You don't call Jerry Falwell a white leader."[33]

Alexis McGill, the political scientist, notes that the media tend
to follow the "representations that they have the easiest access to,"
which happen to be Sharpton and Jackson, and while some may
find their high-profile existence irritating, she believes there is a
place for them.[34] But critics argue that Sharpton and Jackson de-
liberately seek out high-profile issues in an effort to be seen as
spokespeople for the African American community, and that
claims to the contrary are disingenuous. Lauren Williams, editor
of Stereohyped.com, a news and entertainment blog for African

Americans, states emphatically, "Al Sharpton's not my leader. Jesse Jackson's not my leader. They don't speak for me. I don't agree with everything they say. I don't agree with everything they do. I resent the implication that I'm supposed to be following these people when they've decided that they are leaders and the media has bought into it."[35]

This perception appears to be shared by a majority of young black Americans. According to our survey, Jackson and Sharpton are two of the least influential high-profile African Americans. When asked, "Of the following, whose opinion do you value most?" 20 percent of respondents selected Oprah Winfrey, 20 percent selected Barack Obama, and 15 percent chose Colin Powell. Jesse Jackson garnered 7 percent while Sharpton came in last with 4 percent, behind both Russell Simmons and Condoleezza Rice.[36]

In spite of their differing political perspectives and party affiliations, Powell and Obama share one quality that sets them apart from leaders like Jackson and Sharpton: while acknowledging that their race is a part of what defines them, Powell and Obama have chosen not to be defined by racial politics. This has earned them a measure of distinction and admiration among a constituency of young black professionals that eludes Jackson and Sharpton.

"Karl," a young black voter in his thirties, says that when he hears the names Jesse Jackson or Al Sharpton, "I think old-school." Both, he says, have "run their course." (Karl asked that his real name not be used because he maintains close personal and professional ties with prominent Democrats). In contrast, he was ebullient with admiration of Colin Powell and explained that he strongly believes Powell has almost single-handedly reshaped the way both white and black Americans view black Americans.[37] According to a piece in *Time* magazine, "Powell and Obama have another thing in common: they are black people who—like Tiger Woods, Oprah Winfrey and Michael Jordan—seem to have an iconic power over the American imagination because they transcend racial stereotypes."[38]

Regardless of their politics, nearly all of those interviewed expressed admiration for Powell. Many credited him with helping reshape the way white Americans view blacks in leadership positions and consequently building the foundation on which leaders like Obama and Rice now stand. Karl, who formerly worked for a Democratic elected official, says of Powell, "He did for us what Bill Cosby did for us with *The Cosby Show*. He brought us to a level where we could think 'we are GOOD.' Even if you don't agree with him you're like, 'Colin's the man. He should have been president.' If he had run he would have been president. He was good enough to be president. Nobody can knock that."[39] In his stand-up special *Bring the Pain,* Chris Rock wryly observes that speculation about Powell being drafted as a vice presidential candidate was insulting to Powell because "he [would be running] with a guy he could beat."[40]

As simple as it may sound, part of what makes Powell so appealing to this younger generation is his willingness to say and stand up for what he actually believes, without making a political calculation. At the 1996 Republican National Convention, Powell was loudly booed for sharing his unpopular (with that audience) views on hot-button cultural and social issues, stating, "You all know that I believe in a woman's right to choose and I strongly support affirmative action."[41]

Those interviewed felt that he demonstrated similar conviction during his tenure as secretary of state. Whatever role he may have played in our country's march to war appears to have been trumped by the perception that he was not a true believer and as such walked away from a failing policy and a flailing administration. Margo, a self-described liberal, says of Powell, "He seems like a very strong leader. I appreciated the fact that he stood up during the Iraq war and stood his ground." She added that she thinks Powell is "a good person."[42]

"Julius," a business consultant, identifies Powell as the political leader he admires most in the world. (Julius asked that his real name not be used because his company frowns on public discussion of politics.) A first-generation American, he references Powell's modest beginnings as the son of Jamaican immigrants, saying, "I admire Colin Powell for the simple reason that he made his way through the ranks. He started from humble beginnings and he is an example of the American Dream."[43] This admiration for Powell is particularly striking, considering that Julius adamantly opposes the war in Iraq and says that he would never vote for a candidate who supports it. Yet Powell's appeal transcends the issue.

Cary, the Morehouse graduate, says of Powell, "I think he's a wise, wise man who is a true example of what it means to be a political figure . . . at a great cost." He particularly admires the way Powell dealt with Iraq, saying he "did what you are supposed to do" when your conscience puts you at odds with your job. He adds that "I think he's a really smart man." But most of all, he says, he admires Powell for a leadership style that sets him apart from other high-profile, so-called black leaders. "He's soft-spoken but I think those are the strongest leaders sometimes."[44]

In a telephone interview for this book, Powell made himself clear about his feelings regarding the term "black leader": "I consider myself a leader who is black and always have. I have always made it clear that I am a black man, proud to be a black man, I've worked hard all my life as a black man, and I have tried to take advantage of the sacrifices that were made by the black men and women who went before me." But he always found it troublesome when people commended him on being a black secretary of state. "When people would come up and usually put it in the form of 'It's great to have a black secretary of state. You're the black secretary of state.' And I would smile and say, 'Is there a white secretary of state?' I am the secretary of state, period." Powell notes that this type of separate but equal praise has followed him throughout his career. "I'm black and proud of it, but don't put *black* in front of 'secretary of state' or in front of 'general.' When I was a young lieutenant I was once told, 'You're the best black lieutenant I've ever seen' and I accepted the compliment and went away with the position that I've got to convince this guy that I'm the best *lieutenant* he's ever seen." Powell feels this was important for his own career but also for blacks in general. "I didn't want him to confine me and so I have always resisted being confined to a solely black context, and when you look at my career over the last twenty years: first national security adviser who was black; first chairman of the Joint Chiefs of Staff who was black; first secretary of state who was black; first four-star commander of the armed forces who was black; but I always want 'black' to come after so that it doesn't confine me to a particular demographic. That's not what we fought for all these years, to be confined that way or categorized that way." And with a quick laugh, "or to be called 'articulate.'"[45]

To reinforce his point, Powell cites some of his high-profile friends in leadership roles as examples of how being a great leader, period, trumps being a great "black leader." He feels, for instance, that *Newsweek*'s 2002 cover story heralding the rise of people like Richard Parsons of AOL, Stanley O'Neal of Merrill Lynch, and Kenneth Chenault of American Express as "the new black power" was incredibly outdated. Powell notes that these men "have been extremely successful and become extremely wealthy and extremely well regarded not just in the black business community but in the business community. They do not represent black power; they represent power." He calls any thoughts to the contrary "a forty-year-old headline."[46]

Powell's analysis illustrates the long-standing reality that blacks in leadership positions often find themselves under a peculiar cultural microscope. Along with the responsibility of leading, they are also expected to serve as de facto cultural ambassadors who must be ready at any moment to accurately translate their race's culture, language, and opinions. Additionally there is the pressure that comes with being anointed an official representative of your race, whether that is your announced intention or not. This is why Jackie Robinson never publicly reacted to the numerous indignities he faced during his tenure in Major League Baseball. He knew that if he fought back he might not only harm his own career but the career of every black man who came after him.

White male leaders do not face the same level of scrutiny. No pundits or academics gathered to discuss how the impeachment of President Clinton would affect future white candidates for the presidency. But consider what would have happened if the man Toni Morrison called "the first black president" had actually been black. While Americans like to believe in the idealistic notion that prejudice no longer exists, who can doubt that subsequent black candidates would have faced unflattering comparisons to their scandal-plagued predecessor?

A 2006 article in *The Economist* crystallizes the uneasy burden of leadership expectations that blacks in American politics have long faced within their own communities. As the article notes, the need to secure support in primarily black voting districts often causes these leaders to be pigeonholed politically. Later they find that their ability to appeal to more diverse audiences is limited because they have become identified as black leaders and are seen as capable of leading only black constituencies. What makes this burden even more frustrating for black leaders is that their white peers do not face it. No mainstream white elected official has ever been rejected for seeming "too white," yet a black official could easily see his career ended on a national scale for seeming "too black." Unfortunately, the catch-22 is that a black official could have his or her career ended (before it even began) among crucial black voters for seeming "too white" (as Newark Mayor Cory Booker found out in his first run for office).[47]

As *The Economist* notes, the rise of Barack Obama seems to mark a fresh new direction for black leadership in America. "Something about him," the piece says, "fills a gap in American politics: he seems not to be faking when he talks of mending America's religious and racial divides. He is that rare thing, a black politician who addresses the whole nation, not just an ethnic enclave."[48]

Most of the young black Americans interviewed for this book think Jackson and Sharpton represent the past. Obama, with his sterling credentials and charismatic personality, represents their hope for the future.

Obama's meteoric rise perfectly demonstrates the burden that comes with being a black American leader in whom countless numbers—both black and white—entrust their hopes and dreams. He is also an example of the intense hype and scrutiny that inevitably results when America believes it has discovered yet another extraordinary minority. Obama is to politics today what Tiger Woods was to golf ten years ago. The hope, anticipation, and speculation about what he might be tomorrow is even more exciting than watching him today. Like Woods, he is an emerging icon who can make both black and white Americans feel good about themselves.

For black Americans he represents the American Dream; as he said in his career-making speech at the 2004 Democratic National Convention, "the hope of a skinny kid with a funny name that believes America has a place for him too." For white Americans he represents a different kind of ideal. A cover profile of Obama in *Time* quotes Shelby Steele, who is noted for his writings on racial theory, as saying, "White people are just thrilled when a prominent black person comes along and doesn't rub their noses in racial guilt. White people just go crazy over people like that."[49]

Joe Klein, the author of the *Time* piece, observes that "Obama's personal appeal is made manifest when he steps down from the podium and is swarmed by well-wishers of all ages and hues, although the difference in reaction between whites and blacks is subtly striking. The African-Americans tend to be fairly reserved—quiet pride, knowing nods and be-careful-now looks. The white people, by contrast, are out of control. A nurse named Greta, just off a 12-hour shift, tentatively reaches out to touch the Senator's sleeve. 'Oh, my God! Oh, my God! I just touched a future President! I can't believe it!' She is literally shaking with delight—her voice is quivering—as she asks Obama for an autograph and then a hug."[50]

With a multiracial background that includes a white mother and being raised by white grandparents, Obama represents a black man and leader who does not use anger at white America as a political weapon. Combined with his Harvard law degree and his beautiful family, this makes him a leader all Americans can embrace. During an appearance on the *Oprah Winfrey Show* to promote his memoir *The Audacity of Hope*, Obama called his family a "mini United Nations" and said he has relatives who resemble both Bernie Mac, the dark-skinned African American comedian, and Margaret Thatcher, the former prime minister of England. He told Winfrey he considers his diverse family tree an asset that helps him relate to people of all backgrounds. It is therefore not surprising that Obama, a multiracial candidate, has struck such a chord with younger Americans, who have begun to embrace an increasingly multicultural worldview.

Though there have been some high-profile exceptions (most notably in response to the Jena Six), for the most part younger black Americans are more likely to continue the battle for civil rights in corporate boardrooms and on America's college campuses than on the streets of Birmingham. Therefore they have begun to question the effectiveness of traditional protest politics. And they have also begun to question the effectiveness (and sincerity) of the leaders within the black community who rely primarily on the politics of protest (and press conferences). This has left an opening on the opposite end of the leadership spectrum that helps explain why Oprah Winfrey and Barack Obama were both selected by respondents as the most influential among a list of highly influential black Americans.

Winfrey may epitomize what it means today to be an effective black leader (or rather a leader who is black). While she does not sign official product endorsement deals, her indirect endorsement of the books on her program (including those not included in her book club but simply mentioned) was cited by a 2004 study by Brigham Young University as having a greater influence on book sales than anything else in the history of modern publishing.[51] Just imagine the impact she could have if she actually did endorse products, including candidates.

It appears we are about to find out. For the first time ever, Winfrey has decided to toss her hat into the political ring—not as a candidate herself but by endorsing her friend (and senator in her home state of Illinois), Barack Obama. While she has never involved herself directly in a political race, one could argue that she has already played a pivotal role in the outcome of an election. In 2003 she welcomed her longtime friend, newswoman Maria Shriver, onto her program along with Shriver's husband, movie star Arnold Schwarzenegger. At the time, Schwarzenegger was a newly announced candidate for governor and was being dogged by controversial statements regarding women and allegations of inappropriate sexual behavior in the past. These allegations were viewed as particularly damaging among female voters. Shriver and Schwarzenegger put on a united front, but, more importantly, the warmth and camaraderie on display between the three of them was evidence of Oprah's decades-old friendship with the two. (She was a guest at their wedding.) Oprah did not need to endorse Schwarzenegger's candidacy; her body language spoke volumes. To her, clearly, these were two great people she would not only gladly support in a voting booth but gladly welcome (and likely had) into her home. The appearance may not have been Schwarzenegger's magic antidote, but it certainly stopped the hemorrhaging and put his campaign well on the road to recovery.

The goodwill Oprah enjoys among the American people and her nonthreatening persona even allow her to address controversial racial issues in a way that is accessible for white Americans. When Christopher Darden, the former assistant district attorney who prosecuted the O.J. Simpson case, appeared on her program in 2006, they discussed how divided Americans remained over the Simpson verdict even years after the trial. While Oprah made it clear that she considers Simpson guilty, she wondered if Darden could at least understand why some black Americans might perceive the verdict as "evening the score" with white America after all the injustices blacks have experienced, beginning with slavery (a sentiment she made clear she personally does *not* agree with). The moment was stunning because in one sound bite she had managed to articulate the position of countless black Americans more accurately than almost any legal analyst had done, yet without alienating her predominantly white audience.

Would that have been the response had Al Sharpton made the same statement? Would white Americans have even heard him, or would they have tuned out of the conversation before it even began? Would they have done a simple calculation that Sharpton + O.J. Simpson trial = antiwhite tirade = I am not listening?

Similarly, in 2005, when she was denied entry into the exclusive Hermes boutique in Paris and said that she felt race played a role, she forced white Americans to pause and ask themselves: If Oprah Winfrey still faces discrimination today, how bad must it be for the average black American?

With her immense wealth and her enormous contributions to historically black colleges and other programs, Oprah has arguably done more than anyone else to provide educational opportunities for blacks since integration. By honoring black icons such as Rosa Parks and Coretta Scott King in her nationally televised Legends Ball, she introduced more Americans to the importance of those civil rights icons than any black history class ever could.

If being an effective black leader means having the power to make things better for black people and to engage black America,

white America, and all of America, then Oprah is in a class by
herself. What makes her such an effective leader is that she actually spends her time, energy, and resources changing the world
for the better for all Americans, as opposed to spending it trying
to prove to us that she is "the nation's most important black
leader."

When asked to name a social or political leader he admires,
Luke, the stylist, says that no political leader has earned his utmost admiration, but the social leader who has is Oprah Winfrey.
He said he considers her the quintessential leader because "with
her beliefs, her morals, her values and who she is, she's consistent
and a lot of leaders are not consistent. They'll compromise but
she doesn't really compromise."[52]

The comic Chris Rock believes the black community needs to
become more creative in its efforts to find a black leader. In *Bigger
and Blacker,* Rock proposes his nomination for America's most
important black leader. "You know who I think the Black leader
should be? Pat Riley. Coach Pat Riley. No one has brought more
black men to the promised land than Pat Riley. He may not get
us to the mountaintop but he'll get us to the playoffs. That's all
we can ask for."[53]

But maybe not. If Barack Obama's candidacy is successful, all
Americans, regardless of color, could end up with their very own
black leader.

Chapter 6

THE POLI-
TICS OF THE
PULPIT

Does God Endorse
Candidates and
Do Young Black
Voters Care?

In the battleground of American politics, black churches have
long been portrayed as playing Tony Blair to the Democratic
Party's George W. Bush: an ally expected to provide unwavering
support and loyalty while never publicly questioning what he gets
out of the relationship. Over the past two election cycles, however,
cracks have begun to appear in the once unbreakable bond between influential black clergy and Democrats. These cracks have
already begun to influence elections, most notably in 2004. Black
ministers in states like Ohio can claim at least some of the credit
for helping to secure George W. Bush's second term (more on that
later). The evolution of black churches, from a reliable weapon in
the Democratic Election Day arsenal to a weapon of mass destruc-

tion for Republicans, has raised questions about which issues matter most to black voters and whose voices wield the most influence with them. It has also confirmed one undeniable political reality. Traditional Democratic strategy for reaching black voters—which one black pastor described as "showing up the Sunday before the election on Tuesday"—is as dead as Tony Blair's political career.

The church has long played a pivotal role in the black community's social and political movements. Perhaps one of the strongest testaments to the church's importance as a source of empowerment for blacks is the fact that religious gatherings were heavily regulated during slavery. Blacks faced restrictions on when, where, and how they could worship, the concern being that if left unsupervised such gatherings could result in a unity of thought and sense of community that could prove dangerous. Black ministers in the North were active in the movement to abolish slavery.[1] Later, influential ministers like Adam Clayton Powell, Jr., of Harlem's famed Abyssinian Baptist Church, used the power of the pulpit to establish a voice for congregants and the surrounding community on social and political issues. Powell would eventually leverage this power into a legendary political career becoming New York's first black member of Congress.

The civil rights movement solidified the political power of black churches. As one of the few places in most southern towns where blacks could congregate without drawing suspicion, the church often served as a community meeting place and primary source of information, and thus naturally emerged as the centerpiece of the civil rights movement. In an era long before the NBA and NFL (let alone tennis) were dominated by black superstars (and a "rapper" was something you removed from a piece of candy), ministers were the public figures the black community looked up to. They became the movement's defining faces. The Southern Christian Leadership Conference (SCLC), consisting of Martin Luther King, Jr., and fellow pastors like Ralph David Abernathy, Fred Shuttlesworth, and Joseph Lowery, imbued the movement with an aura of moral and spiritual authority over those seeking to defeat it. Equally importantly, the combined efforts of SCLC leaders and their parishioners proved to be an unstoppable force for social change. Pastors and their congregants formed the backbone of one of the movement's defining moments, the Montgomery bus boycott.

Their pivotal role made churches an attractive target to those who opposed civil rights, and eventually a church became the setting of one of the movement's most harrowing tragedies. In 1963 a bomb launched by Ku Klux Klan members tore through the 16th Street Baptist Church in Birmingham, Alabama, killing four young girls (one of whom, Denise McNair, was a childhood classmate of Condoleezza Rice). Even white Americans who opposed integration ideologically were appalled at the idea of children—particularly in a house of worship—becoming collateral damage. Instead of silencing the movement as intended, the bombing served as a galvanizing turning point.

While some black ministers, like Powell, had already clearly aligned themselves with the Democratic Party, others were initially less definite in their party alliances. Martin Luther King, Sr., the pastor of Atlanta's Ebenezer Baptist Church, spent much of his life as a registered Republican. This was not uncommon at a time when many blacks still associated the "Republican" label with Abraham Lincoln and the freeing of slaves. This would change virtually overnight during the 1960 presidential election, after a dramatic series of phone calls placed in October of that year by John F. Kennedy and his brother Bobby.

Just weeks before the election, Martin Luther King, Jr., was arrested during an Atlanta sit-in. Although the charges were dropped, the authorities kept King in jail for an alleged parole violation. John F. Kennedy placed a call to King's wife, Coretta, offering sympathy and support. Shortly thereafter, his brother contacted both the governor of Georgia, S. Ernest Vandiver, and the presiding judge in the case, Oscar Mitchell, to help orchestrate King's release on bail.

In his autobiography, King recounted the impact these events had on his view of the presidential race:

> Senator Kennedy had served as a great force in making my release from Reidsville Prison possible. I was personally obligated to him and his brother for their intervention during my imprisonment. He did it because of his great concern and his humanitarian bent. I would like to feel that he made the call because he was concerned. He had come to know me as a person then. He had been in the debates and had done a good job when he talked about civil rights and what the Negro faces. Harris and others had really been talking with him about it. At the same time, I think he naturally had political considerations in mind. He was running for an office, and he needed to be elected, and I'm

sure he felt the need for the Negro votes. So I think that he did something that expressed deep moral concern, but at the same time it was politically sound. It did take a little courage to do this; he didn't know it was politically sound.

I always felt that Nixon lost a real opportunity to express support of something much larger than an individual, because this expressed support for the movement for civil rights. It indicated the direction that this man would take, if he became president.

And I had known Nixon longer. He had been supposedly close to me, and he would call me frequently about things, seeking my advice. And yet, when this moment came, it was like he had never heard of me. So this is why I really considered him a moral coward and one who was really unwilling to take a courageous step and take a risk. And I am convinced that he lost the election because of that. Many Negroes were still on the fence, still undecided, and they were leaning toward Nixon.[2]

While King was reluctant to endorse candidates publicly, saying he wanted to maintain a nonpartisan stance, his father did endorse candidates and in fact had already endorsed Richard Nixon prior to his son's arrest.

That abruptly changed. King would write, "My father had endorsed Nixon until that call. He knew about my relations with Nixon, and I think he felt that Nixon would do a good job on the civil rights question. I guess deep down within there may have been a little of the religious feeling that a Catholic should not be president. I'm sure my father had been somewhat influenced by this, so that he had gone on record endorsing Nixon. After that call, he changed, and he made a very strong statement."[3]

Not only did King Sr. switch his endorsement, but he used his influence to encourage other black ministers to support Kennedy as well. Kennedy went on to win in 1960 in one of the closest presidential elections in our nation's history (along with that *other* election in 2000), and support from black voters was credited with cementing his victory.

Thus began the storied relationship between the Democratic Party and black churches. As southern Dixiecrats left the party in droves in response to the civil rights legislation championed and signed into law by Lyndon Johnson, the bond between blacks and Democrats solidified. Sunday morning treks to black houses of worship became as commonplace for white candidates seeking black support as kissing babies. Cornell Belcher, pollster for the Democratic National Committee, notes that "if it were not for frequent church-going African American women, the Democratic Party would be in a lot of trouble because they are among the strongest Democratic votes."[4]

It is no coincidence that the last two successful Democratic presidential candidates, Jimmy Carter and Bill Clinton, were both extremely comfortable in black churches, no doubt due in part to their southern heritage. When Clinton gets revved up, his speaking style has drawn comparisons to that of a preacher (and it's probably safe to assume that this is meant as a reference to a black southern preacher as opposed to, say, a white Presbyterian minister).

In any marriage, the honeymoon eventually gives way to the mundane realities of dirty socks, missed anniversaries, and spousal complaints of feeling taken for granted. In the marriage between Democrats and black churches, the churches have become the neglected spouse.

Some would say it's even worse. Bishop Harry Jackson of the conservative High Impact Leadership Coalition likens the treatment black churches receive from Democrats on the campaign trail to the way a married man treats his mistress. Black ministers and parishioners alike feel that Democratic candidates spend the majority of their campaigns with the voters who really matter to them and then creep over to predominantly black churches for a "Sunday morning drive-by" just before Election Day, not to be seen or heard from again until they are in the mood.[5]

This is a rare issue on which Bishop Jackson and Reverend Al Sharpton find common ground. In a speech at the 2005 National Urban League Conference, Sharpton said, "We must stop allowing people to gain politically from us if they're not reciprocating when dealing and being held accountable." He cautioned black voters not to allow politicians to "come by and get our votes 'cause they wave at us on Sunday morning while the choir's singing. And we act like that is reaching out."[6]

This sense of being taken for granted, combined with black Americans' conservatism on social issues, combined to create a perfect storm in 2004, one that left the Democrats with flood damage.

Much of the black community has long been conservative on social issues like abortion, but historically this has not translated into votes for conservatives. Issues like abortion and gay marriage had not entered the political sphere when blacks first secured the right to vote and established their alliance with Democrats. Later, after these issues had entered the national discourse, they were seldom discussed publicly within the black community. This long-standing practice has permitted many black ministers to maintain cozy relationships with Democrats in spite of their disagreement on various social issues. The thinking is that while we may not agree on abortion or gay rights or sexual education, since we're not going to talk about it anyway it needn't color our politics.

That position was easier to maintain in the 1960s when the partnership between Democrats and black churches was still new. Back then abortions were barbaric back ally operations that no one dared discuss. The idea of gay marriage was as laughable as the idea that one day a woman might actually become president and the term "sex education" was an oxymoron. The only issue that really mattered was civil rights, and since the Democrats were (eventually) on the right side of the issue that the ministers *were* publicly talking about, the ones that they weren't simply ceased to matter.

The sexual revolution, *Roe v. Wade,* the crack epidemic, AIDS, and even MTV would change all that.

If it was once a matter of decorum to stay away from taboo topics in the sanctuary, as they grew increasingly visible in the popular culture the silence ceased to seem quaint. Instead it began to seem like denial bordering on insanity. But denial wasn't solely to blame. In 1992 the Democrats stumbled upon a presidential nominee whose charm and charisma evoked comparisons to JFK. It was only fitting that Arkansas Governor Bill Clinton, like Jack Kennedy before him, would make the black clergy a cornerstone of his successful campaign and subsequent presidency.

At the start of the new century, as civil rights struggles over segregated schools gave way to squabbles over affirmative action, social issues it was once acceptable not to discuss had begun to have a devastating impact on the black community. Today nearly two-thirds of black children are born out of wedlock, a statistic often blamed for others that are equally disheartening, most notably the high incarceration and unemployment rates among black men.[7] As a promotional video for Amachi, a mentoring group for children of incarcerated parents, puts it, "You've got to see a man to be a man."[8]

Yet the statistic that is most troubling threatens not only the community's social well-being but its health. According to the Centers for Disease Control, AIDS is now the leading cause of death for black women ages twenty-five to thirty-four.[9]

These issues have made it increasingly difficult for black ministers to maintain a comfortable silence on once taboo subjects, although that hasn't stopped some from trying. Yet at a certain point the silence becomes deafening. To be fair, there are certainly black ministers who are committed to making a difference on these issues. But in stark contrast to their predecessors' stance during the civil rights movement, the present generation of leading black ministers has come to no firm public consensus either that these problems are necessary to talk about or that finding appropriate solutions is just as important to the long-term survival and success of the black community as the civil rights movement was. In fact it was an actor, Bill Cosby, who called attention to some of the most pressing social issues plaguing the black community. His recent controversial comments have done more to bring these subjects into the open than any high-profile members of the clergy have.

One issue on which black ministers do seem comfortable in reaching a public consensus is gay marriage. According to a study conducted by the Pew Forum on Religion and Public Life, while support for gay rights has increased since 2000 among most racial and religious groups (including Catholics and Jews as well as other Protestants), it has decreased among black Protestants. After reaching a high of 65 percent in 1996, it fell to 40 percent in 2004.[10] Many ministers see gay marriage as a threat to black families and therefore the black community at large. (Apparently it is more of a threat than rampant out-of-wedlock births and sky-rocketing AIDS rates.) The possibility of gay marriage becoming a reality struck a nerve among many black ministers and returned the black church to the forefront of political activism.

It is often said that every black person has a gay cousin or uncle who everyone in the family knows is gay but no one talks about it. This "don't ask, don't tell" approach has served as a comfortable cloak for one of the community's dirty little secrets: homophobia. When I asked Julian Bond, chairman of the NAACP, if he believes the majority of the black community is homophobic, he said that while he cannot definitively state that a majority of blacks are, he would say that a great number are.[11] Bond is a part of a small but prominent group of civil rights luminaries, including the late Coretta Scott King and Representative John

Lewis, who have described gay rights as the last remaining civil rights frontier, a perspective that has drawn fire from many in the black community.

Bond says he is "positive" that homophobia has hindered the community's response to the AIDS epidemic, particularly among churches. He adds, "I don't want to condemn all the black churches in America because I think the picture is really mixed, and I don't know to what degree and to what percentage black churches are engaged in the fight against AIDS or are not. . . . I think some are doing great work. But I do think this Bible-based ignorance is devastating to the fight against AIDS."[12]

Al Sharpton echoes that sentiment. "I know that homophobia plays a role. I think the reason that a lot of black ministers, churches, and leaders don't address [AIDS] is because of homophobia. They don't want to identify with an issue that they think is derived in even some remote way from homosexuality. . . . And I think that in that denial our people are dying, and you have epidemic proportions of that among our people, particularly our women who are given HIV [by] men who are infecting them."[13]

Hip-hop mogul Russell Simmons agrees that homophobia has slowed the community's response to AIDS. He calls this a "sad" fact but expresses hope that one day the community will "get past this."[14]

In an article in *Newsweek*, Ellis Cose writes that some religious leaders in the black community are so overwhelmed by the magnitude of problems they are seeking to address, including poverty, that they simply get stretched too thin. But "some of the reluctance also comes from a combination of denial and disgust.

For taking on AIDS means openly talking about things that many people, particularly those who are culturally conservative, find exceedingly distasteful or discomforting," including sex, drugs, and men having sex with men. Cose writes that Jatrice Martel Gaiter, of Planned Parenthood in Washington, D.C., "finds such attitudes not just troubling but profoundly immoral. Religious leaders, in her view, have a responsibility 'to preach about this from the pulpit, to write about it, to have an AIDS ministry.' But more often than not, she believes, the black church is silent. In an age when prostitutes—at least in certain areas of Washington—are paid twice as much for sex without a condom as with, and unsafe sex is rampant among teens, Gaiter argues that reticence can kill." Other experts cited in the piece note that some churches are more comfortable supporting efforts to address the AIDS epidemic in Africa than in the United States because doing so would be an acknowledgment that it actually happens here—and more likely than not has happened to someone they know. According to Gaiter, "I think the black middle class has almost totally rejected this issue—as if they are excluded from it, or embarrassed by these people."[15]

Floyd Flake is one of the most prominent ministers in the nation, black or white. He is also one of the most savvy at bridging religion and politics. Flake received a doctor of ministry degree from the United Theological Seminary in Dayton, Ohio, and served in the House of Representatives from 1987 to 1997. He retired from Congress to spend more time supervising the growth of Greater Allen AME Cathedral, a megachurch that has grown into a megacorporation with an 825-person workforce, an operating budget approaching $24 million, "expansive commercial and residential development, [a] 500-student private school, and various commercial and social service enterprises."[16] When I asked Flake if he believes the black church has abdicated its leadership responsibility on key social issues and if homophobia is at all to blame, his reply suggested that the answer is not as simple as the question. Flake notes that the so-called black church "has many components and many facets. When you say that the black church has abdicated the responsibility, I think it is a failure of people to understand that it is not necessarily monolithic in its approach to all issues. You've got some churches, particularly those that are pastored by older pastors, where they don't deal with AIDS or gays or abortion or anything else. They don't deal with any social issues. You've got others that deal with what they call the issues of justice and that's basically their silo. You've got others, like this church or Potter's House, where you're dealing with the broad band of issues, which is inclusive of AIDS. No church that's going to sustain and survive into the future is going to spend all of its investment on AIDS or anything else."[17]

Luke, the stylist who is in his twenties, says that he "absolutely" believes that the church bears some responsibility for the surging AIDS epidemic. In his own experience, he found that the church's commitment to shunning those that it deems to be sinners outweighs its commitment to providing a nurturing and supportive environment for those in need. He tells a story of a pastor at a church that he attended who would regularly denounce "faggots" from the pulpit. He finally decided to confront the pastor one day after the service. He told him, "I do respect your position as being leader, but if you're going to lead, lead the right way. Lead in love and not hate." The pastor replied, "I'm not leading in hate. God loves us all," before advising him that if he was indeed a "faggot" he needed to change. Luke answered that the appropriate word is "homosexual."[18]

Pastor Dennis Meredith of the historic Tabernacle Baptist Church in Atlanta has learned firsthand just how strong antigay sentiment runs in the black community, particularly in the church. Meredith says he had long taken a more "traditional" approach in the pulpit, espousing the traditional message on homosexuality: it is bad, and so are the people who practice it. When he arrived at Tabernacle in the early 1990s, the once-thriving congregation was struggling. After more than seventy years in existence, the church was down to fewer than two hundred members. Meredith's enthusiastic leadership turned the tide, and by 2002 the church had reached megachurch status with three thousand members.[19]

That all changed nearly five years ago when Meredith's son told him he was gay. Meredith's "traditional" condemnation of gays and lesbians evolved into a message of tolerance. Today when you visit the church's website you find the greeting, "Welcome to Tabernacle Baptist Church: A Place of Love and Acceptance." With this change the church lost more than a third of its membership. Some of those who left said they did not want to be known as members of the "gay church."[20]

Meredith lost personal relationships as well. Longtime friends among the clergy began to ostracize him, and invitations for speaking engagements dried up. When I asked Meredith if he considers the majority of the black community homophobic, he said that homophobia is so pervasive within the black community that it even includes blacks who are themselves gay. Concerning the roots of homophobia in the black community, Meredith observes, "We're not a community that is by and large well read. We typically like for people to tell us things instead of investigating and conducting research for ourselves. . . . Our concept of human sexuality is very conservative and not good, which lends itself to why we have a whole lot of teen pregnancy, why the AIDS epidemic is so prevalent in the African American community, why STDs are out of control. We have a terrible concept of how we approach human sexuality . . . and that's just not healthy."[21]

After a difficult transition, Tabernacle is flourishing again, bolstered by its growing gay population. When asked how he responds to critics of his message and policy of acceptance, Meredith notes that people often try to shape the Bible to their own needs, or their own message rather than God's. "The Bible is not a book about human sexuality," he said. Trying to frame it as such, he added, is like trying to use it as a mechanic's manual. Most of all, Meredith points out, the Bible clearly teaches that "God is love," and that means love for "everybody." Not only did Jesus not specifically discuss sexuality but "the only thing Jesus did not tolerate was *in*tolerance. He was *not* tolerant of that."[22]

Meredith believes the politicization of the gay marriage issue in the 2004 election was nothing more than a "diversion" from more pressing issues, such as the war in Iraq. He admits to knowing a number of pastors who do not care for George W. Bush personally but encouraged parishioners to vote for him because of his support for a ban on same-sex marriage. In his home state of Ohio, he said, a friend who pastors a large black church had welcomed Meredith to use the premises for a gospel recording he was making, but the invitation was rescinded after word spread within the church about Meredith's stance on gays and lesbians.[23]

Clearly Meredith's clergy friends were not alone. Prior to the 2004 election, many were dubious about an Election Day scenario presented by David Bositis of the Joint Center for Political and Economic Studies, asserting that President Bush could garner as much as 18 percent of the black vote. While that figure amounted to little more than wishful thinking for the GOP nationally, as Bositis would later tell the *Village Voice,* the one place where he was *not* wrong was Ohio. There, Bush drew 16 percent of the black vote, more than enough to put him over the top.[24]

Cornell Belcher, the DNC pollster, says that assessments of the impact of the gay marriage issue on the presidential election are exaggerated, noting that previous GOP presidential candidates, like Bob Dole, also received double-digit black support in Ohio.[25] In a recent interview, Bositis told me that while it is true that Ohio has a more GOP-friendly history than some other states, the role of gay marriage should not be underestimated. After all, Bob Dole's double-digit numbers did not stop Bill Clinton from winning the state in that election.[26]

If gay marriage was a mere diversion in 2004, it was an effective one, but Meredith predicts it will not be so in the future. He labels gay marriage an election year issue and muses that some of his clergy friends who once advocated so passionately from the

pulpit on behalf of the president now believe they made a mistake. The church's future on these issues, Meredith points out,
will be shaped by its future leaders—younger parishioners whom
he describes as more open-minded and accepting than their parents and grandparents.[27]

Few individuals have been more influential in shaping the culture and attitudes of younger black Americans than hip-hop icon
Russell Simmons. During a recent interview, he acknowledged
that homophobia is prevalent among black Americans (and has
consequently been a part of hip-hop), but he believes that is
changing. Simmons, who supports gay marriage, believes that
younger black Americans are more accepting than their parents
and that each generation will be more accepting than the last. At
least that is his hope.[28]

The numbers suggest that he is right. In our study of four
hundred randomly selected black Americans ages eighteen to
forty-five, half of all respondents ages eighteen to twenty-four
support either marriage rights or partnership benefits for gays
and lesbians.[29]

Meredith notes that while his congregation lost eight hundred
members due to its controversial policy of inclusion of gays and lesbians, membership remains relatively healthy at 2,200. The biggest
change has been in the makeup of the congregation. Previously,
the church consisted primarily of parishioners between the ages
of forty and sixty. Now, the typical age of its members is twenty
to thirty. While more than half the congregation is made up of
gay men and women, they are joined by young heterosexuals who
simply enjoy worshiping there. Meredith was initially surprised at

how accepting his younger parishioners are. He recalls how he asked a bride scheduled to wed at the church if it bothered her that some people call it the "gay church." She replied, "We live in a world of diversity and I want my church to reflect that."[30]

When asked how he sees the future of the black church's relationship with gays and lesbians, Meredith draws parallels to the church's once fierce opposition to female ministers, which is now a distant memory in most major houses of worship. He likens opposition to gays and lesbians to the way a child stands on the beach, trying to block the waves with his body. As Pastor Meredith sees it, acceptance is the rising tide. "It's inevitable. It's going to happen. God is moving the world towards a place of love and acceptance. Fifteen to twenty years from now, what's happening in my church will be happening in churches all over the country."[30]

While it is easy to think of the GOP's use of gay marriage to draw black votes as the tactics of a flirtatious floozy looking to exploit the cracks in a shaky marriage, the real explanation is more complicated. Cornell Belcher argues that religion has long affected the politics of blacks and whites differently, "The more frequently a white person is in church on a weekly basis, the stronger they are voting Republican. The more frequently an African American is going to church, it is almost the reverse."[31] That could be changing, particularly at America's megachurches.

Alexis McGill, the political scientist and expert on hip-hop voters, explains that the growth of megachurches, with their emphasis on economic issues and the so-called prosperity gospel, taps into "a very strong self-help reliance" philosophy in the black community, one that presents an opening for conservatives. "I think the right is picking up on this in a way that hasn't existed before."[32]

Since his tenure as governor of Texas, George W. Bush has been cultivating close relationships with influential black ministers, among them Bishop T. D. Jakes, pastor of the nearly 30,000 strong Potter's House ministry based in Dallas. Jakes, who was named one of the twenty-five most influential evangelicals by *Time* magazine, has described the president as "someone who takes his faith seriously."[33] His wife, Serita Ann Jakes, and First Lady Laura Bush have been described as good friends. Mrs. Jakes delivered remarks at a White House luncheon for "African American clergy spouses" hosted by Mrs. Bush to commemorate Martin Luther King Day in 2006. The president also enjoys a close relationship with Kirbyjon Caldwell of the 14,000-member Windsor Village United Methodist Church in Houston. Caldwell, who had previously supported Bill Clinton, became so close to President Bush that he even appeared at the 2000 Republican National Convention. He has been dubbed "spiritual adviser to the president."

When I asked Reverend Sharpton why the Bush administration was more successful at making inroads with black ministers than its GOP predecessors, he said simply, "Faith-based initiatives. They're funding them. What the Republicans did is take it away from the social science hustlers that the Democrats had and give it to the church guys."[34]

According to David Kuo, former deputy director of the White House Office of Faith-Based and Community Initiatives, a number of prominent African American pastors supported the president's campaign promise to funnel $8 billion of new funding to support religious, as well as some secular, programs to aid the poor. In his memoir, *Tempting Faith,* Kuo recalls that as of 2003 the promised funds had never materialized, and he found himself in the untenable position of having to explain to these ministers, who had gathered at the White House for a meeting with the president, why. According to Kuo, during a conversation with Bush before the meeting, the commander in chief said of the pastors, "All these guys care about is money. They want money."[35]

Kuo believes the president's religious convictions are unquestionably sincere, but he challenges the notion that his administration's leadership is comprised of true believers. Kuo paints a picture of an administration whose general wore his faith on his sleeve but whose lieutenants mocked it as little more than a campaign tool. He writes that the president's religious conversion was emphasized on the campaign trail and "carried throughout the country by a network of prominent evangelical pastors who had been quietly working since 1998 to recruit thousands of other pastors to join the Bush team. After the election, however, those same pastors became accomplices in their own deception by not demanding that the president's actions in office match their electoral fervor." (Kuo also wryly notes that "this White House is certainly not the first administration to milk religious groups for votes and then boot them unceremoniously back out to pasture.")[36]

Adam Clayton Powell IV, whose father and grandfather were pastors of the famed Abyssinian Baptist Church in Harlem, says that a number of pastors, under the pressure of economic interests, have allowed themselves to become political patsies. "A lot of these pastors or ministers shift and go with the wind, and more power to them. If it works for them, God be with them. But that's basically what it is. George Bush is the only sheriff in town, so they want to support him, and get some of the goody bags. The minute a Democrat goes in, they'll try to support that person."[37]

Despite his friendship with the president, before the 2006 midterm elections Bishop Jakes wrote in an online column for CNN that "members of the black clergy face a challenge in the upcoming political season to refrain from being used by any political party or ideological agenda to further their aims at the expense of the critical issues facing our communities."[38]

While Pastor Meredith is critical of how vocal some ministers were on the issue of gay marriage, he defends the church's involvement in other issues, such as civil rights. "I think that it's important that we do take a position on issues that confront humanity. I don't think we should politicize religion but I do think there are issues that affect humanity [and] that the pulpit has to speak out for people."[39]

The central issue facing the black church today is not whether it will become more inclusive of gays and lesbians but whether its leaders will have the same degree of influence with young black Americans on social and political issues that they had with previous generations.

When asked whether he believes the church plays as central a role in the lives of younger black Americans as it has in those of older black Americans, Reverend Flake points to the demographics at his church, the 18,000-member Greater Allen AME Cathedral, noting that eighteen- to thirty-five-year-olds are driving its growth. The church, he contends, does not play a less relevant role in the lives of younger black Americans, merely a different one. According to Flake, "the church is playing a greater role among younger African Americans, in a different way.[40]

"In the past," Flake notes, "the church was the primary vehicle for the civil rights movement." For him personally, the church instituted "a sense of faith so that I wouldn't give up, even though I was growing up in a segregated society" and helped "to engage us in the past in the civil rights movement to get the laws so that our children can benefit as they do today." But he adds that the needs of his children's generation are very different. While his own generation relied on the church for guidance and strength in the struggle for legal equality, younger black Americans rely on its guidance in their quest for economic equality. They come to hear messages on how to alleviate credit card debt or how to buy their first home—subjects that Flake addresses regularly.[41]

What they do not come to hear, Flake says, is who to vote for.

This revelation may sound surprising coming from a former congressman, but Flake has made a career out of surprising people. Though a Democrat, he has never been afraid to break ranks with his party. His bipartisanship is so well known that when he retired from Congress he was on the short list of candidates for secretary of education in President Bush's cabinet before he withdrew his name from consideration.

According to Flake, the church has a clear role, and that role is not to serve as a political tool. During our interview he spoke on this subject at length, saying, "I think churches should have a clear understanding [of] their role as one that informs, in some instances gives guidance to, the political process. But the church itself cannot be a political entity. It has a voice and that voice must be heard, particularly if its leadership is going to deal with those who get into political power. I think the church has to make that voice very clear in terms of what its expectations are for those who are leaders, as we do from this congregation not from the pulpit."[42] For Flake, this means that the most effective role he can play on behalf of his congregants is not as a former congressman but as a pastor guided not by partisan politics, but by what he calls "the politics of empowerment."[43]

Asked to define the politics of empowerment, Flake responds, "For me it is not a matter of waiting for two to four years for any particular party to be in power because my community suffers if I do that. So what I try to do is evaluate what my community needs are and address those needs through whoever happens to be in power or seeks to be in power, and then shape my responses in terms of endorsements around whether that person can deliver to the needs of the community." He would never under any circumstances endorse within the church because that is not a church's role, but he welcomes candidates of all parties who wish to attend church services. If he feels moved to do so, he will endorse a candidate outside of his church in the role he describes as Floyd Flake "private citizen," not pastor.[44]

Flake does not consider the political wedge issues that many clergy have embraced to be an integral part of the politics of empowerment. Emphasizing hot-button issues like abortion or gay marriage, he says, is hopping on a spiritual roller coaster: the issue is up one minute and down the next, and "because the plethora of issues that define the dynamics of one's life cannot be where you just really focus on one thing. . . . Speaking out on them is one thing, making that your ministry is another thing, and that is not my ministry."[45]

In this perspective Flake has an unlikely ally. Shannon Reeves, an ordained minister and chairman of the Republican National Committee's new African American Policy Council, believes that hot-button issues rarely advance political dialogue but instead are primarily used to stir up the base—something both Democrats and Republicans are guilty of. Noting that he was not in his present position with the RNC when gay marriage was a focus of the 2004 campaign, Reeves says, "I think that a minister has a responsibility to spend the time with their congregation and to analyze the issues and ideas of each candidate, and I don't think they should allow themselves to be used on either side." There may be a fine line between social activism and blatant politicking, but Reeves feels it is an important line, and one that no minister should cross. "You want your members to be socially conscious and absolutely exercise their right to vote, but you want to make sure that it's not a situation where the pastor is going to benefit." You do not want a situation where "the pastor delivers his 5,000 members to the polls so the pastor ends up on a board somewhere."[46]

Flake says that ministers who attach themselves and their ministries to specific issues like gay marriage risk "closeting" themselves and their ministries (he chuckles on realizing the irony in his choice of words), particularly with younger members.[47] This a sentiment shared by Lauren Williams, the editor of Stereohyped.com. She shares a story of a friend who visited a church where the entire sermon was dedicated to denouncing gay marriage. The friend said that she attends church to hear a message of redemption, not condemnation. Williams is more direct: "I feel like going to church where the sermon is only about gay marriage is the equivalent of a hip-hop video with just scantily clad, booty-shaking girls in it. There's no substance and you're appealing to the lowest common denominator."[48]

Based on Flake's analysis of what makes a successful ministry, conservative ministers who emphasize the gay marriage issue above all else are hardly different from those who have aligned themselves with Democrats over the years. Both hinder their ability to reach as many people as possible spiritually by "closeting" themselves politically. Furthermore, as Flake sees it, toeing a particular party line from the pulpit hinders a pastor's ability to advocate effectively on behalf of his congregation and community beyond the pulpit.[49]

This may sound strange coming from someone who made his career as a politician, but on this subject Flake practices what he preaches, having endorsed both Republicans, such as former New York Mayor Rudolph Giuliani, and Democrats, such as Senator Hillary Clinton. As Flake explains, "I believe that churches need to tell their people, as I do, that in any election, if there's a Republican and a Democrat running, both are invited to come and the congregation is introduced to both. I never restrict a Republican from coming because it is a predominantly black church, or [give] a Democrat . . . an invitation that a Republican does not get. I never tell the people how to vote. I let them make up their own minds."[50]

This perspective appears to be shared by younger black Americans. As Pastor Meredith notes, during the civil rights movement "the pulpit was the largest venue where African American people were able to connect and get a voice."[51] This is simply not the case anymore. The rise of the Internet, with its virtual communities of MySpace, Facebook, YouTube, and blogs, and the growing number of black Americans attending college have allowed many of them to connect and find a voice on platforms beyond the confines of the traditional church. Alexis McGill calls the church "still a very important influencer" but thinks that other institutions now have greater reach with younger black Americans. "I think 'Vote or Die' [the voter initiative launched by Sean 'Diddy' Combs] showed that. Russell [Simmons]'s organization showed that." Some of these institutions have no physical location but instead are in the airwaves and on the radio. "We form political identity in different places now than just getting a message from the minister." She adds, "Unless you meet people where they are, which is the essence of politics, you're not going to be able to persuade them and bring them over."[52]

Where they are has diversified. Today, the church may help shape the perspectives of young black Americans, but it is no longer the primary vehicle for doing so, and they no longer consider political edicts of the clergy to be gospel (so to speak). For these younger black Americans, the church is no longer the first place they look to for information or political leadership. In our study of young black Americans, in response to the question,

"Do the opinions of a religious leader that you admire influence the way that you vote?" 76 percent of respondents answered no.[53]

For the post–civil rights generation, it is not that the black church has become irrelevant, although one day it may be. If younger black Americans do not feel they are receiving information and leadership that is relevant to improving their day-to-day lives and communities, then the black church as an institution will cease to be relevant to them.

Today, younger black Americans most need the church to be an institution that harnesses its resources and extensive social networks to educate them on issues that legitimately affect their daily lives: the importance of maintaining good credit, the importance of persuading children to occasionally turn off the television and open a book, and, yes, the importance of discussing sex—its beauty and its dangers—in a way that is open, honest, and frank, not dripping with condemnation, and that acknowledges the realities of a community that is being killed by the silence that surrounds it.

While championing the politics of high-profile issues like gay marriage, abortion, or a particular candidate may maximize a minister's popularity in the short term, doing so does not earn the respect of diverse members of the community needed to successfully lead over the long term.

As long as influential pastors continue doing things as they always have, and as long as they appear more comfortable engaging in photo-ops with powerful politicians than helping the *un*-powerful people in our communities who need it most, they will forfeit their political influence within the community, and may forfeit their influence, period. And that means that a day will come when both Democrats and Republicans will lose their ability to use the black church as a political football tossed only during the Super Bowl of politics, also known as Election Day.

When that day comes, perhaps both parties will finally try to devise a strategy for reaching black voters that goes beyond picking up the phone and calling a few ministers, and in the words of Reverend Sharpton, waving at us as the choir's singing on Election Day.

Chapter 7

THE GREAT COSBY DEBATE

The Class Divide in Black America

The criticisms directed at government officials in the aftermath of Hurricane Katrina could fill a book—and some already have. But the anger directed at one official was unique. This person was criticized not because anyone thought she bore any responsibility for the disastrous response or because anyone thought she didn't "care about black people," as music star Kanye West notoriously said of President Bush. She was criticized because of where she was when the disaster occurred.

As thousands of Gulf Coast residents lay dying and thousands more were stranded on the roofs of their homes, Secretary of State Condoleezza Rice was vacationing in New York. Like any high-powered female visitor to the Big Apple, she took in a Broadway show and did some shoe shopping, but not just any shoe shopping. She hit the legendary shoe sanctuary of the well-heeled: Ferragamo. Within hours the media crucifixion began. Gossip columns reported that another shopper accosted the secretary of state at the store and had to be forcibly removed by security, an account Rice denied. As she would later note, domestic issues do not fall within her purview as secretary of state.[1] Her job is to manage the nation's affairs abroad, not here at home. So why did her absence from Washington strike such a nerve?

One could argue that Rice became an easy target for the public to vent their rage, fear, and sense of helplessness because she is a part of the administration that many deemed responsible. One could even argue that most New Yorkers simply don't like Republicans—at least not ones who don't have the last name Bloomberg or Giuliani. But the truth is more complex.

For some, Rice's ill-timed vacation perfectly crystallized their sense that the president and the people he surrounds himself with are out of touch with the needs of everyday Americans due in part to their bubble-like existence—on vacation on a ranch in Crawford or living it up with a glam getaway in the Big Apple. While this criticism is nothing new for the president himself, during the Katrina crisis it was hurled at Rice like a grenade. She was not targeted simply because of her GOP label. The passionate anger came from someplace deeper. No one actually thought Condoleezza Rice failed at doing her job. But many thought the administration itself failed to demonstrate any semblance of humanity. For others, Rice became fair game because at that key moment she failed to demonstrate that she is politically black enough.

The criticism surrounding Condi's Katrina trip was not just about Condi herself. It struck a chord because it perfectly illustrated an uncomfortable divide that has been quietly emerging in black America. The idea that in 2005 there were black Americans so poor that they could not afford to flee a city to save themselves and their families proved a disturbing backdrop for imagery of the most powerful black woman in the world buying shoes that 99 percent of Americans cannot afford. Rice found herself caught in the crossfire of an increasingly contentious debate among black Americans that is beginning to ripple throughout the political sphere: does every black American who makes it have an inherent responsibility for those black Americans who have not?

On a June 2007 episode of the *Oprah Winfrey Show,* Henry Louis Gates, director of the W.E.B. Du Bois Institute for African and African American Research at Harvard University, called the widening gap between "blacks who are making it and those who are not" one of the biggest divides in our nation's history, and one of the most damaging to our nation's future. The divide itself is nothing new. Even during slavery, there were wealthy, free blacks, some of whom even owned slaves. At the height of segregation there were communities of black doctors, funeral directors, ministers, and educators whose families comprised black America's social elite. But today the class divide is having far greater ramifications among black Americans of the post–civil rights generation. The reason is simple. One hundred or even fifty years ago, two black Americans from different socioeconomic backgrounds were united in the singular experience of second-class citizenship.

Therefore it was only natural that their social and political goals would be steeped in a common purpose.

Today there is no longer such a thing as a universal black American experience. For this reason, there is no longer a single black political agenda. Can anyone really argue that Michael Jordan and Tiger Woods inhabit the same America that African immigrant Amadou Diallo lived in when New York police officers fired forty-one shots at him, simply because they all happen to be black? Fifty years ago the answer would have been an unequivocal yes.

Dorothy Dandridge, the first black woman to be nominated for an Academy Award for Best Actress, was forbidden to use the swimming pools at some of the swanky hotels in which white patrons paid top dollar to see her perform, for fear she would contaminate them. In spite of her fame (not to mention her legendary beauty), she wasn't treated much differently than the black maids who worked in the same hotels. Today one would be hard-pressed to find a hotel owner, white or black, who wouldn't be thrilled to see Halle Berry, the actress who portrayed Dandridge on screen, take a dip in any pool anywhere. Halle Berry's American experience is likely to be quite different from that of the black Americans working in any hotel in which she stays. In Dandridge's day, race trumped class. Today, class largely trumps race.

Comedian Chris Rock has tackled this issue as it relates to his own fame: "Yeah, I love being famous. It's almost like being white, y'know? People are nice to ya, they give you the benefit o' the doubt. . . . You drive a flashy car down the freeway and the cops'll pull y'over and before they even look they like 'What the f**k are you doing?' and then they see it's you and they like 'Awww man, it's Chris Rock, it's okay, man we thought you was a nigga.'"

Fifty years ago, it did not matter if your name was Nat King Cole or Emmett Till (or Chris Rock or O.J. Simpson). More than where you lived or your economic and class status, to be black and to live in America meant to be defined most significantly by the limitations that were placed on you by race. Cole enjoyed worldwide acclaim as a beloved entertainer, yet when he moved with his family into the all-white Hancock Park neighborhood in California in 1948, his dog was poisoned, a cross was burned on his lawn, and someone shot a bullet through his window.[2] The legendary entertainer Sammy Davis, Jr., in spite of being a superstar and friends with future President John F. Kennedy, received death threats after he married the white Swedish actress May Britt in 1960.[3] Heavyweight boxing champion Jack Johnson had his career destroyed by a 1920 prison sentence stemming from a sexual relationship with a white girlfriend. Emmett Till was murdered in 1955 for whistling at a white woman. For these and other reasons, racial identity alone has overwhelmingly defined the politics of black people in America. But as the main pillars of Jim Crow have come down, the walls dividing black Americans along class lines have gone up.

While the benefits bestowed upon celebrities are obviously exceptional, in many ways the gulf separating upper- and middle-class black Americans from poor ones has become as wide as the one separating celebrities from the rest of us. As a result, younger black Americans increasingly question the idea that it is their race that most defines their American experience and therefore that it should most define their politics.

This is a generation that does not remember Emmett Till or that his killers were allowed to go free despite their later confessions to the crime. But it does remember when O.J. Simpson was acquitted of the murder of his white ex-wife and her white male friend. Regardless of one's thoughts on his guilt or innocence, one thing on which everyone can agree is that Simpson got off because he could afford legal representation that most of us cannot. In his stand-up special *Bring the Pain,* Chris Rock cites class, not race, as the deciding factor in the Simpson case. "If O.J. drove a bus, he wouldn't even be O.J.—he'd have been Orenthal the bus-driving murderer."[4]

When asked whether class or race has greater influence on how they are treated in society, the black Americans surveyed for this book were evenly divided, with most respondents ages eighteen to twenty-nine selecting class and those thirty to forty-five selecting race. It's not surprising that class distinctions were evident among the responses as well.[5] For instance, 59 percent of respondents with an annual income of $100,000 to $249,000 selected class, while 58 percent of respondents with an annual income of $25,000 to $49,000 selected race.

This shift in perspective is one of the most significant developments in politics in the last half century. If there is a group of black Americans who believe that American society defines individuals—including them—based on what they achieve, not what color they are, then race is no longer the primary player in their political dialogue. And if race is moved off the table, it completely alters the way American politics have worked for the past forty years. Suddenly the issues that have long been used to bring black voters to the polls—such as the role of government programs or even the idea that one party is inherently more racist than the other—no longer automatically trump other issues.

If you believe your class status determines how you are treated in society, then you are more likely to believe that you have some control over how you are treated. Those born poor may contemplate the possibility—no matter how remote—that their circumstances could change. It is possible to get a job, start a business, marry someone with money, even win the lottery. But race is permanent. If you believe you have some control over how you are treated, you are less likely to believe that whites have an insurmountable head start that will be a permanent obstacle for success for black Americans—or that such a notion should color your politics.

This idea that any American can control his or her own destiny is the cornerstone of the American Dream, but historically this dream was not always within reach for black Americans. Now that this has changed, the political outlook of some younger black Americans has begun to change as well. Instead of feeling they automatically share political common ground with people of their skin tone, they may instead share common ground with people in their tax bracket.

Accentuating this shift is the fact that income and educational level are strong indicators of voter participation. According to the United States Census Bureau, in November 2004 the voting rates of citizens who hold bachelor degrees are almost twice as high as those who do not have a high school diploma (78 percent to 40 percent, respectively). Nineteen percent of voters live in families with incomes of $100,000 or more, compared with only 16 percent of the total citizen population in this bracket.[6] Additionally, marriage rates are a strong indicator of voter registration and participation. Married individuals have the highest voter registration rates of any demographic at 78 percent and the highest voting rates at 71 percent. This is compared to voting rates of 58 percent for those who are divorced and 52 percent for those who have never been married. On average, black men and women with advanced degrees are more likely to marry than those who are less educated and poor. This means that as the gap between black Americans who are advancing and those who are not continues to increase, the ability of those who are making it ultimately to decide elections will increase as well.

Julius, a consultant in his thirties, says he can personally attest to the role of class in shaping his political beliefs. He says that before achieving the success he now enjoys in his very lucrative job for a major global consulting firm, he was less focused politically on economic issues. "I don't think I was too concerned about tax cuts and incentives and all of that good stuff, and now I realize that I work very hard and I want to see more of my money stay in my pocket." He says economic issues played a key role in his evolution from Democrat to registered independent.

According to Michael Steele, the former lieutenant governor of Maryland, voters like Julius represent the Republican Party's greatest opportunity for growth. Steele recounts how during his campaign for the Senate a young black man in his twenties or thirties approached him and said, "I'm going to vote for you, not because of the social stuff, because I don't feel you guys on abortion. I couldn't care less about that. But I love your message on money." The young man then reiterated, "I love your message on money. I love your ideas of empowerment." Steele argues that economic empowerment represents the next step of the civil rights struggle, and he believes that the Republican Party has been more adept at evolving to reflect that. "What people are beginning to realize is that this generation has a greater opportunity than any other to do it because we have stepped back from the civil rights march to recent history," says Steele. "As I look at the future, you see this transition from getting a seat at the lunch counter, which is what Dr. King was all about, to individuals like myself and others who are saying now it's time to own the diner."[7]

The controversy that erupted over comments made by comedian Bill Cosby highlights just how significant the class issue has become in the growing political divide in black America. Cosby single-handedly revived the great bootstrap debate by arguing that it is primarily individual behavior that has handicapped some black Americans, not institutional racism. His remarks, known as "The Pound Cake Speech," were delivered in May 2004 at a celebration of the fiftieth anniversary of *Brown v. Board of Education*. Cosby challenged both black youth and their parents:

> These people are not parenting. They are buying things for their kids—$500 sneakers for what? And won't spend $200 for "Hooked on Phonics". . . . They're standing on the corner

and they can't speak English. I can't even talk the way these people talk: "Why you ain't," "Where you is". . . . And I blamed the kid until I heard the mother talk. Then I heard the father talk. . . . Everybody knows it's important to speak English except these knuckleheads. . . . You can't be a doctor with that kind of crap coming out of your mouth.[8]

Cosby's comments immediately sparked passionate debate among Americans in general and black Americans in particular. Professor and author Michael Eric Dyson dedicated an entire book to the subject, titled *Is Bill Cosby Right? Or Has the Black Middle Class Lost His Mind?* In addition to labeling Cosby's comments both classist and elitist, in a *New York Times* interview Dyson dubbed them part of Cosby's "Blame-the-Poor Tour."[9] He added that Cosby should "pick on someone in his own class," arguing that "if he had come out swinging at Condi Rice or Colin Powell, they could defend themselves. But he's beating up on poor black people, the most vulnerable people in this nation. And why jump on them?"[10]

Dyson acknowledged that the furor over Cosby's comments represented much more than a mere ideological debate among black Americans. It was a watershed moment. In his book Dyson writes, "It is clear that Cosby has touched a raw nerve of class and generation in black America." The controversy "also embodies the different visions put forth by older and younger members of the race." Dyson argues that Cosby's remarks dismissed the realities facing many poor black Americans: "Cosby also contends that black folk can't blame white folk for our plight. His discounting of structural forces and his exclusive focus on personal responsibility, and black self-help, ignore the persistence of the institutional racism Cosby lamented in his dissertation."[11]

This vehement criticism represented more than a simple ideological disagreement between two high-profile black cultural critics. Their debate was the embodiment of ideological class warfare. While today he is a successful author and academic, Dyson was once a teen father on welfare. With his brother currently serving time in prison for second-degree murder (a crime for which Dyson believes he was wrongfully convicted), Cosby's comments represented much more than an ideological disagreement. They were personal.[12]

For many critics, however, the substance of Cosby's comments was not nearly as shocking as the source. In publicly criticizing his fellow black Americans, Bill Cosby broke a long unspoken commandment within the black community: thou shalt not air thy community's dirty laundry. Cosby's response was simply, "I haven't even started on dirty laundry" and he added that keeping such problems quiet was analogous to whispering "about a small-pox epidemic in your apartment building when bodies are coming out under the sheets."[13]

Some high-profile black Americans weighed in with support, including Reverend Al Sharpton, who said that while he felt Cosby's delivery could have used some polish, "the core of what he said was correct, that we have to be honest about our lowering our standards, our bringing down our values, and our criminal element, and almost a glorification of thug life. He's right about that."[14]

As the debate regarding the fairness and accuracy of Cosby's comments rages on, reaction to them has shed light on a widening class schism in the black community. For most, including the working class and middle class as well as the affluent, Cosby's criticism not only made sense but was long overdue. Of the four hundred respondents surveyed for this book, more than 80 percent agreed with Cosby's remarks.[15]

Joel, a twenty-three-year-old South Carolina native interviewed for this book, was the first person in his family to attend college. He argues that many people did not read or hear Cosby's speech in its entirety and thus missed the big picture. "I believe the substance is that we have to be more aggressive in how we pull ourselves up by our bootstraps." Joel also credits *The Cosby Show* with providing positive images of black Americans that inspired him—and others from poor backgrounds—to believe that they too could become successful doctors, lawyers, or other professionals. According to Joel, Cosby's contributions to black America on-screen, as well as his many contributions to black institutions off-screen, are a testament to his commitment to all black Americans. For these reasons, Cosby's remarks should be taken as they were intended, as much-needed tough love.[16]

Margo, the self-described liberal Democrat, also embraces Cosby's view. She says that in her current capacity as a director of a nonprofit that works with at-risk and disengaged youth, she sees firsthand many of the obstacles facing low-income minorities. Still, she says, "I think personal responsibility is important and I think at the end of the day, whether things are fair or not, we have to make a choice as to what we're going to do about it."

She adds that while minorities, particularly poor ones, face a variety of challenges, the need for personal responsibility cannot be forgotten. "What he [said] is that there is personal responsibility and we've abdicated that responsibility for the most part, and I don't see that being talked about enough. There is a choice when you live in an apartment on public assistance, you're getting welfare and you're buying $100 sneakers. That's a choice and I think some of it comes from shortsightedness. I think there are a lot of factors that go into it but there is also personal responsibility involved."[17]

Cosby's remarks reignited the debate over whether a lack of personal responsibility is to blame for the plight of black Americans who have still not captured the American Dream, or whether lingering institutional racism is. Yet in some ways this oversimplifies Cosby's larger point, which is that it should not be an either/or proposition. Lingering racism is not an excuse for irresponsible behavior.

One issue that captures the complexities of this debate is the staggering unemployment rate among black men, particularly in major metropolitan areas. In 2004, a *New York Times* headline sent shockwaves through black America: "Nearly Half of Black Men Found Jobless."[18] The accompanying story described the troubling findings of a report by the Community Service Society, a nonprofit group for the poor, which used data from the federal Bureau of Labor Statistics to show that "just 51.8 percent of black men ages 16 to 64 held jobs in New York City in 2003."[19] The findings set off a cultural panic in the black community. Community leaders, cultural critics, academics, and activists all weighed in on possible causes and solutions. Al Sharpton led a march on city hall. Former New York City Council member Charles Barron was joined by two hundred concerned citizens in what was billed as the Emergency Leadership Summit on Black Male Unemployment. The summit morphed into a task force, aptly named New Yorkers for Jobs and Justice.

Various possible culprits were suggested for the staggering statistics. Some felt that inequity in the school's educational system produced unskilled young black men who were unable to compete in the job market. Some cited the outsourcing of low-skilled middle-class jobs such as factory work. Some argued that elected officials could make a tangible difference by simply navigating the city's labor relations landscape more effectively. Columnist Errol Louis wrote, "The politicians could also be negotiating with the building trades unions, including the carpenters, painters, electricians, plumbers, and sheet metal workers. Many of the unions remain racially segregated, and it is still far too rare to see a workforce at most construction sites that reflects New York City's diversity."[20]

Others blamed institutional racism. This theory would appear to be bolstered by a 2005 study conducted by Princeton University that showed that white high school graduates received twice the number of positive responses from potential employers as black high school graduates. The study also noted that "a criminal record reduced positive responses from employers by about 35 percent for white applicants and 57 percent for black applicants." The most disturbing finding was that a black applicant *without* a criminal record received the exact same responses from employers as a white applicant *with* a criminal record.[21]

Many of the black Americans interviewed for this book acknowledged that there are barriers, particularly when it comes to stereotypes and racial profiling, that hinder black men in their daily lives. But they also felt strongly that when it comes to poverty and employment, personal responsibility plays a large role. According to our survey, this belief is shared by a majority of younger black Americans. In response to the question, "When it comes to issues of joblessness and economic inequality within the black community, what do you believe is most likely the cause?" only 7 percent of respondents selected "institutional racism." More than twice that number, 19 percent, selected "personal responsibility." Sixty-four percent selected "a combination of the factors above."[22]

Charizma, the registered independent in her twenties, says that institutional racism and lack of personal responsibility are both to blame, noting that "black men in general have it rough out there." She cites inequity in the educational system and the disproportionate number of black men in the criminal justice system as examples of institutional racism. But she adds, "In another respect you have people—and this is not by any means most people—who decided they want to just use the system for what it's worth and get whatever money they can out of it and just be lazy and I say that because I know people like that. I definitely don't think it's a majority but there are some out there." She shares a story regarding someone she knows whose experience demonstrates the complex factors at play in black male unemployment.[23]

The individual is romantically involved with someone close to Charizma, and yet throughout the relationship he has been only sporadically employed and relies on his girlfriend to be the primary breadwinner. He was working when he met his girlfriend but then was laid off. His girlfriend helped him get another job, but then he was injured and began receiving worker's compensation. In spite of assurances from doctors that he is well enough to begin working again, he has declined to do so. Charizma declares him "so complacent. He is completely fine living off of a woman, not supporting himself. He is absolutely okay with that. I just don't get it."[24] Charizma believes a number of young black men learn this attitude from growing up in fatherless households. "They're like 'my mom did everything. So you can do everything. My mom raised the kids on her own. She didn't have a man helping her.'"[25]

Floyd Flake explains that many young black men do not believe they have the skill set to succeed, and this becomes a self-fulfilling prophecy. Flake himself was born into poverty along with twelve siblings, but he persevered and eventually wrote a book called *The Way of the Bootstrapper,* which outlines principles for overcoming adversity. He says that when he counsels young black men in prison—many of them sent there for drug offenses—he speaks of their capabilities in a way they can relate to. He explains that the skill set they used to work their way up the ladder of an illegal drug operation is no different from the skills needed to sell a product legally. He tells them that they can "blow the minds of these kids coming out of Yale and Harvard because they come out with theory, you've had firsthand experience."[26]

Many of the black men interviewed for this book felt strongly that personal responsibility is the ultimate deciding factor in the class divide. Ondre attended a public high school in the Bronx, New York, where he lives today. He says, "Even where I live I come home from a business trip and I see the same people hanging out in the lobby. These are guys—some of them I went to high school with—so you're seeing them, not working, and able, it's not like they're handicapped or something. We went to the same high school. We had a lot of the same classes so they're not stupid. They're able to do things and they're choosing not to. That isn't the police. That's not politicians. That's not your mama. That's you. You're doing it. I would say that 90 percent of that 50 percent unemployment here in the city is self-imposed." He adds that even those who did not finish high school and college still have options, such as financial aid to attend trade school. At the end of the day, he says, the most important factor is that "you have to have the drive to do it."[27]

When asked whether the government bears any responsibility for the plight of unemployed black men, he says no. "I wouldn't say that at all. I think over time we've gotten to a point where we've become complacent and kind of forgotten the gains made in the '60s and '70s in terms of movement to get into higher education, to get into corporate America, to break into the middle class. We've forgotten about that so that's why we're at the place we are now."[28]

Cecil, a consultant, echoes that sentiment. When asked if he thinks institutional racism plays any role in the plight of black men, he says, "I think institutional racism is an excuse that many use. When you look at immigrants, they find a way to work." The son of Nigerian immigrants, he argues that black immigrants are more ambitious than native-born blacks, and their work ethic reflects that, a theory shared by several other young black Americans I interviewed.[29]

Camille, the twenty-five-year-old southern native who is not an immigrant, sees a clear distinction between the goals and priorities of native-born African Americans and black immigrants. "With immigrants who come to this country, there is this sense that you should do better than your parents and the generation before you. [But] black folks here are kind of pacified by the things that they can do to get by every day. . . . I believe that you can see a difference in terms of how many of them [black immigrants as opposed to black Americans] fill spots at top universities. There are so few black Americans there."[30]

On this claim she is backed up by a *New York Times* piece entitled "Top Colleges Take More Blacks, But Which Ones?" According to the article, "While about 8 percent, or about 530, of Harvard's undergraduates were black . . . the majority of them—perhaps as many as two-thirds—were West Indian and African immigrants or their children, or to a lesser extent, children of biracial couples." The article went on to say, "Researchers at Princeton University and the University of Pennsylvania who have been studying the achievement of minority students at 28 selective colleges and universities (including theirs, as well as Yale, Columbia, Duke and the University of California at Berkeley), found that 41 percent of the black students identified themselves as immigrants, as children of immigrants or as mixed race."[31] The gap between black immigrants and native-born black Americans has become an increasing source of tension, particularly as black

Americans see many of the young men from this country fall ever farther behind.

Cecil argues that the educational gap is one of the starkest differences between black immigrants and native-born black Americans, resulting in a lifetime class divide. "In other countries being a celebrity is not a big deal; everything is about school. Everyone wants to be a doctor or an engineer," as opposed to a rapper or an athlete. He adds that this emphasis on education, as opposed to academic superiority, is the reason why so many immigrants (Asian as well as black) succeed in a way that many native-born black Americans do not.[32]

Julius, the consultant, notes that in his native country all white-collar professionals are black. Consequently all young blacks grow up knowing not only that they have the opportunity to become white-collar professionals, but that it is expected of many of them.[33]

Perhaps the most significant difference between the way young black professionals, immigrants as well as U.S. natives, view the intersecting roads of race, class, and politics, can be summed up by the philosophy that Cecil says his African-born parents instilled in him. He says in Africa there is definitely inequity, but there is also an acceptance that life isn't fair. You deal with it, work hard, and move on. "This concept that everything has to be an even playing field is nonsense. It's not an even playing field among white people. What makes you think it's going to be an even playing field for anyone else?"[34]

In addition to the young black professionals I interviewed, Cosby has another ally on the subject of personal responsibility in the black community: Chris Rock. Though Rock's provocative subject matter and racy language are the antithesis of Bill Cosby's clean-cut, family-friendly routines, when it comes to class differences and personal responsibility among black Americans, the two share common ground. Nearly ten years before Cosby tripped a cultural live wire with his comments, Rock drew controversy with a routine outlining the differences between "black people" and "niggas."

Rock boldly announced, "There's like a civil war going on with black people. There are two sides: there's black people, and there's niggas. And niggas have got to go." *Time* magazine said of the routine, "It was a caustic comic commentary that contrasted the values of upwardly mobile blacks with those who had given in to a kind of gangsta nihilism. . . . Niggas, in Rock's view, were a source of ignorance, violence, family dysfunction. It was a riff that resembled traditional stand-up comedy in the way that an open wound sometimes resembles a smile."[35]

Dyson also weighed in on the Rock "controversy," telling *Time* that Rock's willingness to flout the "dirty laundry rule" was symptomatic of a growing generational divide. "The taboo he shattered was exposing the secret, closeted discourse among black Americans about their own," Dyson said, adding, "Rock signifies an unwillingness among the younger black generation to abide by the dirty-laundry theory. That theory suggests you don't say anything self-critical or negative about black people where white people can hear it. But the hip-hop generation believes in making money off the publication of private pain and agony."[36]

The disconnect between black Americans of different socio-economic levels *and* different generations translates into an obvious disconnect on various political issues, such as welfare and taxes. Taxes have long been the ultimate rich-versus-poor political battle, and the refrain "the rich get richer" has long served as a battle cry to drive millions of middle- and working-class Americans to the polls. This refrain used to be one of the most reliable rallying cries to motivate black voters, most of whom occupied the bottom rungs of America's economic ladder. But today, as the ranks of wealthy black Americans continue to grow, many are not afraid to break political ranks to see their interests protected.

Bob Johnson, the founder of Black Entertainment Television, has been a longtime supporter of Democratic candidates (including presidential candidate Hillary Clinton), but in 2004 he helped organize a group of black millionaires to support a Republican-backed measure to repeal the estate tax. Johnson was joined by other black multimillionaires, including Earl Graves, the founder of *Black Enterprise* magazine.[37]

The influence of the growing population of wealthy black people is beginning to have political ramifications within the halls of Congress. While it once voted as a solidly Democratic unit, the Congressional Black Caucus has recently begun to lose some of its cohesiveness—particularly when it comes to economic issues. Eight of the forty-one caucus members bucked the party line by supporting the estate tax legislation. Ten supported the controversial Republican-backed bankruptcy bill. Five members supported both, including 2006 Democratic Senate candidate Harold Ford,

Jr., of Tennessee, whose conservative credentials made him a viable contender in his increasingly red home state. In a *Washington Times* interview, Congressman Charles Rangel, a founding member of the caucus, argued that the autonomy of a few members did not represent a seismic shift. "Why any member would be voting for the bankruptcy bill or estate-tax repeal or for making the tax cuts permanent or any of those things is just stupid, but it doesn't tear us apart because whether it is a speaker or a member, we only have one vote. . . . We have to be very, very tolerant of a person that votes stupid, because they may think they have a good reason . . . you may think the vote is stupid but they know what they are doing."[38]

Rangel's comments are representative of the disconnect that exists between different generations *and* different classes of black Americans on social and fiscal issues. What Rangel now dismisses as a mere blip—the political equivalent of a paper cut—has the potential to become a hemorrhage.

The four other members who joined Ford in voting for both measures all hold degrees from elite universities. Three of them—Ford, Congressmen David Scott (D-MD), and William Jefferson (D-LA)—received degrees from Ivy League universities (Penn, Penn, and Harvard, respectively). Congressman Sanford Bishop holds a law degree from Emory, while Congressman Albert Wynn (D-MD) has one from Georgetown.

At first glance it may seem that educational background is not wholly relevant to an elected official's political philosophy, but controversial former Congressman Earl Hilliard sees it as tied directly to political beliefs. He believes that where a black official attended college is indicative of just how black he or she is.

After being defeated by Artur Davis, a Harvard Law School–trained former federal prosecutor, in 2002, Hilliard gave an interview in the *Black Commentator* denouncing the new generation of black politicians "who have gone to predominantly white elementary and high schools, and have graduated from predominantly eastern universities. . . . They have not had the experience with the Black community that the elders had. They are black in skin tone but, philosophically, they are not. So, whites understand them better than we do."[39] Al Sharpton tapped into that sentiment while stumping on the campaign trail on behalf of Hilliard when he said, "Everybody that's our color is not our kind. Everybody that's our skinfolk is not our kinfolk."[40]

What seems to make Hilliard especially bitter is his feeling that younger blacks from elite universities are merely puppets of white puppet masters, unlike the black leaders of his generation, who held to their own beliefs and philosophies (and did not hold elite degrees). Hilliard blames his defeat not on his own ineptitude or his opponent's stellar credentials, but on Jewish organizations he believes used a younger black with a fancy Ivy League degree to target him for defeat:

> One Jewish organization wrote me and said that I ought to stop whimpering because, after all, they didn't replace me with a white [laughter]. They know that they couldn't get away with that. That's going too far. But does it make a

difference, if the guy's from Harvard, went to predominantly white schools, like my opponent, replacing someone from South Side High School, Booker T. Washington High School, Alabama State undergrad school and Howard Law School . . .

So, when you have these people who have gone to predominantly white elementary and high schools, and have graduated from predominantly eastern universities, they have not had the experience with the Black community that the elders had. They are black in skin tone but, philosophically, they are not. So, whites understand them better than we do.[41]

Hilliard then outlines why he considers it dangerous that a generation of young black elected officials has seemed to achieve the American Dream by attending America's premiere colleges alongside children with names like Kerry and Bush: they forsake their own race and start to think like white people. Of the alleged white puppeteers he blames for orchestrating his defeat he says,

They don't go to Howard, or Morehouse, or Alabama State to get people to run against the Mayor of Newark, or Andy Young, or Craig Washington. They go and get those from the eastern schools who have a white-oriented philosophy. Or, who have been educated to compete on an individual level. So that, when the tally is in, they think: I did it. I made it through Harvard and Yale and Princeton on my own. I'll make it in life on my own. I don't need the tribe, I

don't need the group, I don't need the race. So you have a
Condoleezza Rice: I made it because I'm smart, and because of myself. I didn't need affirmative action, I don't believe in it. If I can make it, everybody else can make it.[42]

Most people would argue that the civil rights generation
fought so that their children and grandchildren could go to some
of the nation's best universities, but in Hilliard's eyes, if you are
young and black, signing a letter of intent to Harvard, Yale, or
any comparable institution is no different from signing your official sellout papers.

In an interview for this book, Congressman Artur Davis, who
defeated Hilliard, dismissed his tactics as not uncommon in the
black community and typical of "black on black racists." He
notes that his election shows that this tactic is losing its effectiveness.[43] Today, "it's impossible for a significant number of people
to have marched in '65. They weren't born then. So as we move
further in time from the 1960s, it's impractical to apply that standard, 'Well were you a part of the movement? Did you march?'
As a practical matter that standard's collapsing."[44]

It would be easy to dismiss Hilliard as just one bitter man still
wallowing in defeat, yet he notes that a number of colleagues from
his generation faced similar threats from Ivy League upstarts.

The gulf between blacks of different generations and educational backgrounds, and the animosity it can fuel, was thrust into
the national spotlight in the epic battle in 2002 between Cory
Booker and incumbent Sharpe James for the Newark mayor's office. The race entailed so much drama, including name-calling

and physical confrontations, that it became the subject of an Academy Award–nominated film, *Street Fight*.

Booker embodies everything Hilliard considers wrong with black America's future. Raised in affluent Bergen County, New Jersey, by his parents (the first blacks to integrate their neighborhood), Booker attended Stanford University and then Yale Law School, interrupting his ascent to study at Oxford University as a Rhodes Scholar.

Booker had some solid Democratic credentials, including a stint volunteering on Jesse Jackson's presidential campaign in 1988 and being named one of the top 100 to watch by the Democratic Leadership Council, but James and his supporters did not hesitate to level the puppet master accusation against him. Booker acknowledged that he supported the idea of school vouchers and certain faith-based initiatives, evidence of a political philosophy unencumbered by traditional party labeling. His diverse stable of supporters, which included Barbra Streisand and former New Jersey Senator (and Democratic presidential candidate) Bill Bradley, who cosponsored an event for Booker with former Republican presidential candidate Jack Kemp, reinforced this idea. While the media described him as Clintonesque, a Democrat with centrist leanings, this was not enough to assuage Booker's critics. At a campaign event, James called Booker "a Republican who took money from the KKK."[45] However, the greatest vitriol exchanged during the race was not over political affiliation but over race, more specifically over which of the two black candidates was "black enough" to be mayor. The *Washington Post* noted the campaign's symbolic importance: "The question embedded in Booker's candidacy is here to stay, as it is nationally: 'What defines urban leaders in a post-riot, post-movement generation?'"[46]

James, casting the race as a choice between an authentic black and an "inauthentic" one, was fond of saying of Booker, "You have to learn to be an African American. And we don't have time to train you." In the *New York Times*, African American historian Clement Price said of the criticisms levied in the race, "As black people, we have our own notions of racial authenticity . . . Cory Booker, because he has pedigree, because he came from the suburbs and because he's generating white support, he's being portrayed as if not nonblack, he's unblack."[47] (It is no coincidence that Harvard law graduate Barack Obama faces similar criticisms.) Price was later quoted in the *Washington Post* as saying the race would likely be the last "so focused on blackness, with blacks less and less of a majority."[48]

Booker attempted to take the high road, by paying homage to James and others who came before him. "It was Sharpe James's generation of leaders in America that broke down barriers." He also made it clear that he did not take for granted the struggles that his forebears endured: "My parents were sitting at lunch counters. My parents were integrating schools. So when I came along, I could go to Stanford or Yale; I could get a Rhodes scholarship. I could really benefit from all the fights that they fought."[49]

The campaign was about as close to a political civil war as black America has ever fought, with Ivy League Professor Cornel West and film director Spike Lee—two of America's most recognized arbiters of black culture—throwing their support behind Booker, and Al Sharpton and Jesse Jackson lining up behind James. Jackson perpetuated the "puppet master" theory by likening Booker to a "wolf in sheep's clothing." Floyd Flake said of the contest, "The younger guys are going to have to make their way, because what's really most threatening to [their elders] is that here is a generation of kids that are not locked up in the struggles of the civil-rights era. And the older generation is saying, 'They're not ready because they're not black enough?' It's a sad indictment on us as a race."[50]

The *New York Times* described the two candidates as representing "generational differences between the old and new black political guards that may become only more pronounced as both generations age." David Bositis, noted expert on African American voters, was quoted as saying, "What makes these generational differences so striking is that there was a time when the difference between the young politician and the old politician was just age. Now you have different experiences and different viewpoints." The *Times* then added a note of civility that was mostly lacking in the campaign itself: "Despite those differences . . . both candidates share similar core beliefs—a concern for civil rights and social justice and a belief in using government to improve the lives of their black African-American constituents."[51]

Though defeated by James in 2002, Booker was elected mayor of Newark when James retired in 2006. Four years earlier, Bositis had said, "To people from the segregated South, the oppressor was the white world. When they were growing up, there were very few black Americans who were embraced by the white world. So it's very easy to slip into the 'Cory Booker is white-centered' or 'Conservatives have brought him in.' But, let's face it, in another 20 years you're not going to find another black politician who will have had the experience of segregation, even in the South."[52]

I asked Booker if he believes leadership is moving away from the racial politics of the civil rights movement. He replied, "I don't look at the struggles of the past from my parents' generation, my parents' parents' generation . . . in terms of them struggling for race issues, race politics. Rather, I see them struggling to add a deeper meaning to what it means to be an American, to try to help this country live up to itself and its ideals. I did not see the civil rights movement as a black struggle; I saw it as an American struggle. Every generation of African Americans has been trying to pull this nation to be more fully itself. As Langston Hughes says in a poem, 'America never was to me, but I swear this oath, America will be.' And so I understand my historical African American struggles as struggles to try to make this country live up to itself."[53]

Most people agree that one of the most profound instances of America's not living up to itself occurred in the aftermath of Hurricane Katrina. As other countries looked on, parts of America, the greatest country in the world, devolved into a third world nation. While much of the analysis focused on the race of the victims, Katrina really became the ultimate symbol of the class divide in America. A black American with the means to relocate would have waited out the tragedy in a hotel far away from the godforsaken Superdome. Though the media heavily emphasized black Americans' conviction that race played the defining role in the government's inadequate response, most polls showed that black Americans felt class was equally significant. A September 2005 *Time* magazine poll found that "about three-quarters (73 percent) of blacks believe race and income level played a role" in the government's response.[54] Similarly, a USA Today/CNN/Gallup poll showed that while 60 percent of black Americans believed race played a role, slightly more (63 percent) believed that the victims' poverty played a significant role.[55]

According to our survey among younger black Americans, the opinions on who and what were to blame for the disastrous response reflect the lack of a universal perspective. In answer to the question, "Of the following, which do you believe played a role, if any, in the response to Hurricane Katrina?" respondents were nearly equally split, with 23 percent selecting government incompetence, 22 percent selecting the race of the residents, 22 percent selecting the class status of the residents, and 25 percent selecting all of the above.[56]

Katrina brought together every complicated ideological contradiction that the American Dream entails for black Americans. The idea that no matter who you are or what you do or how much you make, your single vote is worth as much as that of the richest and most powerful person in this country, is one of the nation's great democratic principles. It reinforces the notion that democracy and the American Dream are ultimately in the hands of the individual. Since these ideals have not always been accessible to black Americans, believing in the promise of either can be a challenge, particularly for those who feel that the true benefits of both remain beyond their reach.

This struggle to form an individual identity based on who you are and what you do, not your last name or your skin color, has faced every ethnic group in this country. At one point or another, Irish, Italian, and Jewish immigrants all confronted the same idea: if you come to the United States and work hard, the American Dream—success and eventually equality—will follow. The idea that every American has an equal chance of making it became sufficiently believable for white Americans that when neighbors or distant relatives didn't make it, their failures were solely their own burden. After all, if you made it, and if your father and grandfather before you also made it—despite the language barrier—then anyone could who really wanted to.

For black Americans, making peace with this version of the American Dream is not always so easy. Hurricane Katrina magnified an uncomfortable and largely unspoken reality: no matter how successful we become or how far we go, we are constantly reminded that for every Barack Obama, there are thousands of black men who are unemployed. While white Americans who live in Greenwich, Connecticut, may know that there are children who look like theirs who go to bed hungry each night, it is unlikely that such children are within their own extended families; and therefore even less likely that the thought of hungry children keeps them up at night.

Successful black Americans don't always find it easy to sleep so soundly.

You can have a degree from a competitive university, a 401K, even stock options, and all of the other things that the civil rights generation fought for you to have, but there may still be members of your family or people in your neighborhood for whom those things are not within reach. And unlike white Americans, who may look at relatives who aren't "making it" with a guilt-free conscience and know that they simply aren't trying hard enough, for some black Americans a question mark is likely to hover above their success like a guilty cloud: just because I made it, does that really mean the rest of my people can if they simply want to badly enough? Or is the fact that fifty years ago we were still second-class citizens still a barrier to the American Dream? In other words, are people who look like me who are not making it the exceptions, or am I?

For some the answer is simply: They didn't work as hard as I did. They don't want the dream as badly as I do. For others the answer may be: I am lucky I had two parents at home.

Black Americans no longer share a universal perspective on this question. Therefore they no longer share a universal political identity. According to Mayor Booker, "This country, incredible as it is and as boldly idealistic, as audacious in its accomplishments, on how much it's afforded [me] even to be where I am right now, we still have unfinished business to do. My generation is still trying to make real on those promises, often where you can judge it best: at the most disadvantaged people in your country. Judge a nation by the least of its people in terms of the opportunity they're enjoying, socioeconomic status, and the like. So I think that black America will always be a lens to look through [which] to judge the success of our nation."[57]

Chapter 8

CAN THE PARTY OF LINCOLN BECOME THE PARTY OF 50 CENT?

Young Black Voters and the GOP

If you were asked to name the black American most likely to inspire a generation of young black Republicans, Colin Powell might come to mind, or even Condoleezza Rice. Jesse Jackson . . . not so much. But that is exactly who helped launch the career of one of the nation's most influential young black conservatives.

At forty, Shannon Reeves does not fit the popular stereotype of a black Republican. A self-proclaimed member of the Hip-Hop Generation, he cites listening to Doug E. Fresh and Run DMC as highlights of his youth in Oakland, California. His childhood resembles that of thousands of other young black men. He was raised fatherless in a tough neighborhood where opportunities were scarce, temptation was plenty, and the most popular career for black men led to a jail cell. "I had a clear opportunity to sell drugs," says Reeves, "to be a lookout guy when I was thirteen years old to make $100 a week. My grandmother gave me an allowance of $20 a week. I could have clearly quadrupled my allowance by standing on the building in the housing projects, looking for the police and hollering from building to building."[1]

"Sometimes people make the characterization that just because you're poor, all of a sudden your judgment is clouded. Like you don't know the difference between right and wrong. Poor people know that stealing is wrong. Poor people know that murder is wrong. Poor people know that drug dealing is illegal."[2]

Reeves considers the culture of victimhood, in which those from poor backgrounds are seen as helpless and destined for failure, to be one of liberalism's most offensive (and historically effective) political tools. But his journey from Oakland to the upper reaches of Republican leadership did not follow a simple, up-by-your-bootstraps story line. Just as his background differs greatly from your average fiscal conservative's, so does his story about what brought him to the Republican Party.[3]

At nineteen, Reeves was already a veteran civil rights activist, having begun volunteering for his local NAACP branch as an adolescent. The first person in his family to go to college, Reeves selected historically black Grambling State University. The year was 1988, a presidential election year, only this election was expected to be like none before it. Civil rights activist Jesse Jackson was a candidate. While not the first black candidate for president, Jackson in his second run was by far the most serious and certainly the first to create such excitement. Through his contacts at the NAACP, Reeves was able to secure a position on the campaign. He describes the experience as life-changing in the way that only those who have experienced the intensity, insanity, and (usually) heartbreak of a presidential campaign can really understand.[4]

Heartbreak eventually came when Jackson, despite a strong (and much better than expected) showing in a number of states, lost the primary. From Reeves's vantage point, that should not have been the end of the story. "The Democratic party was never serious, in my view, about Reverend Jackson getting the nomination, or even being placed on the ticket, even though he got 7 million votes in the primary across the country." According to Reeves, "The Democratic Party saw Reverend Jackson as one who could harvest a black crop, [so] that he could bring in all of these black Democrats. And in doing so, the Democratic Party would be better off. But they would discard him after it was over." Reeves believes that "Reverend Jackson's 7 million votes earned [him] a spot on the ticket with Dukakis."[5]

The excuses he heard for why Jackson was not named to the ticket varied, he says, but hinged primarily on the "not ready" argument. "I think that's exactly what the Democratic national leadership said, that the country was not ready for a black candidate on a major party ticket." When I asked Reeves if, looking back, he believes they were right, he was circumspect. "Whether Dukakis . . . picked Jackson [or] Bentsen, the ticket would have lost. Well, at least lose doing the right thing."[6]

For Reeves, the snub was a turning point. "I began to really see the devaluing of the African American voter."[7]

Following the 1988 primary season, Reeves returned to college, where for the first time he began to question why he was a Democrat. He shared his frustration with a professor who asked Reeves if he had ever thought about being a Republican. It was a question he had never really pondered. He was black; his family members were Democrats and so was he. His political science professor, a staunch liberal, explained that the majority of class papers Reeves had submitted conveyed a conservative bent, and he suggested that Reeves research for himself which party best represented him politically. He found that the party where his ideology felt most at home was the GOP.

Shortly after his switch, Reeves founded the Grambling chapter of the College Republicans. Not surprisingly, the move generated some controversy at the historically black college, but between its inception and Reeves's graduation the chapter flourished, with fifty active members.[8]

While no GOP for Jackson '88 alumni support groups have popped up, apparently Reeves's eventual abandonment of the Democratic Party is not the only switch to have been inspired by Jackson's run for office. In his book *The Hip Hop Generation,* Bakari Kitwana interviews political commentator Lee Hubbard, who credits Jackson with inspiring the political activism of many young black conservatives. Jackson's campaigns in '84 and '88 spurred their first political involvement, he says, and many "were energized by Jesse's talk of forming a third party, but became disillusioned when there was no follow-through and Jesse was a full-fledged Democrat. A lot of the issues like less government, less welfare, and anti-abortion sentiment resonate with core sectors of the black community, so it shouldn't be surprising that you see young Blacks jumping on conservative politics."[9]

Maryland's former Lieutenant Governor Michael Steele, who, despite his aversion to labels, currently heads the Republican political action committee GOPAC, considers the growth of young black conservatives a natural political evolution. "At the end of the day, the political home for African Americans is the GOP. It is where we started politically and I believe it is ultimately where we will end up politically."[10]

Though usually viewed today through the lens of such racially inflammatory moments as Hurricane Katrina or the infamous Willie Horton ad from the 1988 presidential election, the relationship between blacks and Republicans was once a cozy one. Through the early part of the nineteenth century, the "Democratic-Republicans" were one of America's dominant political parties. This would be the last time that Democrats and Republicans would share much of anything. In the 1820s the party split into two with one faction becoming known simply as Democrats and the other faction (comprised largely of the party's National Republican branch) known as the Whigs. The Whig Party would die out in the 1850s and in its place the modern-day Republican Party would rise.

In 1860, the Republican Party ran its first successful presidential candidate, an Illinois legislator who opposed the expansion of slavery by the name of Abraham Lincoln. Lincoln took the helm of a nation deeply divided. While race, and more specifically the issue of slavery, had always caused friction in the young nation, it was now on the verge of tearing the country apart. On January 1, 1863, in the midst of the Civil War, Lincoln issued the Emancipation Proclamation, an executive order declaring freedom for all slaves.

The end of slavery precipitated an even more shocking development in southern race relations. After losing the right to own blacks as property, southern whites faced an even more unthinkable reality: black elected (or appointed) officials. Reconstruction ushered in the first black elected officials in our nation's history—all Republicans. Lincoln's legacy inspired generations of black Republicans, including Edward Brooke III of Massachusetts, who in 1996 became the first African American elected to the United States Senate since Reconstruction.[11]

The GOP's early political identity was firmly entrenched in its antislavery roots. In addition to being the guiding force of Reconstruction, later Republican presidents would take a more aggressive position on early-twentieth-century civil rights issues such as lynching. According to presidential historian Al Felzenberg, Republican President Warren G. Harding was far more progressive on civil rights issues than his Democratic predecessor, Woodrow Wilson. Felzenberg, who rates the successes and failures of various administrations in his forthcoming book *Leaders We Deserved and Some We Didn't*, notes that in addition to denouncing lynching in a State of the Union Address, Harding supported making it a federal crime.[12]

While Wilson maintained cordial relations with some black Democrats, including W.E.B. Du Bois, he had a less than stellar record on important civil rights issues, including segregation, downplaying its impact on black Americans.

Democrats were further hurt by the emergence of a vocal Dixiecrat wing in the mid-twentieth century. Officially known as the States' Rights Democratic Party, Dixiecrats gained strength on the basis of one key issue expressed in their campaign slogan: "Segregation Forever." Founded by Democrat Strom Thurmond (whose public opposition to integration masked his private life as the involved father of his mulatto daughter), the Dixiecrats caused infighting among the Democrats that forced the party to find its conscience on civil rights. At the 1948 Democratic convention, future Vice President Hubert Humphrey delivered a rousing speech intended to reinforce the importance of the party's commitment to civil rights. In a moment that would provoke outrage from states' rights proponents, Humphrey stated:

> My friends, to those who say that we are rushing this issue of civil rights, I say to them we are 172 years late. To those who say—To those who say that this civil-rights program is an infringement on states' rights, I say this: The time has arrived in America for the Democratic party to get out of the shadow of states' rights and to walk forthrightly into the bright sunshine of human rights. People—People—human beings—this is the issue of the 20th century. People of all kinds—all sorts of people—and these people are looking

> to America for leadership, and they're looking to America
> for precept and example.[13]

Thurmond and other Dixiecrats, fed up over the issue of civil rights, would eventually desert Democrats for the greener pastures of the GOP.

Being recognized as "the party that freed the slaves" had been one of the most effective political messaging strategies in the history of U.S. politics—at least until the civil rights movement came along. President Franklin Roosevelt began laying the groundwork for wooing black voters over to the Democratic side with his New Deal government programs during the Great Depression, but it was the civil rights movement that brought black voters firmly into the Democratic Party.[14]

When President Lyndon B. Johnson signed the 1964 Civil Rights Act into law, he famously said, "I think we just delivered the South to the Republican Party for a long time to come."[15] He was right. Southerners, outraged at the northern wing of the Democratic Party for supporting civil rights for blacks, finally revolted and crossed the political aisle. And with that came a role reversal in American politics that has lasted forty years.

As older segregationist Democrats like Senator James Eastland and Senator John Stennis passed from the scene, and others like Strom Thurmond became Republicans, in the minds of black Americans the most disturbing images of the civil rights movement—Confederate flag–waving mobs, attack dogs, and fire hoses—became indelibly linked to what was no longer considered such a Grand Old Party. These images were further solidified when the more conservative Barry Goldwater defeated the more moderate Nelson Rockefeller for the Republican nomination in 1964. Though known for supporting earlier civil rights measures, Goldwater opposed the Civil Rights Act of 1964. The highly effective branding of "GOP, the party that freed the slaves" was essentially trumped by even better branding: "Democrats, the party that actually believes you are a citizen and should have equal rights."

Richard Nixon was the last Republican presidential candidate to remain somewhat competitive in the contest for black voters. Nixon earned 32 percent of the black vote in his race against Kennedy in 1960, yet in 1968 he helped solidify the party's negative reputation among blacks by employing what became known as the southern strategy. Facing a threat by avowed segregationist George Wallace, Nixon attempted to neutralize Wallace's candidacy by taking a middle-of-the-road approach on civil rights. While avoiding Wallace's extreme race baiting, the southern strategy was steeped in subtle racism in a troubling effort to placate southern whites. After Nixon, the GOP had other moments that demonstrated serious racial insensitivity, or at best questionable judgment, that reinforced its unflattering reputation among black voters.

One of the most infamous moments came during the 1988 presidential race: an attack ad that criticized Democratic nominee Michael Dukakis for supporting a program that allowed convicted felon Willie Horton to leave his Massachusetts prison on a weekend furlough. While out, Horton attacked a white couple, raping the woman. The advertisement drew controversy due to its racially inflammatory imagery, but it was highly effective.

Though the ad was based in fact, it was also steeped in racial stereotypes playing into some white Americans' worst fears—a big, bad, dangerous black man unleashed on good, wholesome, taxpaying Americans and, worst of all, a white woman.

Another ad, run by Senator Jesse Helms's campaign in 1990, featured such blatant race baiting that it almost made the Horton ad seem tame. Titled "Hands," it opens with an image of two white male hands as a voice-over begins: "You needed that job. You were the best qualified, but they had to give it to a minority because of a racial quota. Is that really fair?" One of the most deplorable yet brilliant ads executed in modern politics, "Hands" helped clinch Helms's reelection.

This was the party that George W. Bush had the challenging task of trying to portray as welcoming of minorities when he ran for president in 2000. Many doubted it could be done, but Bush worked hard to establish himself as a different kind of a Republican—a "compassionate conservative." While this term struck many as an oxymoron, Bush had established some enduring relationships with prominent black Americans during his tenure as governor of Texas, relationships that helped him in his quest for the White House. As mentioned earlier, one was with Kirbyjon Caldwell, pastor of the 15,000-member Windsor Village United Methodist Church in Houston, Texas. Caldwell, who had long been thought a Democrat, surprised many when he enthusiastically threw his support behind Bush in 2000 and even, at Bush's request, appeared at the 2000 Republican National Convention. He has since become known as the president's spiritual adviser. That year's convention lineup also included candidate Bush's foreign policy adviser, Condoleezza Rice, and the popular former chairman of the Joint Chiefs of Staff, General Colin Powell. Many journalists pointed out that despite all the diversity on the convention stage, the crowd was still overwhelmingly white, with blacks making up only 4.1 percent of convention delegates.[16]

On the campaign trail, Bush struggled to reconcile his compassionate conservatism with old-school conservatism, with mixed results. He gave a speech at Bob Jones University that helped him woo the religious right but did not necessarily bolster his image among minorities, since the university had a rule banning interracial dating.[17] For the most part, however, he found himself in an interesting position. In any other modern election it might have seemed laughable for a Republican presidential candidate to make a play for any portion of the black vote, but this was not any other election. The man Toni Morrison called "the first black president" was leaving office, and his anointed successor, Vice President Gore, didn't exactly scream second black president. It was widely rumored that tension lingered between Gore and Clinton because Gore felt the impeachment and subsequent fallout had cast a permanent cloud over his own run for the White House. This was believed to be the reason the Gore campaign limited Clinton's presence on the campaign trail, a strategy that may have impressed some constituencies but not many black voters. Bush, meanwhile, found himself buoyed by a contingent of black ministers who supported his idea of funding faith-based initiatives to address many of the community needs long addressed by the government. (Still, his share of the black vote ended up in the single digits.)[18]

We all know what happened. The weeks following the election became a blur of hanging chads, court rulings, and protests. And the first generation of black voters to grow up knowing voting as a truly inalienable right learned a valuable lesson, but what lesson they learned is in the eye of the beholder. Some learned that every vote really does count. Others learned that the system is flawed, so maybe their vote doesn't matter after all. The latter thought was bolstered by the disenfranchisement of thousands of voters, some who were convicted felons and others who, for reasons ranging from inept voter registration records to inept (some alleged blatantly partisan) poll workers, were simply shut out.

George W. Bush won the recount, but many believed he hadn't actually earned the right to govern them—at least not in his first four years. Ken Mehlman, the former chairman of the Republican National Committee, says that the 2000 election damaged this administration's image with many black voters out of the gate. "In my honest opinion, if we hadn't had a recount in 2000, I think you would have had a very different situation with respect to the administration. I think the recount made it really hard."[19]

The president had his share of high-profile missteps, such as when he declined invitations to speak before the NAACP convention throughout his first term. Defenders of the president argued that the civil rights organization had engaged in partisan name-calling, but critics argued that the snub demonstrated how out of touch the president remained with black voters. He also elicited strong criticism for his involvement in a high-profile Supreme Court case regarding affirmative action. In 2003, the Bush White House filed an amicus brief arguing that the University of Michigan's undergraduate admissions procedures were unconstitutional for its use of a complex point system that ultimately benefited minority applicants. The move was seen by some merely as an attempt by Bush to prove his conservative bona fides before an election year. The idea that a man who many believed had glided into the nation's elite universities on the strength of his family's name and connections, was now challenging admissions procedures as "unfair" was an irony lost on very few. He also, however, made two decisions that were historic for black Americans. In his first administration he appointed Condoleezza Rice national security adviser and Colin Powell secretary of state. One young woman interviewed for this book, a former Democrat turned registered independent, said her reaction to the appointments at the time was, "Say what you will about Republicans but it seems like with them we go everywhere and with Democrats we don't go anywhere. After all, it's not like he appointed them to some lame ambassador post or secretary of the Interior. These were two of the most powerful positions within his cabinet and those types of roles are not given to tokens."[20] (It is worth noting that both Powell and Rice voiced dissent with the administration's position on affirmative action with both issuing statements regarding the University of Michigan case.)

In 2002 the president got an opportunity to show off just how different "compassionate conservatives" are from old-school conservatives. At a 100th birthday celebration for Senator Strom Thurmond, who had campaigned for president in 1948 on a segregationist platform, Senator Trent Lott of Mississippi noted that Thurmond had carried Lott's home state that year and added, "We're proud of it. And if the rest of the country had followed our lead, we wouldn't have had all these problems over all these years either." The comment triggered a firestorm.[21]

Prominent Republicans and conservative groups denounced Lott's remarks, but the most damning criticism came from President Bush, who said, "Recent comments by Sen. Lott do not reflect the spirit of our country. He has apologized and rightly so. Every day that our nation was segregated was a day our nation was unfaithful to our founding ideals." Bush also called the comments "offensive."[22] Though the president never publicly said Lott should resign his post as Senate majority leader, many believe that he privately pulled the trigger. The repugnancy of Lott's remarks aside, many Republicans were said to be incensed that he had set back any strides the party had made with black voters.

Bush's very public denunciation of Lott helped limit the hemorrhaging—at least with some black voters. For others, Lott's comments were proof that the GOP of 2002 was not so different from the race-baiting GOP of 1968, and that they represented what most Republicans thought but were too smart to say. But there was an entire generation of black voters who had not been born in 1968 and had no recollection of Nixon's southern strategy or the not so good old days of Thurmond's Dixiecrat-turned-Republican heyday. This generation instead saw that the mainstream Republican establishment considered racially inflammatory comments so unacceptable that they could cost you your job. In 2005 the president had to grapple with another example of foot-in-mouth disease demonstrated by a well-known conservative. William Bennett, an appointee in the administration of the first President Bush, said on a radio program:

> If you wanted to reduce crime, you could—if that were
> your sole purpose, you could abort every black baby in this
> country, and your crime rate would go down. That would
> be an impossible, ridiculous, and morally reprehensible
> thing to do, but your crime rate would go down.[23]

As conservatives found themselves facing yet another racially tinged media firestorm, the second President Bush denounced the comments as "not appropriate." Prior to the next election, Republican National Committee chair Ed Gillespie organized an African American economic empowerment tour headlined by high-profile black Americans like Erika Harold, the 2003 Miss America (and Harvard law student), and boxing promoter Don King. When I spoke with her, Harold described the tour as an opportunity for members of the black community to hear what other options are out there. From Harold's vantage point, when one party assumes that it will win nearly all of the black vote, and another accepts that it will never win it, black voters end up disenfranchised by default.[24]

More than fifty gatherings were organized nationwide for the empowerment tour. At the time, Gillespie said of the tour, "It is not in my interest, as Chairman of the Republican National Committee, for 90% of black voters to support Democratic candidates in every election. More important, it is not in the interest of black voters."[25] How successful they were at winning over new black voters remains to be seen, but one thing is certain. The Bush campaign's effort in 2004 has become the gold standard for any GOP candidate looking to make serious inroads with black voters. The model basically consists of the following:

1. Exploit discontent within the Democratic Party.
2. Find a wedge issue—preferably one that is on the ballot.
3. Hope and pray the Democrats nominate a candidate black voters like even less than you.

The 2004 election served up all three criteria on a silver platter. While the war in Iraq was increasingly unpopular—particularly with black Americans—for some it was trumped by the issue of gay marriage. The president's support among black voters nationally barely cracked the double digits, but in Ohio it was a whopping 16 percent, enough to win him the election.[26] This goes back to an important point raised by the anonymous Democratic political operative interviewed for this book. The Bush campaign did not focus on trying to win the black vote from Democrats but on winning *enough* black votes in key areas. According to this operative, that's what makes the burgeoning independent movement among younger black voters potentially so threatening. If Republicans target those voters on specific issues that resonate with them, they have a chance to win them.

In 2005, Ken Mehlman succeeded Ed Gillespie as chairman of the RNC and made efforts to increase the party's diversity a hallmark of his tenure. In an interview for this book, he credited his upbringing with influencing his commitment to diversity. Mehlman, who is Jewish, notes that historically the Jewish and black communities have worked together on a variety of issues.

Both of his grandfathers were a part of that tradition, with one being a card-carrying member of the NAACP dating back to the 1940s and the other a member of the National Urban League. Mehlman calls bigotry the greatest immorality of all. "There can be no greater immorality than treating somebody a certain way or thinking about someone a certain way because of the color of their skin, or their gender, or their religion. I was raised to believe that bigotry and racial prejudice are incredibly immoral and that racial reconciliation is right, and if you have the platform of being the chairman of the party, then you ought to act on that based on how you were raised."[27]

Mehlman immediately began building on the groundwork laid by Gillespie, traveling the country in an effort to reach out to black voters. His message, he said, was rooted in one simple theme, "Give us a chance and we'll give you a choice." When asked to identify the issues where the GOP offers a better alternative for black voters than the Democratic Party does, Mehlman cites educational issues such as school choice, as well as economic issues including Republican-backed measures to promote home ownership and entrepreneurship.[28] As part of his efforts to begin repairing the party's image among black voters, in 2005 Mehlman appeared before the NAACP, something President Bush had not done since being elected. Mehlman's remarks signaled a more aggressive effort by Republicans to begin rebuilding their reputation among black voters. At one point he said, "Some Republicans gave up on winning the African-American vote, looking the other way or trying to benefit from racial polarization. I am here as Republican chairman to tell you we were wrong."[29]

This apology garnered extensive media attention. A writer for the *Pittsburgh Post-Gazette* labeled it "a stunning case of political candor."[30] While some felt the moment reeked of political opportunism, at least one person thought Mehlman's effort to extend an olive branch was genuine. NAACP Chairman Julian Bond, who had been criticized by some conservatives for his comments about the administration, said of Mehlman's speech, "I thought it was sincere, but the problem is that having given this mea culpa, the organization he represented kept on doing the very things he was apologizing for. The most recent election in Maryland, the Republican Party tried to suppress black votes. So you can't come to me and tell me you want my vote and then find ways to keep me from casting it for fear I'm going to cast it for the other people."[31]

When asked about Bond's remarks, Mehlman replied that he respects Bond and the two have gotten to know one another, but he simply disagrees with Bond's characterization of the party.[32] Unfortunately for Mehlman, just one month after he delivered his groundbreaking speech before the NAACP, his ambitious effort to rebrand the Republican Party among black Americans took a severe hit. It wasn't a candidate or a political party that inflicted the damage but a hurricane.

The images of Hurricane Katrina were more powerful than any political attack ad ever could be. While most Americans agree that government itself failed the victims of Katrina, the White House and the Republican president absorbed much of the criticism. The level of disappointment, anger, and sometimes rage felt by many black Americans was epitomized by Kanye West's now infamous comment during a televised fund-raiser to benefit the victims. West looked into a camera and said, "George Bush doesn't care about black people." When I asked Mehlman about West's remarks, he called them "appalling" but admitted that the handling of Katrina "reinforced the image of [Bush] being out of touch and it reinforced the notion that the government wasn't responding in the way it should."[33]

One young black voter interviewed for this book had a more measured perspective. He pointed out that West said the president "doesn't care about black people, not that he hates them," an assessment this voter considered a very big distinction and one he agreed with. He argued that when a tsunami devastated Asia in 2004, there were some Americans who sympathized but were not moved to take action—not because they didn't like the victims but because it didn't affect them directly so they weren't really aware and didn't really care. From his perspective, the president had a similarly ambivalent attitude about poor black Americans.[34]

When asked how Katrina affected any inroads the GOP had made with people of color, General Colin Powell was candid: "Katrina was bad." Powell joined others in noting that New Orleans had a black mayor at the time, the implication being that the Katrina blame game is more complex than the race-based claims of critics like Kanye West. Powell added that "the inadequate response to it and the inadequate handling of it certainly didn't enhance the view of African Americans, or frankly the world, toward the administration."[35]

Mehlman admits that the fallout from Katrina was "horribly damaging" to GOP efforts, but he optimistically distinguishes between horribly damaging and hopelessly damaging. "I don't believe in hopeless," he says. From his vantage point, the bigger lesson of Katrina is not simply the need for better communication and preparation among governments at all levels, but the need for voters of all ethnic, racial, and class backgrounds to be invested and engaged in the process. Katrina "certainly exposed that government at every level—local, state, and federal—was not up to the challenge," he says, but "it also exposed the effect of a generation of policy that is the result of one-party rule. It's a result of where one party takes you for granted and the other party doesn't try hard enough for the vote." That result is "what always happens in a natural disaster, which is the people who can afford to help themselves the least get hurt the worst and too many of them were black."[36]

But he called the idea that Katrina would set the GOP back with black voters for years to come, "incredibly condescending and patronizing toward the black community. The question is who comes up and what you offer as a solution, and that's why I think the candidates this year have to seriously offer solutions."[37]

David Bositis, a national expert on black voters, says that the fundamental problem for Republicans is that their reputation among this group has been so bad for so long that to make any serious strides, the party has to put forth a concerted effort to change what it stands for and who represents it.[38] It attempted to do just that before the 2006 midterm elections, running three high-profile African American candidates in hotly contested midterm races. The candidates included Kenneth Blackwell, the secretary of state in Ohio who was seeking to become governor;

former football star Lynn Swann, who was running to unseat Ed Rendell as governor of Pennsylvania; and Maryland Lieutenant Governor Michael Steele, who was running to replace retiring Democrat Paul Sarbanes in the U.S. Senate. Their races drew much fanfare, including a *Washington Post* article entitled, "The Year of the Black Republican?"[39]

Steele's candidacy garnered particular attention because his support for raising the minimum wage and opposition to the death penalty earned him endorsements from a diverse group of high-profile black Americans—many of them Democrats. In addition to hip-hop mogul Russell Simmons, Steele was endorsed by five Democratic members of the Baltimore City Council, as well as the Democratic county executive, Wayne Curry.[40] One political consultant was quoted in the Associated Press as saying, "If Michael Steele got 25 percent of the African American vote, he would probably win."[41]

Yet Steele got 25 percent of the black vote and still didn't win. When I asked him why not, he said simply, "Because I lost 20 percent of my base. My base stayed home." He added that he had a lifelong Republican in his seventies tell him, "I voted straight Democrat. I wanted to send a message that I was fed up, that we have forgotten who we are as Republicans; we have forgotten what the Contract with America was all about."[42]

But Steele's campaign was successful in peeling a significant number of black voters—including many young ones—away from Democrats. His race has been labeled "a national model" for Republicans on how to win black voters.[43] When I asked Cornell Belcher at the Democratic National Committee if it is fair to say that Steele's support among black voters likely would have carried him to victory had President Bush's approval rating not been at an all-time low, Belcher responded, "You can't completely divorce the Republican brand from Bush. The Republican brand is not one that's been particularly great in the black community, and Bush has encapsulated for them all that they dislike about the Republican brand."[44]

But based strictly on the numbers, had turnout among conservatives been higher, it is very likely that Michael Steele would be running his own Senate office today instead of a political action committee. His campaign and a handful of others nationwide demonstrated that GOP candidates can successfully win over a sizable share of the black vote—particularly younger ones—if they are genuinely committed to doing so.

The common model for doing so—exploiting discontent with the Democratic Party, highlighting a wedge issue, and hoping the Democrats put up an unappealing candidate—helped two Republicans win high-profile races in this decade. Michael Bloomberg, a billionaire political novice, won a close election to become New York City's mayor in 2001. Known for his liberal positions on issues such as gun control and abortion (and for having previously been a Democrat), Bloomberg was widely viewed as a RINO—Republican in name only. He was not considered a serious contender and then two things happened. The first was 9/11, which occurred the day New York's primary elections were originally scheduled. By the time the primary was rescheduled, Mayor Giuliani, who on September 10 had pretty much worn out his welcome, had been transformed into "America's mayor" and was supporting Bloomberg, his fellow Republican. The second factor—and arguably the one with the greatest impact on the election's outcome—was the bruising primary battle between the two leading Democratic primary candidates, which devolved into an epic falling out over a campaign tactic with racial overtones. As described in Chapter 5, the campaign of Mark Green, a white candidate, was accused of disseminating a racially inflammatory flier in predominantly white neighborhoods that depicted his opponent Fernando Ferrer, who is Puerto Rican, kissing a cartoonishly enlarged posterior of Al Sharpton. Charges and countercharges ensued. Ferrer lost the Democratic nomination to Green. Unfortunately for Green, the flier—which he disavowed any knowledge of—ended up costing him significant numbers of black and Latino voters and ultimately the mayoralty.[45] While the city's last Democratic mayor, David Dinkins, had drawn 64 percent of the Latino vote, Green and Bloomberg ended up splitting it, 49 percent to 47 percent, respectively. Green was not only hammered by those who showed up at the ballot box but by those who did not. It was reported that significant numbers of Latino voters simply stayed home. Black voters, meanwhile, also dealt Green a significant blow. According to the *New York Times*, "The fallout from the runoff may have also played a role in Mr. Green's weaker-than-expected support among black New Yorkers. Black voters were still Mr. Green's strongest supporters, but the 71 percent of the black vote that he won, according to the voter surveys, fell far short of the 90 percent Democrats have won in the past." The *Times* went on to explain, "Mr. Bloomberg benefited. In Bedford-Stuyvesant,

Brooklyn, he won 21 percent of the vote, compared with 16 percent for Mr. Giuliani in 1997 and 2 percent for Mr. Lazio [Hillary Clinton's Senate opponent] in 2000. In Fort Greene, Brooklyn, he won 27 percent of the vote, compared with 19 percent for Mr. Giuliani and 4 percent for Mr. Lazio."[46]

After his win Bloomberg spent much of his first term working to strengthen his relationships with the black community, and to ensure that his first election would turn out to be more than simply a fluke of disgruntled voters. He established relationships with prominent black ministers, including Calvin Butts of Harlem's famed Abyssinian Baptist Church, and the pastor and former Congressman Floyd Flake, both of whom subsequently endorsed him. He also appointed Terence Tolbert, a well-known African American political consultant, to a prominent position on his reelection team, and received the support of high-profile black Americans who called themselves African Americans for Bloomberg; the group included celebrities such as Magic Johnson and the supermodel Iman.

But most of all yet again Bloomberg benefited from a clumsy misstep by his Democratic opponent. Only this time it was Ferrer, who sparked a backlash with racial overtones. On the campaign trail for the 2005 mayor's race, Ferrer said he did not believe that the shooting of unarmed African immigrant Amadou Diallo, whose death became a rallying cry for many black New Yorkers on the issues of racial profiling and police brutality, was a crime. The comment would haunt him throughout the campaign. Mayor Bloomberg was easily reelected, his victory labeled a "K.O." by the *New York Daily News*.[47] It was not surprising that

Bloomberg won, but that he won a whopping 47 percent of the black vote.[48]

Basil Smikle, Jr., a political consultant based in New York, says that the Bloomberg/Ferrer race presents an excellent study in contrasts regarding effective strategies for reaching out to black voters. He notes that while Bloomberg ran advertisements featuring African Americans like basketball legend Magic Johnson in a suit and tie discussing Bloomberg's commitment to economic empowerment for black communities, Ferrer ran an ad that featured Al Sharpton dancing. Smikle notes that while Ferrer's ads were entertaining and portrayed the campaign's lighter side, one can't help being struck by the profound contrast between the messages the two candidates conveyed to the community. In essence the Ferrer ad said that the most effective way to reach black voters is not to tell them how you have benefited and can continue to benefit their community, but to invoke stereotypes by showing a well-known figure from that community dancing. It demonstrated a measure of disconnect that bordered on insulting.[49]

Though not quite as effective as Bloomberg, Arnold Schwarzenegger is another Republican who has made inroads with black voters. Schwarzenegger's celebrity (not to mention his image as a moderate, bolstered by his wife Maria Shriver's Kennedy family ties), helped position him as someone different from a tried-and-true conservative. He also benefited by a significant screwup by a Democrat. Schwarzenegger ended up as one of more than a hundred candidates on the ballot to succeed California Governor Gray Davis, who was forced to leave office after a majority of Californians supported a 2003 recall effort. Schwarzenegger's closest competition was Lieutenant Governor Cruz Bustamante. Unfortunately for Bustamante, only two years before he had the kind of verbal slip politicians have nightmares about. At a black history event before four hundred attendees, Bustamante used the infamous N-word. The timing, not to mention the location, could not have been worse. Reportedly a quarter of the audience walked out in protest. Though Bustamante apologized and referred to it as a "slip," many simply didn't buy it. One attendee remarked, "I was appalled he would even say it as a slip. You don't make a slip like that unless it is something you say normally. It simply shouldn't have been said. In any context, it shouldn't have been said."[50] Two years later, during the recall, the comment hung like a cloud over Bustamante's candidacy. While some polls had him in a statistical dead heat with Schwarzenegger, "rock solid" support among black voters was going to be crucial to his success.[51] He didn't get it. Schwarzenegger, like Bloomberg, was able to earn double-digit support among black voters and ultimately won.[52]

After his election, Schwarzenegger took a page from the Bloomberg playbook and worked to nurture relationships within the black community. It paid off and in 2006 he was reelected with 27 percent of the black vote.[53]

Shannon Reeves points to Schwarzenegger's victories, along with his favorability ratings among black voters, as proof that when Republicans put in the time and effort reaching out to a specific demographic, they will see returns. Reeves explains that at this early point in his tenure as chairman of the African American Policy Council for the RNC, he is focusing on what he calls "in-reach," as opposed to "outreach." From his perspective, outreach refers to people you consider outsiders. "My role is to make sure that the members of my party have a good understanding of the community I grew up in, so that when policy is shaped, that can be a consideration. When relationships are built, that can be a consideration." Part of his "inreach" effort involves "working inside the party to train state party officials and county party officials, leaders within the party, to get a basic understanding of the African American community." Reeves explains that it's extremely difficult to ask people to reach out to a group they don't really know and expect positive results. "You have to spend the internal time getting the relationship. Make sure they understand the community. Then you can start doing some outreach. And that is the huge step that has never been in place [for the modern-day GOP]."[54]

To David Bositis of the Joint Center for Political and Economic Studies, the idea that Republicans can make significant inroads on a national level with black voters seems highly unlikely, at least with the current crop of candidates. "You're not going to have Mitt Romney setting any black hearts on fire . . . or McCain or of course not Giuliani. You would have to start to have some Republicans who basically didn't march in lockstep with the Bush wing of the party."[55]

Tara Wall remains optimistic that black voters will return to the party of Lincoln—someday. Wall, who is African American and a member of the post–civil rights generation, is the former director of outreach communications for the Republican National Committee. According to her, one of the key factors in

determining how soon the GOP will become competitive in vy-
ing for the support of black voters will be the commitment
demonstrated by the party leadership. "We need more guys like
Ken [Mehlman]," Wall says. [56]

Former Secretary of State Colin Powell is cautiously optimistic
about the potential for a shift among black voters: "I think the
possibility is there for a shift, but I have been looking at this possibility for years and it hasn't happened. I think it's because the
Republican Party still has an image—even though you'll find
people like me and Condoleezza Rice and Secretary [Alphonso]
Jackson and so many others—the Republican Party still does not
have an image that it is sensitive to the concerns of blacks at the
lower end of the scale in our country."[57]

Ken Mehlman, former RNC chair, says, "In the short term,
the tragedy of this last administration has been the combination
of the recount and Katrina—iconic images that unfortunately
had negative impact." But Mehlman adds that voters can sense
which candidates are genuine and sincere in terms of reaching
out to them. He admits that for GOP candidates to gain real
traction, "It's going to take a long time and it's not going to happen overnight. . . But if they do it over enough elections, we'll
make real inroads."[58]

The anonymous Democratic political operative I interviewed
said it could take as little as a decade for a real shift to begin—particularly if Democrats have a disaster on a national scale comparable to the meltdowns that put Bloomberg and Schwarzenegger in
office. "Honestly, if the GOP is smart and Obama gets screwed
out of the nomination, if I were them I would bottle that and sell

that to younger black voters and ask them, 'Why are you staying over there? What's in it for you?'"[59]

Depending on how the 2008 presidential race turns out, that might not be hard to do. If the Democratic primary includes any serious controversies, particularly with racial overtones, it could provide a legitimate opening for Republicans, if not this election cycle then the next. For instance, hypothetically speaking, what happens if President Clinton (the second) and Vice President Bill Richardson find themselves running against candidates Powell or Rice in 2012?

That's not the only possible scenario. David Bositis says that for the black independent voter movement to really shake up American politics, either Republicans would have to make a concerted effort to change their image "or there could be a new rise in third party politics, [if] somebody like Bloomberg runs."[60] Shortly after I talked with Bositis, Michael Bloomberg announced that he was changing his party registration from Republican to independent.

Bloomberg, should he decide to run, has more than enough money to make himself a force in the race, and he has already proved twice in New York that he should not be underestimated. He could be this election's Ross Perot, only less grating and more qualified. As we all know, Perot had a profound impact on the 1992 election. (Some argue that President Clinton owes him, more than anyone else, a thank you for his election.) Bloomberg could provide an alternative for younger black voters should they decide they are not pleased with the choices available from either major party.

Perhaps Michael Steele is correct when he says that the GOP's greatest opportunity for growth among black voters lies with economically ambitious young black men.[61] If rapper 50 Cent is any indication, Steele is on to something. In addition to being a rapper, "Fitty," as he is known (real name Curtis Jackson), has also proven to be a savvy businessman, making a cool $400 million off of his investment in Glaceau vitamin water. Jackson, who has been shot nine times, would seem to have little in common with the current commander in chief's patrician upbringing, yet he surprised many by defending George W. Bush in the wake of Katrina and later drawing comparisons between himself and the president. Calling President Bush "incredible . . . a gangsta," in *GQ* magazine, he said that he wanted to meet Bush "and tell him how much of me I see in him." (It may come as a shock to First Lady Laura Bush that she married 50 Cent's alter ego.) Fitty then added that he would have voted for Bush in 2004, had his felony conviction not prevented him from doing so.[62] (If only the president had a nickel for every time he's probably heard *that* excuse from supporters.)

Colin Powell believes that economic advancement is likely to spur more black Americans to seek out the GOP. He predicts that "over time, as more blacks enter the middle class; as more blacks become of means, and that is happening—they will vote their interests, which may not be the same as blacks used to do in the past when they were worried about affirmative action." He notes that as the times change, so do the issues that matter. "These are people who are already in successful positions in America so affirmative action may not have the same pull. Tax policy and how much they pay in taxes and how their newfound wealth and better standard of living is protected by a political party" are the issues more likely to influence their politics.[63]

No doubt 50 Cent will agree with him.

Acknowledgments

There are so many people to thank for their help with this book.

First, I owe a tremendous debt of gratitude to the Suffolk University Political Research Center and its director, David Paleologos, for their contributions to the survey research portion of this book. I could not have asked for better research partners.

I am also extremely appreciative of all of the interview subjects who participated in this project on and off the record, without whom this book would not have been possible.

And to my wonderful editor, Bill Frucht. All of the qualities I could ever dream of finding in an editor—wisdom, patience, fortitude, and a terrific sense of humor—Bill has in spades. I am very lucky to have had the opportunity to work with you and the rest of the team at Basic Books. Thank you for giving this project a home.

Words cannot express how grateful I am to my literary agent and dear friend Michele Rubin. She made every step of this process such a joy and reminded me to enjoy the ride whenever I was in danger of forgetting to do so. I would also like to thank the entire team at Writers House, including Talia Shalev, Kelly Riley, and Michael Mejias, for making me feel like a member of the family.

A special thank you to my research assistant, Scott Olster. His extraordinary attention to detail and tireless work ethic were invaluable to this project.

Also, sincerest thanks to SheSource.org for supporting this book and my work as a political analyst, and for championing women experts everywhere. Additionally, I would like to thank Lauren Williams of Stereohyped.com for being an early and enthusiastic supporter of my blog.

There are so many friends I must thank for cheering me on when the writing got particularly tough, and for telling me that I could do it when I began to doubt whether I actually could.

First, to my "kitchen cabinet," the friends who endured late-night phone calls to listen to me read four different versions of the same paragraph and pretended not to mind: Jenna Bond-Louden, Gwen Cooper and Laurence Lerman, James Fou, Andrea Woodhouse, and David Madden. You have no idea how grateful I am for your friendship, constructive criticism, and patience.

A special thank you to David B. Katz for being a wonderful person and an even better friend, but also for starting me on this journey in the first place. This book never would have happened were it not for him introducing me to Dan Lazar, who in turn guided me to my literary agent, the fabulous Michele Rubin.

And to my other friends, family, and cheerleaders, including Alice and Diogo Bustani, Eileen deParrie, Tyler Doran, Michael Goldman, Jeremy Heimans, Janessa Hoyte, Cary Jordan, Josh Mann, Camille Nixon, Ron Oppenheim, Cecil Orji, Anthony

Paduano, Erica Perkins, Dave Pollak, Alex Price, Sara Roccisano, Ilana Rosenbluth, Basil Smikle, Jr., Dr. Todd Sinett, Robert Smith, Terence Tolbert, Tiffany Townsend, Eisa Nefertari Ulen, Kevin Wardally, Leonard Weintraub, Amber Winsor, Zulma Zayas, and my many extended family members who are too numerous to name but whose support has been very much appreciated . . . a million thanks.

If I have accidentally missed someone, I hope you will forgive me and know that I will be forever filled with gratitude for *all* of the love, support, and encouragement that helped me reach the finish line.

Many wonderful teachers and professors have inspired me over the years, but I want to extend a special thank you to my high school English teacher Paula Jay—for being so tough on me. You were right, Mrs. Jay. I wasn't writing up to my potential then but at least I'm trying to now.

Lastly I would like to thank my grandmother Katherine Hill Venable for instilling in all of the Venable women an indomitable spirit, one that has inspired me to always follow my dreams.

Notes

Introduction

1. Chris Rock, *Never Scared*, HBO, April 17, 2004.

2. Chris Rock, *Bigger and Blacker*, HBO Home Video, 1999.

3. John Swansburg, "Chris Rock: The William F-ing Buckley of Stand-up," *Slate*, February 24, 2005, www.slate.com/id/2113952.

4. Rock, *Never Scared*.

5. David Bositis, *The Political Perspectives of Young African Americans: A National Opinion Poll Report*, Joint Center for Political and Economic Studies, 2001.

6. Keli Goff, Suffolk University Political Research Center, May 2007.

7. Anonymous source A, interview by author, Spring 2007.

8. Mark Leon Goldberg, "Non-Native Son," *American Prospect*, August 13, 2004, www.prospect.org/cs/articles?article=nonnative_son.

9. Colin Powell, telephone interview by author, March 28, 2007.

10. Al Sharpton, interview by author, New York City, April 7, 2007.

Chapter 1

1. Bakari Kitwana, *The Hip Hop Generation* (New York: BasicCivitas, 2002), 148.

2. "Hip Hop Generation Agenda: 'More Than Music and Style,'" *Black Commentator*, July 1, 2004, www.blackcommentator.com/97/97_cover_hh_convention.html.

3. Kitwana, *Hip Hop Generation*, 22.

4. Nick Marino, "Talkin' Hip Hop: Women Look at Thin Line Between Love, Hate," *Atlanta Journal-Constitution*, November 1, 2005, E1, www.proquest.com.

5. The original air dates for this episode of "The Oprah Winfrey Show" were April 16–17, 2007. Shaheem Reid, "Hip-Hop Hits Back at Imus, Critics: T.I., Snoop, Fat Joe, Common Weigh In," *MTV News*, April 23, 2007, www.mtv.com/news/articles/1557857/20070423/t_i_.jhtml.

6. Steve Jones, "Can Rap Regain Its Crown?" *USA Today*, June 14, 2007, www.usatoday.com/life/music/news/2007–06–14-rap-decline_N.htm.

7. Keli Goff, Suffolk University Political Research Center, May 2007.

8. Kitwana, *Hip Hop Generation*, xiii.

9. Alexis McGill, interview by author, New York City, June 11, 2007.

10. Bakari Kitwana, telephone interview by author, June 16, 2007.

11. Kitwana, interview by author, June 16, 2007.

12. Cornell Belcher, telephone interview by author, June 7, 2007.

13. Basil Smikle, Jr., interview by author, New York City, June 21, 2007.

14. Adam Clayton Powell IV, interview by author, summer 2006.

15. Belcher, interview by author, June 7, 2007.

16. B.J. Bernstein, "Out in the Open," CNN, October 29, 2007.

17. Kitwana, interview by author, June 16, 2007.

18. Michael H. Cottman, "National Urban League Targeting Plight of Jailed Black Men," *Black America Web*, March 27, 2005, www.blackamericaweb.com/site.aspx/bawnews/nul328.

19. Kitwana, interview by author, June 16, 2007.

20. Kitwana, interview by author, June 16, 2007.

21. "New Survey Reveals Unexpected Duality in Attitudes of Black Youth in America," University of Chicago press release, February 1, 2007, www-news.uchicago.edu/releases/07/070201.blackyouthproject.shtml.

22. "Hip-hop Stars Lead Jena 6 Activism," Associated Press, October 5, 2007, http://news.enquirer.com/apps/pbcs.dll/article?AID=/20071005/ENT/710050347/1025/LIFE.

23. "Last Minute Appeal in Teen Sex Case Sparks Outrage," CNN.com, June 11, 2007, www.cnn.com/2007/US/06/11/teen.sex.case.

24. Scott Farwell, "North Texans Marching Behind 6 Young Men in Jena," *Dallas Morning News,* September 20, 2007, www.dallasnews.com/sharedcontent/dws/news/texassouthwest/stories/092007dnmet jenasetup.3645e08.html#.

25. Kitwana, interview by author, June 16, 2007.

26. Russell Simmons, *Do You* (New York: Gotham, 2007), 275–276.

27. Russell Simmons, telephone interview by author, May 29, 2007.

28. Simmons, interview by author, May 29, 2007.

29. Simmons, interview by author, May 29, 2007.

30. Helen Kennedy, "Dems Facing a Rap: Hil and Obama Got Help from Foul Musicians," *New York Daily News*, April 15, 2007, www.nydailynews.com/news/wn_report/2007/04/15/2007–04–15_dems_facing_a_rap.html.

31. Kitwana, interview by author, June 16, 2007.

32. Shannon Reeves, telephone interview by author, June 6–7, 2007.

33. McGill, interview by author, June 11, 2007.

34. Simmons, interview by author, May 29, 2007.

35. Goff, Suffolk University Political Research Center, May 2007.

36. Al Sharpton, interview by author, New York City, April 7, 2007.

37. Kitwana, interview by author, June 16, 2007.

38. McGill, interview by author, June 11, 2007.

39. Cory Booker, interview by author, Newark, NJ, April 10, 2007.

40. Colin Powell, telephone interview by author, March 28, 2007.

41. Adam Clayton Powell IV, interview by author.

42. McGill, interview by author, June 11, 2007.

43. Simmons, interview by author, May 29, 2007.

44. McGill, interview by author, June 11, 2007.

45. Chisun Lee, "Political Prisoners," *Village Voice*, October 13–19, 2004, http://proquest.com.

46. Smikle, interview by author, June 21, 2007.

Chapter 2

1. Matthew Mosk, "Angling for Hip-Hop Appeal," *Washington Post*, August 25, 2006, B1, www.washingtonpost.com/wp-dyn/content/article/2006/08/24/AR2006082401676.html.

2. Russell Simmons, *Do You* (New York: Gotham, 2007), 278–279.

3. David A. Bositis, "The Political Perspectives of Young African Americans: A National Opinion Poll Report," Joint Center for Political and Economic Studies, 2001.

4. Keli Goff, Suffolk University Political Research Center, May 2007.

5. Goff, Suffolk University Political Research Center.

6. Lynette Clemetson, "Younger Blacks Tell Democrats to Take Notice," *New York Times*, August 8, 2003, www.nytimes.com.

7. Clemetson, "Younger Blacks."

8. Cornell Belcher, telephone interview by author, June 7, 2007.

9. Shannon Reeves, interview by author, June 6–7, 2007.

10. Russell Simmons, telephone interview by author, May 29, 2007.

11. Charizma, interview by author, New York City, August 10, 2006.

12. Camille, interview by author, New York City, July 25, 2006.

13. David Bositis, telephone interview by author, June 18, 2007.

14. Ruth La Ferla, "The Changing Face of America: With Help from Hollywood and Madison Avenue, Generation Y Is Challenging the Way America Thinks About Race and Ethnicity," *New York Times,* February 2, 2004.

15. Cory Booker, interview by author.

16. Floyd Flake, "Interview: Floyd Flake," *Religion and Ethics Newsweekly*, September 24, 2004, www.pbs.org/wnet/religionandethics/week804/interview.html.

17. Erika Harold, telephone interview by author, February 12, 2007.

18. Alexis McGill, interview by author, New York City, June 11, 2007.

19. Al Sharpton, interview by author, New York City, April 7, 2007.

20. Sharpton, interview by author, April 7, 2007.

21. Bakari Kitwana, telephone interview by author, June 16, 2007.

22. Kitwana, interview by author, June 16, 2007.

23. Amaya Smith, telephone interview by author, June 7, 2007.

24. Jeff Johnson, telephone interview by author, October 9, 2007.

25. Michael Steele, telephone interview by author, April 24, 2007.

26. Booker, interview by author, April 10, 2007.

27. Booker, interview by author, April 10, 2007.

28. Harold, interview by author, February 12, 2007.

29. Mosk, "Angling for Hip-Hop Appeal."

30. Robin, telephone interview by author, June 29, 2006.

31. Clyde, interview by author, New York City, Fall 2006.

32. Clyde, interview by author, Fall 2006.

33. Johnson, interview by author, October 9, 2007.

34. Bositis, interview by author, June 18, 2007.

35. Camille, interview by author, July 25, 2006.

36. Robin, interview by author, June 29, 2006.

37. Adam Clayton Powell IV, interview by author, New York City, July 2006.

Chapter 3

1. Adam Nagourney, "Biden Unwraps '08 Bid with an Oops!" *New York Times*, February 1, 2007.

2. Julian Bond, telephone interview by author, February 8, 2007.

3. Colin Powell, telephone interview by author, March 25, 2007.

4. Toni Morrison, "Talk of the Town," *New Yorker*, October 5, 1998, 31–32.

5. William Jefferson Clinton, remarks to the Arkansas Black Hall of Fame, October 19, 2002, www.clintonfoundation.org/101902-sp-cf-rr-usa-sp-wjc-at-arkansas-black-hall-of-fame.htm.

6. "Bill Clinton Inducted into Arkansas Black Hall of Fame," *Jet*, November 11, 2002, www.proquest.com.

7. William M. Welch, "Welfare Bill Rouses Liberal Clinton Allies but They're Still Supporting Him," *USA Today*, August 22, 1996, 4A, www.proquest.com.

8. Clinton, remarks, October 19, 2002.

9. Dewayne Wickham, *Bill Clinton and Black America* (New York: Ballantine, 2002), 24.

10. Floyd Flake, interview by author, Jamaica, NY, May 7, 2007.

11. Keli Goff, Suffolk University Political Research Center, May 2007.

12. Russell Simmons, telephone interview by author, May 29, 2007.

13. Alexis McGill, interview by author, New York City, June 11, 2007.

14. Artur Davis, interview by author, Washington, DC, May 9, 2007.

15. Goff, Suffolk University Political Research Center, May 2007.

16. Bond, interview by author, February 8, 2007.

17. Bill Clinton, *My Life* (New York: Alfred A. Knopf, 2004).

18. Ondre, interview by author, New York City, September 23, 2006.

19. Roger Simon, "Black Like Kerry," *Jewish World Review*, March 9, 2004, www.jewishworldreview.com/cols/simon030904.asp.

20. "Civil Rights Leader Wants Apology from Kerry," MSNBC.com, March 10, 2004, www.msnbc.msn.com/id/4490974.

21. Hannah Fairfield, "Is There a Family Resemblance?" *New York Times*, August 7, 2007, 2, www.proquest.com.

22. John Kerry, "John Kerry: Your Questions, His Answers," interview by Gideon Yago, MTV.com, *Choose or Lose*, undated, www.mtv.com/chooseorlose/features/john_kerry_033004/index2.jhtml.

23. Rush Limbaugh, "Pathetic Hip-Hop Pandering," *Rush Limbaugh Show*, April 5, 2004, www.rushlimbaugh.com/home/menu/fstack/pathetic_hip_hop_pandering.guest.html.

24. "Is Kerry Being Truthful or Just Pandering to the Youth Vote?" http://forums.sohh.com/showthread.php?t=451273.

25. "Sister Souljah Moment," *Wikipedia*, http://en.wikipedia.org/wiki/Sister_Souljah_moment.

26. Charizma, interview by author, New York City, August 10, 2006.

27. Joel, interview by author, New York City, August 5, 2006.

28. Ondre, interview by author, September 23, 2006.

29. David Brooks, "Bush and Dean: To the Manor Born," *Milwaukee Journal Sentinel*, September 16, 2003, http://findarticles.com.

30. "Dems Battle Over Confederate Flag," CNN.com, November 2, 2003, www.cnn.com/2003/ALLPOLITICS/11/01/elec04.prez.dean.confederate.flag.

31. "Dems Battle Over Confederate Flag."

32. "Dean's Comment on Confederate Flags, Pickups Sparks Iowa Dust-up," *USA Today*, November 2, 2003, www.usatoday.com/news/politicselections/nation/2003–11–02-dean-flag_x.htm.

33. Howard Dean, Democratic Debate, *Newshour with Jim Lehrer*, transcript, November 5, 2003, www.pbs.org/newshour/bb/politics/july-dec03/dean_bg_11–05.html.

34. Dean, Democratic Debate.

35. David M. Halbfinger, "Dean's Flag Remarks Thrill and Repel in South," *New York Times,* November 8, 2003, A12, www.proquest.com.

36. Howard Dean, interview by Bill Hemmer, *American Morning: Interview with Howard Dean,* CNN.com, November 6, 2003, http://transcripts.cnn.com/TRANSCRIPTS/0311/06/ltm.03.html.

37. Halbfinger, "Dean's Flag Remarks."

38. "Adam Clayton Powell IV Endorses Sharpton," *Port of Harlem*, January 16–29, 2004, www.portofharlem.net/jan292004.html.

39. Al Sharpton, Black and Brown Forum, *Newshour with Jim Lehrer*, transcript, January 12, 2004, www.pbs.org/newshour/bb/politics/jan-june04/iowa_01–12.html.

40. Byron York, "Educating Dr. Dean," *National Review*, January 12, 2004, www.nationalreview.com/york/york200401120838.asp.

41. Anne E. Kornblut, "Democrats Elect Dean as Committee Chairman," *New York Times*, February 13, 2005, sec. 1, p. 22.

42. Hazel Trice Edney, "Howard Dean: Democrats Need to Develop Book Sense," *Minnesota Spokesman-Recorder*, February 21, 2005, http://spokesman-recorder.com.

43. Amaya Smith, telephone interview by author, June 7, 2007.

44. Cornell Belcher, telephone interview by author, June 7, 2007.

45. Ryan Grim, "Black Consultants Still Overlooked," *Politico*, May 8, 2007, www.politico.com.

46. Anonymous source A, interview by author, Spring 2007.

47. Ryan Grim, "Black Consultants Still Overlooked."

48. Anonymous source A, interview by author, Spring 2007.

49. Anonymous source B, interview by author, Spring 2007.

50. Anonymous source B, interview by author, Spring 2007.

51. "Democratic Hopefuls Seek Diversity in Advisers: '08 Presidential Election Campaigns Remain Largely Homogenous," http://www.msnbc.msn.com/id/18716194.

52. Anonymous source A, interview by author, Spring 2007.

53. Anonymous source B, interview by author, Spring 2007.

54. Artur Davis, interview by author, May 9, 2007.

55. Russell Simmons, *Do You* (New York: Gotham, 2007), 279.

56. Russell Simmons, interview by author, May 29, 2007.

57. "Biden Says He's Best Prepared, Stumbles When Talking on Schools," *Washington Post*, October 24, 2007.

58. Anonymous Source A, interview by author, Spring 2007.

59. Anonymous Source A, interview by author, Spring 2007.

60. Anonymous Source A, interview by author, Spring 2007.

61. Davis, interview by author, May 9, 2007.

62. Belcher, interview by author, June 7, 2007; Smith, telephone interview by author, June 7, 2007.

63. Al Sharpton, interview by author, New York City, April 7, 2007.

64. Lloyd Grove and Hudson Morgan, "Dissing Dean," *New York Daily News*, June 7, 2005, www.dailynews.com.

65. Anonymous source A, interview by author, Spring 2007.

66. "Laura Bush Knocks 'Plantation' Quip," CBS News, January 18, 2006, www.cbsnews.com/stories/2006/01/18/politics/main1218015.shtml.

67. *Saturday Night Live,* season 31, episode 11, January 21, 2006.

68. Raymond Hernandez, "On Podium, Some Say, Mrs. Clinton Is No Mr. Clinton," *New York Times*, February 13, 2006, B3, www.proquest.com.

69. Hernandez, "On Podium."

70. Patrick Healy and Jeff Zeleny, "Clinton and Obama Unite in Pleas to Blacks," *New York Times*, March 5, 2007.

71. Anonymous source B, interview by author, Spring 2007.

72. Eric Boehlert, "Did Blacks Stay Home?" Salon.com, November 9, 2002, www.salon.com.

73. Boehlert, "Did Blacks Stay Home?"

74. Cory Booker, interview by author, Newark, NJ, April 10, 2007.

75. Toni Morrison, "Talk of the Town."

76. Bakari Kitwana, telephone interview by author, June 16, 2007.

Chapter 4

1. "Don't Misunderestimate Bushisms," CNN.com, January 15, 2003, http://edition.cnn.com/2003/EDUCATION/01/15/offbeat.bushisms.reut.

2. Keli Goff, Suffolk University Political Research Center, May 2007.

3. Nedra Pickler, "Obama Says He Can Turn Out Black Voters," AP News, August 20, 2007, http://apnews.myway.com/article/20070821/D8R53QRO0.html.

4. Anonymous source A, interview by author, Spring 2007.

5. Bakari Kitwana, telephone interview by author, June 16, 2007.

6. Fredreka Schouten, "Wealthy Blacks Back Obama's Campaign," *USA Today*, June 13, 2007, www.usatoday.com/news/politics/election 2008/2007-06-13-obama-donors_N.htm.

7. Schouten, "Wealthy Blacks Back Obama's Campaign."

8. Anonymous source A, interview by author, Spring 2007.

9. Goff, Suffolk University Political Research Center, May 2007.

10. Anonymous source A, interview by author, Spring 2007.

11. Anonymous source A, interview by author, Spring 2007.

12. Barack donor in her twenties, interview by author, New York City, March 2007.

13. Lizzy Ratner and Anna Schneider-Mayerson, "Baby Bundlers Feed Democrats," *New York Observer*, August 2, 2004, www.observer.com/2004/baby-bundlers-feed-democrats.

14. Ratner and Schneider-Mayerson, "Baby Bundlers Feed Democrats."

15. Anne Michaud, "New York's African American Bundlers," *New York Observer*, March 30, 2007, www.observer.com.

16. "The Ladies Love Barack," *Bossip*, April 30, 2007, http://bossip.com/1721/the-ladies-love-barack; "Halle Berry Wants Barack Obama," *Bossip*, April 25, 2007, http://bossip.com/2007/04/halle-berry-wants-barack-obama.html.

17. Bill Schneider, "Obama's Money Puts Clinton's 'Inevitable' Nomination in Doubt," CNN.com, July 2, 2007, www.cnn.com/2007/POLITICS/07/02/campaign.money.schneider/index.html.

18. Anonymous source A, interview by author, Spring 2007.

19. Lauren Williams, interview by author, New York City, May 22, 2007.

20. Alexis McGill, interview by author, New York City, June 11, 2007.

21. Bakari Kitwana, telephone interview by author, June 16, 2007.

22. Karl, interview by author, New York City, August 6, 2006.

23. Stanley Crouch, "What Obama Isn't: Black Like Me," *New York Daily News*, November 2, 2006, www.nydailynews.com/opinions/2006/11/02/2006–11–02_what_obama_isnt_black_like_me_on_race.html.

24. Debra J. Dickerson, "Colorblind," Salon.com, January 22, 2007, www.salon.com/opinion/feature/2007/01/22/obama.

25. "Jesse Jackson: Obama Needs to Bring More Attention to Jena 6," CNN.com, September 19, 2007.

26. Julian Bond, telephone interview by author, February 8, 2007.

27. Kitwana, interview by author, June 16, 2007.

28. Anonymous source A, interview by author, Spring 2007.

29. Anonymous source A, interview by author, Spring 2007.

30. Kitwana, interview by author, June 16, 2007.

31. Anonymous source A, interview by author, Spring 2007.

32. Colin Powell, telephone interview by author, March 28, 2007.

33. Ken Mehlman, interview by author, Washington, DC, May 8, 2007.

34. Mehlman, interview by author, May 8, 2007.

35. Artur Davis, interview by author, Washington, DC, May 9, 2007.

Chapter 5

1. Will Lester, "Poll: Jackson, Rice Are Top Black Leaders," *Breitbart*, February 15, 2006, www.breitbart.com/article.php?id=D8FPNMSO0&show_article=1.

2. Lester, "Poll: Jackson, Rice Are Top Black Leaders."

3. Keli Goff, Suffolk University Political Research Center, May 2007.

4. Bakari Kitwana, telephone interview by author, June 16, 2007.

5. Jake Tapper, "Cracker Barrel May Face Another Lawsuit," *ABC News*, October 17, 2006, http://abcnews.go.com/US/story?id=2577627&CMP=OTC-RSSFeeds0312.

6. Chris Rock, *Bigger and Blacker*, HBO Home Video, July 10, 1999.

7. Julian Bond, telephone interview by author, February 8, 2007.

8. Carmen Wong Ulrich, "The Oprah Effect," *Essence*, October 2006, 190, www.proquest.com.

9. Cory Booker, interview by author, Newark, NJ, April 10, 2007.

10. Booker, interview by author, April 10, 2007.

11. Bond, interview by author, February 8, 2007.

12. Sylvester Monroe, "Does the Rev. Jesse Jackson Still Matter?" *Ebony*, November 2006, 170, www.proquest.com.

13. Erica, interview by author, New York City, Fall 2006.

14. Cary, interview by author, New York City, August 29, 2006.

15. Lester, "Poll: Jackson, Rice Are Top Black Leaders."

16. Floyd Flake, "Interview: Floyd Flake," *Religion and Ethics Newsweekly*, September 24, 2004, www.pbs.org/wnet/religionandethics/week804/interview.html.

17. Monroe, "Does the Rev. Jesse Jackson Still Matter?"

18. Goff, Suffolk University Political Research Center, May 2007.

19. Stephen Ward, "Living for Change: The Jena 6 and Black Leadership," *Black Agenda Report*, October 10, 2007, http://blackagendareport.net.

20. Margo, interview by author, New York City, August 8, 2006.

21. Camille, interview by author, New York City, July 25, 2006.

22. Camille, interview by author, July 25, 2006.

23. Cary, interview by author, August 29, 2006.

24. Kristen, interview by author, New York City, Fall 2006.

25. Charizma, interview by author, New York City, August 10, 2006.

26. Alexis McGill, interview by author, New York City, June 11, 2007.

27. Diane Caldwell, "Racial Politics of 2001; Unhealed Wounds in 2005," *New York Times*, May 8, 2005, sec. 1, p. 33, www.proquest.com.

28. Cary, interview by author, August 29, 2006.

29. Luke, interview by author, New York City, September 2006.

30. Clyde, interview by author, New York City, Fall 2006.

31. Erica, interview by author, Fall 2006.

32. Al Sharpton, interview by author, New York City, April 7, 2007.

33. Sharpton, interview by author, April 7, 2007.

34. McGill, interview by author, June 11, 2007.

35. Lauren Williams, interview by author, New York City, May 22, 2007.

36. Goff, Suffolk University Political Research Center, May 2007.

37. Karl, interview by author, New York City, August 6, 2006.

38. Joe Klein, "The Fresh Face," *Time*, October 15, 2006, www.time.com/time/magazine/article/0,9171,1546362–2,00.html.

39. Karl, interview by author, August 6, 2006.

40. Chris Rock, *Bring the Pain*, HBO, June 1, 1996.

41. Colin Powell, "August 12, 1996: General Powell Speaks at the GOP National Convention," *Online Newshour*, www.pbs.org/newshour/convention96/floor_speeches/powell.html.

42. Margo, interview by author, August 8, 2006.

43. Julius, interview by author, New York City, Fall 2006.

44. Cary, interview by author, August 29, 2006.

45. Colin Powell, telephone interview by author, March 28, 2007.

46. Powell, interview by author, March 28, 2007.

47. "Faith, Race, and Barack Obama," *The Economist*, July 8, 2006, 52, www.proquest.com.

48. "Faith, Race, and Barack Obama."

49. Klein, " Fresh Face."

50. Klein, "Fresh Face."

51. Richard J. Butler, Benjamin W. Cowan, and Sebastian Nilsson, "From Obscurity to Bestseller: Examining the Impact of Oprah's Book Club selections," *Publishing Research Quarterly*, Winter 2005, 23.

52. Luke, interview by author, September 2006.

53. Rock, *Bigger and Blacker.*

Chapter 6

1. Henry H. Mitchell, *Black Church Beginnings: The Long-Hidden Realities of the First Years* (Grand Rapids, MI: Eerdmans, 2004).

2. Martin Luther King, Jr., *The Autobiography of Martin Luther King, Jr.,* chap. 15, www.stanford.edu/group/King/publications/autobiography/chp_15.htm.

3. Martin Luther King, Jr., *Autobiography,* chap. 15.

4. Cornell Belcher, telephone interview by author, June 7, 2007.

5. Bishop Harry Jackson interviewed on "Tony Brown's Journal," May 26, 2007.

6. Marc Morano, "Sharpton Slams Blacks for Blindly Supporting Clinton, Democrats," CNSNews.com, July 29, 2005, www.cnsnews.com/ViewPolitics.asp?Page=%5CPolitics%5Carchive%5C200507%5CPOL20050729c.html.

7. Joyce A. Martin, Brady E. Hamilton, Paul D. Sutton, Stephanie J. Ventura, Fay Menacker, and Sharon Kirmeyer, *National Vital Statistics Reports* 55, no. 1 (September 2006): 61, table 20.

8. Amachi Promotional Video, Big Brothers Big Sisters of Greater Memphis, Hands on Productions Inc., FedEx Corp., 2006.

9. "HIV/AIDS Among Women," *CDC HIV/AIDS Fact Sheet,* June 2007, www.cdc.gov/hiv/topics/women/resources/factsheets/women.htm.

10. "The American Religious Landscape and Politics, 2004," *Pew Forum on Religion and Public Life,* 2004, September 9, 4–5, 30–31, http://pewforum.org/docs/index.php?DocID=55.

11. Julian Bond, telephone interview by author, February 8, 2007.

12. Bond, interview by author, February 8, 2007.

13. Al Sharpton, interview by author, New York City, April 7, 2007.

14. Russell Simmons, telephone interview by author, May 29, 2007.

15. Ellis Cose, "Crisis: The Devastating Impact of AIDS on Black Communities Demands a Much Stronger Response at All Levels," *Newsweek,* May 15, 2006, www.msnbc.msn.com/id/12666386/site/newsweek.

16. Floyd Flake, Manhattan Institute for Policy Research website, www.manhattan-institute.org/html/flake.htm.

17. Floyd Flake, interview by author, Jamaica, NY, May 7, 2007.

18. Luke, interview by author, New York City, September 2006.

19. Dennis Meredith, telephone interview by author, May 29, 2007.

20. Meredith, interview by author, May 29, 2007.

21. Meredith, interview by author, May 29, 2007.

22. Meredith, interview by author, May 29, 2007.

23. Meredith, interview by author, May 29, 2007.

24. Ta-Nehisi Coates, "Bloc Like Me," *Village Voice*, November 10–16, 2004, 40.

25. Belcher, interview by author, June 7, 2007.

26. David Bositis, telephone interview by author, June 18, 2007.

27. Meredith, interview by author, May 29, 2007.

28. Simmons, interview by author, May 29, 2007.

29. Keli Goff, Suffolk University Political Research Center, May 2007.

30. Meredith, interview by author, May 29, 2007.

31. Belcher, interview by author, June 7, 2007.

32. Alexis McGill, interview by author, New York City, June 11, 2007.

33. David Van Biema, Cathy Booth Thomas, Massimo Calabresi, and John F. Dickerson, "The 25 Most Influential Evangelicals in America," *Time*, February 7, 2005, 34, www.proquest.com.

34. Sharpton, interview by author, April 7, 2007.

35. David Kuo, "Why a Christian in the White House Felt Betrayed," *Time*, October 15, 2006, www.proquest.com.

36. Kuo, "Christian in the White House."

37. Adam Clayton Powell IV, interview by author, New York City, July 2006.

38. Bishop T. D. Jakes, "Jakes: No Political Party Can Contain Us," CNN.com, October 20, 2006, www.cnn.com/2006/US/07/05/jakes .commentary/index.html.

39. Meredith, interview by author, May 29, 2007.

40. Flake, interview by author, May 7, 2007.

41. Flake, interview by author, May 7, 2007.

42. Flake, interview by author, May 7, 2007.

43. Flake, interview by author, May 7, 2007.

44. Flake, interview by author, May 7, 2007.

45. Flake, interview by author, May 7, 2007.

46. Shannon Reeves, telephone interview by author, June 6–7, 2007.

47. Flake, interview by author, May 7, 2007.

48. Lauren Williams, interview by author, New York City, May 22, 2007.

49. Flake, interview by author, May 7, 2007.

50. Flake, interview by author, May 7, 2007.

51. Meredith, interview by author, May 29, 2007.

52. McGill, interview by author, June 11, 2007.

53. Goff, Suffolk University Political Research Center, May 2007.

Chapter 7

1. Marcus Mabry, *Twice As Good: Condoleezza Rice and Her Path to Power* (Emmaus, PA: Modern Times/Rodale, 2007).

2. "American Masters: 'The World of Nat King Cole,'" *PBS Previews 2007*, www.pbs.org/previews/americanmasters_natkingcole.

3. Jason Ankeny, "Sammy Davis, Jr.," *All Media Guide*, www.allmusic.com/cg/amg.dll?p=amg&sql=11:gvfqxq85ld6e~T1.

4. Chris Rock, *Bring the Pain*, HBO, June 1, 1996.

5. Keli Goff, Suffolk University Political Research Center, May 2007.

6. Kelly Holder, "Voting and Registration in the Election of November 2004," *U.S. Census Bureau*, March 2006, www.census.gov/prod/2006pubs/p20-556.pdf.

7. Michael Steele, telephone interview by author, April 24, 2007.

8. Bill Cosby, address at the NAACP on the 50th Anniversary of *Brown v. Board of Education*, May 17, 2004, at Constitutional Hall, Washington, DC, in *American Rhetoric*, www.americanrhetoric.com/speeches/billcosbypoundcakespeech.htm.

9. Felicia R. Lee, "Cosby Defends His Remarks About Poor Blacks' Values," *New York Times*, May 22, 2004, B7, www.proquest.com.

10. Deborah Solomon, "Bill Cosby's Not Funny," *New York Times Magazine*, March 27, 2005, 15, www.proquest.com.

11. "Responding to a Controversial Debate About Race in America." Article contains excerpts from Michael Eric Dyson, *Is Bill Cosby Right? Today Show*, May 3, 2005, www.msnbc.msn.com/id/7681419.

12. Solomon, "Bill Cosby's Not Funny."

13. Bill Cosby, interview, *Paula Zahn Now*, November 11, 2004, http://transcripts.cnn.com/TRANSCRIPTS/0411/11/pzn.01.html.

14. Al Sharpton, interview by author, New York City, April 7, 2007.

15. Keli Goff, Suffolk University Political Research Center, May 2007.

16. Joel, interview by author, New York City, August 5, 2006.

17. Margo, interview by author, New York City, August 8, 2006.

18. Janny Scott, "Nearly Half of Black Men Found Jobless," *New York Times*, February 28, 2004, B1, www.proquest.com.

19. Scott, "Nearly Half of Black Men Found Jobless."

20. David R. Jones, "The Urban Agenda: Combating Black Male Unemployment," *New York Amsterdam News*, June 24–30, 2004, 5, www.proquest.com.

21. "Many New York Employers Discriminate Against Minorities, Ex-Offenders," *News@Princeton*, April 1, 2005, www.princeton.edu/main/news/archive/S11/23/70K64/index.xml?section=newsreleases.

22. Goff, Suffolk University Political Research Center, May 2007.

23. Charizma, interview by author, New York City, August 10, 2006.

24. Charizma, interview by author, August 10, 2006.

25. Charizma, interview by author, August 10, 2006.

26. Floyd Flake, interview by author, Jamaica, NY, May 2007.

27. Ondre, interview by author, New York City, September 23, 2006.

28. Ondre, interview by author, September 23, 2006.

29. Cecil, interview by author, New York City, October 14, 2006.

30. Camille, interview by author, New York City, July 25, 2006.

31. Sara Rimer and Karen W. Arenson, "Top Colleges Take More Blacks, But Which Ones?" *New York Times*, June 24, 2004, A1, www.proquest.com.

32. Cecil, interview by author, October 14, 2006.

33. Julius, interview by author, New York City, Fall 2006.

34. Cecil, interview by author, October 14, 2006.

35. Christopher John Farley, "Seriously Funny," *Time*, September 13, 1999, www.time.com.

36. Farley, "Seriously Funny."

37. "Trojan Horse Watch," *Black Commentator*, October 17, 2002, www.blackcommentator.com/14_thw.html.

38. Brian DeBose, "Black Caucus Shows Constituent Changes," *Washington Times*, May 6, 2005, A1, http://web.ebscohost.com.

39. "Hilliard Calls for New Institutions to Protect Black Interests," *Black Commentator*, July 25, 2002, www.blackcommentator.com/8_hilliard_interview.html.

40. Bill Schneider, "Voters Send a Message in Alabama," CNN.com, July 1, 2002, http://archives.cnn.com/2002/ALLPOLITICS/07/01/pol.play.israel/index.html.

41. "Hilliard Calls for New Institutions."

42. "Hilliard Calls for New Institutions."

43. Artur Davis, interview by author, May 9, 2007.

44. Davis, interview by author, May 9, 2007.

45. Seth Mnookin, "The New Natural," *New York*, April 22, 2002, 64, www.nymag.com/nymetro/news/politics/newyork/features/5921.

46. Dale Russakoff, "In Newark Race, Black Political Visions Collide," *Washington Post*, May 14, 2002, A1, www.proquest.com.

47. Richard Lezin Jones, "Race, Writ Large," *New York Times*, May 5, 2002, 14, www.proquest.com.

48. Russakoff, "Newark Race."

49. Mnookin, "New Natural."

50. Clarence Page, "A Great Black Hope," *P.O.V.*, PBS.org, www.pbs.org/pov/pov2005/streetfight/special_analysis.html.

51. Richard Lezin Jones, "As Civil Rights Battles Recede, Generational Fights Replace Them," *New York Times*, May 15, 2002, B6, www.proquest.com.

52. Jones, "Civil Rights Battles."

53. Cory Booker, interview by author, Newark, NJ, April 10, 2007.

54. Ty Trippet, "Time Poll Results: Hurricane Katrina," *Time*, September 10, 2005, www.time.com/time/nation/article/0,8599,1103504,00.html.

55. USA Today/CNN Gallup Poll, *USA Today*, September 12, 2005, www.usatoday.com/news/polls/2005–09–12-poll-blacks.htm.

56. Goff, Suffolk University Political Research Center, May 2007.

57. Booker, interview by author, April 10, 2007.

Chapter 8

1. Shannon Reeves, telephone interview by author, June 6–7, 2007.

2. Reeves, interview by author, June 6–7, 2007.

3. Reeves, interview by author, June 6–7, 2007.

4. Reeves, interview by author, June 6–7, 2007.

5. Reeves, interview by author, June 6–7, 2007.

6. Reeves, interview by author, June 6–7, 2007.

7. Reeves, interview by author, June 6–7, 2007.

8. Reeves, interview by author, June 6–7, 2007.

9. Bakari Kitwana, *The Hip Hop Generation* (New York: Basic*Civitas*s, 2002), 151.

10. Michael Steele, telephone interview by author, April 24, 2007.

11. "Breaking New Ground: African American Senators," U.S. Senate Art and History website, www.senate.gov/pagelayout/history/h_multi _sections_and_teasers/Photo_Exhibit_African_American_Senators.htm.

12. Al Felzenberg, telephone and e-mail interview by author, September 16–17, 2007.

13. Hubert H. Humphrey, 1948 Democratic National Convention Address, July 14, 1948, www.americanrhetoric.com/speeches/ huberthumphey1948dnc.html.

14. Dan Balz and Matthew Mosk, "The Year of the Black Republican?" *Washington* Post, May 10, 2006, A1.

15. Bill Moyers, "Second Thoughts: Reflections on the Great Society," *New Perspectives Quarterly*, Winter 1987, www.digitalnpq.org/ archive/1987_winter/second.html.

16. Sean Loughlin, "Blacks Comprise 4.1 Percent of Delegates at GOP Convention," CNN.com, July 28, 2000, http://archives.cnn.com/ 2000/ALLPOLITICS/stories/07/28/blacks.gop.

17. "Bob Jones University Ends Ban on Interracial Dating," CNN.com, March 4, 2000, http://archives.cnn.com/2000/US/03/04/bob.jones.

18. Balz and Mosk, "Year of the Black Republican?"

19. Ken Mehlman, interview by author, Washington, DC, May 8, 2007.

20. Robin, telephone interview by author, June 29, 2006.

21. John Mercurio, "Lott Apologizes for Thurmond Comment," CNN.com, December 10, 2002, http://archives.cnn.com/2002/ALLPOLITICS/12/09/lott.comment.

22. "Bush Calls Lott Comments 'Offensive,'" CNN.com, December 13, 2002, http://archives.cnn.com/2002/ALLPOLITICS/12/12/lott.comment.

23. "Bennett Under Fire for Remarks on Blacks, Crime," CNN.com, September 20, 2005, www.cnn.com/2005/POLITICS/09/30/bennett.comments/index.html.

24. Erika Harold, telephone interview by author, February 12, 2007.

25. Tara Wall, "RNC Chairman Gillespie Addresses African American Business Leaders," GOP.com news releases, June 2, 2004, www.gop.com/News/Read.aspx?ID=4260.

26. Clarence Page, "Blacks Hearing a New Gospel from GOP," *Chicago Tribune*, March 6, 2005, 11, http://proquest.umi.com.

27. Mehlman, interview by author, May 8, 2007.

28. Mehlman, interview by author, May 8, 2007.

29. Anne E. Kornblut, "Bush and Party Chief Court Black Voters at 2 Forums," *New York Times*, July 15, 2005, A12, http://proquest.umi.com.

30. Tony Norman, "What Color Is Your Hypocrisy?" *Pittsburgh Post-Gazette*, October 27, 2006, www.post-gazette.com/pg/06300/733389-153.stm.

31. Julian Bond, interview by author, February 8, 2007.

32. Mehlman, interview by author, May 8, 2007.

33. Mehlman, interview by author, May 8, 2007.

34. Joel, interview by author, New York City, August 5, 2006.

35. Colin Powell, telephone interview by author, March 28, 2007.

36. Mehlman, interview by author, May 8, 2007.

37. Mehlman, interview by author, May 8, 2007.

38. David Bositis, telephone interview by author, June 18, 2007.

39. Balz and Mosk, "Year of the Black Republican?"

40. Alexander Mooney, "Steele Endorsed by African-American Democrats," CNN.com, October 30, 2006, www.cnn.com/POLITICS/blogs/politicalticker/2006/10/steele-endorsed-by-african-american.html.

41. Tom Stuckey, "Black Voters Consider Steele, but Say Race Is Not Paramount," Associated Press State and Local Wire, July 28, 2005.

42. Steele, interview by author, April 24, 2007.

43. Wiley Hall, "Former Md. Lieutenant Governor to Chair Republican GOPAC," Associated Press, January 26, 2007, http://gopac.org.

44. Cornell Belcher, telephone interview by author, June 7, 2007.

45. Diane Caldwell, "Racial Politics of 2001; Unhealed Wounds in 2005," *New York Times*, May 8, 2005, 1, http://proquest.umi.com.

46. Michael Cooper and Josh Barbanel, "Gains Among Hispanic, Black, and Liberal Voters Helped Push Bloomberg to Victory," *New York Times*, November 10, 2001, www.proquest.com.

47. Lisa L. Colangelo and David Saltonstall, "Bloomberg Wins by a K.O., Crushes Ferrer by Nearly 20-Point Margin," *New York Daily News*, November 9, 2005, 3.

48. Jackie Salit, "The Bloomberg Story," Independentvoting.org, May 30, 2007, www.independentvoting.org/Bloomberg.html.

49. Basil Smikle, telephone interview by author, June 21, 2007.

50. Lynda Gledhill, "Lieutenant Governor Uses Racial Slur in Black History Speech," *San Francisco Chronicle*, February 13, 2001, A1.

51. Earl Ofari Hutchinson, "Bustamante, Blacks and the 'N' Word," Pacific News Service, August 22, 2003, http://news.pacificnews.org/news/view_article.html?article_id=7a44bcc443947a8a5ed9d7d7f47c1d21.

52. Mortimer B. Zuckerman, "Arnold Rides a Tiger," *US News & World Report*, October 12, 2003, www.usnews.com/usnews/opinion/articles/031020/20edit.htm.

53. Daniel Weintraub, "Exit Poll Entrails," *California Insider*, November 8, 2006, www.sacbee.com/static/weblogs/insider/archives/2006_11_08.html.

54. Reeves, interview by author, June 6–7, 2007.

55. Bositis, interview by author, June 18, 2007.

56. Tara Wall, interview by author, Washington, DC, May 8, 2007.

57. Powell, interview by author, March 28, 2007.

58. Mehlman, interview by author, May 8, 2007.

59. Anonymous source A, interview by author, Spring 2007.

60. Bositis, interview by author, June 18, 2007.

61. Steele, interview by author, April 14, 2007.

62. "For the Record: Quick News on 50 Cent, Kanye West, Irv Gotti, Beyonce, Zack De La Rocha, Alice in Chains & More," MTV.com, November 23, 2005, www.mtv.com/news/articles/1514482/20051123/50_cent.jhtml.

63. Powell, interview by author, March 28, 2007.

Index